T0375350

Full Industry Equilibrium

This highly original book develops a systematic zero-net-profit comparative statics theory of the firm that challenges many widely held views in microeconomics. It builds a bridge between the marginalist long-run theory of the firm and Sraffian theory to create a unified theoretical framework that explains how firms react to exogenous shocks resulting in new equilibrium positions of the whole economy. The central message of the book is that too often economists expect more from the microeconomic laws of input demand and output supply than they can really give. The authors show that the zero-net-profit condition requires a more articulated analysis that sometimes yields qualitative results contrary to those of familiar economic laws. Written for academic researchers and graduate students, the book will be of particular interest to those working on the microeconomics of industry equilibrium, comparative statics and Sraffian economics.

ARRIGO OPOCHER is Full Professor of Economics at the University of Padua. He has published in leading economics journals on the topics of economic theory and its history and has written books on long-run growth and trade theory. He is co-editor of the journal *Metroeconomica*.

IAN STEEDMAN is Emeritus Professor of Economics at Manchester Metropolitan University. He is the (co-)author or editor of 14 books and over 140 articles. Until his retirement he was very active in editorial work for the *Cambridge Journal of Economics*, the *European Journal of the History of Economic Thought* and *Metroeconomica*.

Full Industry Equilibrium

A Theory of the Industrial Long Run

ARRIGO OPOCHER AND IAN STEEDMAN

CAMBRIDGE
UNIVERSITY PRESS

CAMBRIDGE
UNIVERSITY PRESS

University Printing House, Cambridge CB2 8BS, United Kingdom

Cambridge University Press is part of the University of Cambridge.

It furthers the University's mission by disseminating knowledge in the pursuit of education, learning and research at the highest international levels of excellence.

www.cambridge.org
Information on this title: www.cambridge.org/9781107097797

© Arrigo Opocher and Ian Steedman 2015

First published 2015

A catalogue record for this publication is available from the British Library

ISBN 978-1-107-09779-7 Hardback

To
Antonella
and
Xiaoling

Contents

Figures

Tables

Preface

The late 1960s saw the growth of the new long-run theory of the firm, many of the contributions to this literature appearing in the *American Economic Review*. At about the same time, capital theory flourished, as a sequel to Sraffa's famous book, *Production of Commodities*. Each of these theories emphasized that the forces of free competition lead to positions of zero extra-profit and each, in its own way, involved a rejection of over-partial reasoning. At the heart of the new long-run theory of the firm lies the idea that if a zero extra-profit equilibrium is disrupted by, say, an increase in the price of one factor, that price increase must be compensated by an increased product price if such an equilibrium is to be restored. (See, for example, Ferguson and Saving, 1969; Silberberg, 1974; Braulke, 1987.) This need to change more than one price at a time is the very basis of the revised comparative statics. It was also central to Sraffa's arguments, focused on the economy as a whole, that between any two alternative positions of the economy, corresponding to a different real wage, all relative prices would be different.

However, this common emphasis on changing relative prices in a way consistent with maintaining zero extra profits did not lead to any interactions between the two theories. The present authors, having made some contributions to each of these theories, came to think that both theories could benefit from recognizing the other. This book is our attempt at a systematic discussion of the implications of such a mutual recognition, built upon the central concept of full industry equilibrium (the term is adapted from Wicksell's *Lectures*, Vol. 1).

Any attempt to build a bridge between two different theories stemming from different traditions is liable to encounter terminological challenges (if no others!). For example, contributors to the new long-run theory of the firm tend to speak of long-run equilibrium, while contributors to Sraffian theory generally speak of long-period positions. Similarly, while the former would tend to refer to a rate of interest and to extra profits (as we have done above), the latter would usually refer to a uniform rate of profit. Because this book is focused on the theory of both the firm and the industry, it has seemed advisable to follow the more conventional terminology of long-run equilibrium. For the same reason, we refer throughout to free competition, not perfect competition. As to the second distinction, we shall always use the term zero net profit. In the matter of expositional style, we have leaned toward simplicity rather than generality. One whole chapter and two other chapter sections which are perhaps either somewhat more demanding or unnecessary for later arguments are therefore marked with asterisks; some readers may wish to skim or even skip this material on a first reading.

In Sections 4.9 and 5.5 we have drawn on material previously published in *Metroeconomica* in 2013. We benefited greatly from the opportunity to present a short course of lectures on our subject matter to graduate-level students and staff at the Joseph Schumpeter Centre, University of Graz, in October 2011. The writing of this book took a big step forward after these lectures and we thank all the participants for their stimulating questions and suggestions. We are most grateful to Heinz Kurz, both for inviting us to lecture in Graz and for his extensive comments on various versions of the book, and to Edwin Burmeister, Geoff Harcourt and Neri Salvadori for their useful comments on some selected chapters.

A.O. and I.S.

Introduction

This book concerns the full, long-run reaction of the firm and the industry to a price shock, be it autonomous or determined in a predictable way by productivity increase, by a change in taxation, or by a change in the conditions of international trade. By full reaction we mean the adjustment of the input mix and of the output(s), under the condition that net profits are null, both before and after the shock, in every industry. For simplicity, we ignore firm heterogeneity; we also ignore the possibility of external economies or diseconomies and leave aside the impact of the shock on the size of the industry and the number of firms.

Within this field of investigation, the most familiar tools of analysis in the economist's toolbox are no doubt the partial equilibrium 'laws' of input demand and output supply. Our central message is that too often economists expect from these 'laws' more than they can give: in relevant economic circumstances they are too simple to provide correct predictions. The zero-net-profit condition, in particular, requires a more articulated analysis that sometimes yields qualitative results contrary to those of the familiar 'laws'.

We recognize, of course, that a cavalier, simplistic use of the 'laws of input demand' has been criticized during the Cambridge capital theory debates. However, such criticisms were focused on the economy as a whole or on vertically integrated sectors, not on individual industries. Their central finding was that a change in the rate of interest may modify the *aggregate* capital/labour and capital/output ratios in a direction opposite to that expected on the basis of a simple 'law of input demand' (a contribution giving a distinct flavour of those debates is Garegnani, 1970). By contrast, we are concerned here with 'micro' productive choices and often assume an identically zero rate of interest.

Almost 30 years ago, when the intellectual appeal of the debates was perhaps declining, one of the present authors (Steedman, 1985, 1988) presented an early analysis of the input use/input price relationship in

1

an industry belonging to a Sraffa-type system characterized by many primary inputs and a zero rate of interest. In a series of examples, it was found that at a micro level there can still be unconventional comparative statics *for both* primary and produced inputs *and without* any interest being paid on capital. This perhaps unexpected result raised a series of questions that stimulated further articles (Steedman, 1998, 2005, 2006; Opocher, 2002; Opocher and Steedman, 2008a, 2009, 2011) and, eventually, shaped the present book. If not interest and capital – which are notoriously tricky matters – what *is* responsible for the violation of a simple law of input demand at the micro level, where it is generally believed to be most reliable? Is the comparative statics of firms whose maximum profit is null qualitatively different from the conventional partial equilibrium comparative statics? Is a consistent zero-net-profit comparative statics more interesting for the applied microeconomist than a crude partial equilibrium analysis? What relevant applications can be built on that theoretical basis? In answering these questions, we share with the canonical Sraffian literature the assumption of many industries which earn zero net profits, have input–output relations and have some inputs in common. As compared with that literature, however, we pay more attention to the presence of many primary inputs and less attention to the presence of a positive and variable rate of interest. We also lean towards the conventional description of production by assuming in most of the book twice-differentiable cost functions and U-shaped average cost curves; we do this simply in order to make it clear that our findings do *not* derive from the rejection of these conventional assumptions.

Our search for an elementary 'sufficient reason' (to use one of Sraffa's favourite phrases) explaining why the law of demand referred to an individual firm is a crude representation of reality led us to reconsider, in the light of our findings, a long tradition of mainstream literature, including the so-called long-run theory of the firm mentioned in the Preface. A microeconomic analysis of production which was less partial than that implied by the conventional demand and supply curves surfaced many times and in many different ways in a vast literature, owing to the fact that a shock hitting the industry can hardly exhaust its effect by changing just one price.

Despite the frequent simplifications in textbooks and in applications, the theory of multi-input use by the firm and the industry is extremely varied and rich. One might even question the existence of single 'laws' of input demand or of output supply: different waves of studies specified the *ceteris paribus* stipulation, the relationship between the firm and the industry, and that between the industry and the economy in different ways, according to different judgements as to which indirect, collateral effects may reasonably be ignored.

The microeconomics of production developed in London and Chicago at the end of the 1930s (Hicks, 1937, 1939; Allen, 1938; Mosak, 1938; also Samuelson, 1947, had been drafted at the end of the 1930s) refined a strict partial equilibrium method as a sensitivity analysis of productive choices in reaction to an individual price change; it also adopted a bottom-up conception of the industry in which the equilibrium of the firm was completely independent from that of the industry. The resulting analytical kernel, so simple and elegant, has been very powerful and influential in the subsequent decades – becoming indeed *the* fundamental tool of partial equilibrium analysis.

Yet that analytical kernel by no means exhausted the variety of questions addressed before, during and after this sudden upsurge of studies. The short-run relationships between input demand and the output market (the so-called 'derived demand' theorized by Marshall and Pigou) were analysed, for instance, by Hicks (1932), Allen (1938) and by later authors such as Saving (1963), Winch (1965) and Heiner (1982). The long-run tendency to zero net profits (or uniform normal profits) due to competitive forces – which featured so prominently in both the classical and the early neoclassical economists – was (re-)introduced against the background of the Hicks–Mosak–Samuelson theory by such authors as Ferguson and Saving (1969), Bassett and Borcherding (1970a), Silberberg (1974), Braulke (1984, 1987), Chavas and Cox (1997); see also Steedman (1998).

These contributions theorized their own input use–input price relationships, involving a specific list of what was given and what changed along with an 'original' price change. It perhaps did not aid clarity that these different relationships have all been called 'input demand curves', like that of the conventional theory.

No less varied are the analyses under the heading of an 'output supply curve'. The old Marshallian theory of supply incorporated many connections between an industry's output level and the supply prices of a variety of inputs and outputs (e.g. Marshall, 1920, pp. 371, 415; Pigou, 1928; Harrod, 1930). Within this broad tradition, we find different supply curves, each involving that many prices changed at once, as in Barone (1992 [1894]), Robinson (1941), Viner (1953), Samuelson (1971).

All these contributions are good examples of the wisdom of Schumpeter's remark that there is no sharp borderline between partial and general equilibrium methods (Schumpeter, 1954, pp. 990–98). They also confirm how far-reaching were Sraffa's famous 1925 and 1926 articles, pointing precisely to the fact that a movement along an upward-sloping supply curve involves a change in many prices; equally far-reaching was his research programme on the 'production of commodities by means of commodities', initiated in 1927, which implied long-run price interdependence outside any rigid scheme of either partial or general equilibrium.

This book reflects our own judgement about the connections between the firm, its industry and other industries that no micro analysis, we think, should ignore. An aspect on which we particularly insist is the great importance of intermediate inputs. We completely agree with the 'long-run theory of the firm' on the fact that a (nominal) change in a wage rate determines, by long-run adjustments in the industry, also a (nominal) change in the output price; but it affects in a like degree the prices of other commodities too, including perhaps the produced commodity inputs of the firm/industry under consideration. All such effects must be taken into account simultaneously. We also insist on the presence of a variety of primary inputs, which are taken to be either land and labour, as in much theoretical literature, or different kinds of labour, as in many applications.

An outline of the book

Chapter 1 introduces the reader to our definition of a full industry equilibrium (FIE) and to the general properties of an FIE comparative statics. We also make it transparent how our FIE analysis relates to both the mainstream 'long-run theory of the firm' and the Sraffian 'long-period theory of production'. In the next chapter we lay some analytical foundations of FIE with reference to a hypothetical isolated industry, as if all inputs could be primary and industry-specific. We first present the main analytical findings of the 1970s long-run theory of the firm; our main reference here is Silberberg's (1974) 'dual' version based on the firm's minimum-average cost-function. The only refinement that we make to this version consists in shedding full light on the underlying structure of relative prices; to say that a parametric increase in an input price is accompanied by an endogenous increase in the output price is, in a sense, to remain on the surface of the phenomena brought about by competition, the deeper roots consisting of a changing relative price structure. Our shift of emphasis also paves the way to further developments in which the change in relative input prices is more complex than that implicitly considered by the above-mentioned literature. Then, remaining in the simple context of Chapter 2, we introduce some issues which were absent in that literature but which play a significant role in the rest of this book, notably the presence of produced inputs and of discontinuities in profit-maximizing input use. Concerning the first issue, the simple case of 'own input use' suffices to generate some peculiarities of produced input use (as opposed to primary input use) in relation to the input price; later chapters generalize the argument to more realistic multi-industry contexts. Concerning the second issue, we shall here step outside the traditional 'smoothness' assumption by admitting that the cost function may be *almost* everywhere twice-differentiable; this single modification is enough to generate significant qualitative changes in the input price–input use relationships, which, again, later chapters will place in the setting of more complex models. The appendices to Chapter 2 present two digressions from the main argument: one deals with some alternative concepts of Hicksian input substitution, while in the other we point out that some long-established results of trade theory are in fact examples of FIE analysis.

Most of the book, including Chapter 2, concentrates for simplicity on single-output firms/industries. Yet, as it can hardly be denied that firms are in fact generally multiproduct, we should at least indicate how our analysis can be extended to joint production; besides, both contestable markets theory and Sraffian theory have devoted much attention to this case. This is done in the starred Chapter 3*, which presents a full-length zero-net-profit comparative statics of multiproduct firms; we shall show that the case with one input and many outputs yields results which exactly mirror those for a multi-input, single-output firm and that some theorems of the long-run theory of the firm can indeed be generalized to the multiple-output, multiple-input case. We retain the isolated industry framework by assuming all *outputs* to be industry-specific, but it should not be too difficult for the reader to envisage the additional complications that non-disjoint groups of commodities would involve.

In the remaining chapters we revert to the single-output case. In Chapter 4 we place a particular industry into its wider industrial context, in which there are input-providing industries as well as industries which compete for the use of the same inputs, both primary and produced. All industries will be assumed to yield maximum net profits of zero. In short, the zero-net-profits comparative statics of a firm belonging to a certain industry should take into account an economy-wide adjustment which provokes a complex change in the structure of relative prices. In order to facilitate the analysis, we assume smooth cost functions, everywhere twice-differentiable, and the absence of input complementarities throughout this chapter. We consider the effect of two main shocks: a change in one primary input price relative to all the others and a change in the rate of interest (while the proportions between primary input prices remain constant); in both cases, *commodity* prices adjust relative to each other and relative to primary input prices, under the forces of competition. The main message of the chapter is that, irrespective of the shock considered, primary inputs and commodity inputs react very differently; the former obey the qualitative restrictions which would be predicted by conventional partial equilibrium analysis, the latter do not – and it is indeed very doubtful that any significant input use–input price relationship can be formulated for produced inputs.

Chapter 5 removes the assumption of everywhere-twice-differentiability and focuses mainly on *primary* input use per unit of gross output in an industry which has relations with other industries; in most of this chapter the rate of interest is assumed to be null. It is shown that labour use per unit of output in a particular industry may be positively related to the real wage; interestingly, this may happen even though we have a conventional inverse relationship at the semi-aggregate level of the vertically integrated sector. This is found in many different specifications of the industrial structure – whether Wicksellian, or of the 'corn-tractor' (Samuelson-Surrogate) variety, or characterized by general input–output relations. We remark that even a single 'jump' may undermine the regularity in primary input use that was obtained in Chapter 4. This finding is particularly relevant in all cases in which a small change in the structure of input prices prompts a change in the very nature of the commodity inputs that are used; the inputs included in some technologies and not in others will be referred to as 'on/off inputs'. The subtitle of Chapter 5, 'Some aftershocks from capital theory', may encourage the reader to find connections with the Sraffian critique of marginalist theory and, of course, it is not coincidental that we have employed a series of models which featured prominently in the famous capital theory debates. Our main interest here, however, is *not* in capital theory paradoxes as such, but in the general properties of FIE comparative statics, of which such paradoxes are, perhaps, simply a particular aspect.

The next three chapters are devoted to some applications of FIE analysis. A given price change can normally be traced back to a specific shock either in the industry under consideration or in other industries. In particular, we analyse some price effects of a change in taxation and productivity increase (exogenous changes in the 'terms of trade' are analysed in the second Appendix to Chapter 2). Our main endeavour will be to relate the industrial patterns of the two 'shocks' to the changing structure of relative prices and real wages, under the assumption that the relative wages of different kinds of labour remain constant; on the basis of our results, we provide a rational method for separating an observable change in a real input price into two components, one due to the direct impact of the shock, the other due to an induced change in relative wages.

As indicated above, our FIE analysis is intended to be a further step in a long theoretical evolution. Rather than supplementing each individual chapter with a series of footnotes on historical matters, we present a compact historical narrative in Chapter 9. Some general conclusions are set out in Chapter 10.

1 | Taking seriously the tendency to zero net profits

The tendency of firms to earn zero net (or 'pure', or 'extra') profits is a salient feature of a capitalist, market economy, for a firm can hardly make permanent losses, unless it is subsidized; nor can it indefinitely make net profits, unless it enjoys legal protection. The regulating effect of competition in a market regime tends to eliminate profits and losses in a variety of different cases. The traditional long-run theory of Wicksell (1934) [1901], Flux (1923) [1904], Edgeworth (1913) and Pigou (1928) tells us that free entry and exit at the margin of the market ensures that output prices are always such as to allow for maximum net profits equal to zero, there being numerous firms, each operating as a price taker at the bottom of its U-shaped long-run average cost curve. The limit-cost pricing theory originated by Bain (1956) predicts that the mere threat of entry may lead firms to set a price equal to average cost; the contestable markets theory of Baumol (1982) and Baumol et al. (1988) [1982] describes the industrial structure in terms of efficient firms earning zero net profits, the number of firms (perhaps only one) depending on the size of the market. Game theory (Tirole, 1988, pp. 209–11) tells us that, in oligopoly, price competition among the existing firms may lead to an equilibrium with properties similar to equilibria with free entry and exit (Bertrand equilibrium). Needless to say, finally, the early theorizations of the classical economists argued for the same tendency, in terms of inter-industry capital movements and vanishing deviations from a uniform rate of profit.

For very good reasons, then, the study of production under ideal conditions of vanishing net profits is a permanent item on the economist's agenda.

The long and multi-faceted theoretical work done in this field can perhaps be said to be conclusive concerning the characterizations of given equilibria, but it is certainly still incomplete and open to debate concerning their *comparative statics*.

Whatever the market context, a fundamental problem arises when we compare different equilibria of an individual firm. Any single shock disrupting a given equilibrium necessarily creates either profits or losses; in order that a new permanent equilibrium be reached, the original shock must therefore be accompanied by some compensating changes. For example, an exogenous reduction in the wage of one kind of labour (say, due to selective immigration) creates profit opportunities and must be accompanied, as time goes on and competition exerts its full effects, by either a reduction in the output price, or by an increase in the wage of another kind of labour, or by an increase in the interest rate, or by yet another change. It is not possible in this case to follow through the simple logic of the familiar partial equilibrium analysis, because there cannot be a parametric change in just one variable under a strict *ceteris paribus* stipulation. At least two variables must differ as between alternative zero-net-profits equilibria. Or to put it more formally, two distinct equilibria on the zero level set of a profit function (i.e. maximum profit as a function of prices) can never differ in just one price. Consequently, the traditional qualitative restrictions concerning choices in the new equilibrium, as compared to the old, should be entirely reconsidered. (Of course, *constancy* of net profits would be sufficient to create the same problem, but we shall always focus on constant *and zero* net profits.)

This book coordinates and takes further different strands of literature which have done this kind of comparative statics, aiming at a unified framework, able to identify the regularities (and lack thereof) of the 'final' reaction of a firm to a given shock, when market mechanisms have eliminated profit opportunities or losses throughout the system. Such a framework of analysis we call 'full industry equilibrium' (or FIE). It should be remarked from the outset that we focus on the *consequences* of processes leading to vanishing profits rather than on the processes themselves. We do not commit ourselves, therefore, to any specific context, or market structure, or competitive process. For brevity, however, the general context leading to null profits will be referred to as 'free competition' and the time within which null profits tend to prevail will be referred to as the 'long run'.

1.1 The long-run theory of the firm, the industry and the economy

A series of articles in the late 1960s and 1970s, mainly in the *American Economic Review* (including Ferguson and Saving, 1969; Bassett and Borcherding, 1970a; Portes, 1971; Silberberg, 1974; Panzar and Willig, 1978), criticized the comparative statics of the classical works of Allen (1938), Hicks (1939) and Samuelson (1947) on the ground of the 'inconsistency of holding output price constant in the face of changing costs through changing factor prices' (Silberberg, 1974, p. 734). They shaped the fundamentals of a proper long-run theory of the firm and very explicitly introduced a comparative statics that was 'less partial', so to speak.

Many results in this book can be considered as further generalizations and extensions of this long-run theory of the firm. Because it can hardly be denied that the older (and simpler) comparative statics still prevails in economics courses, textbooks and applications, a few words of introduction on this strand of literature may be in order. (A more complete narrative of the making of this literature is presented in Chapter 9; its main formal results are discussed in Chapter 2.)

The topic which first aroused interest in the 'new' comparative statics was the long-run scale adjustment of the firm in the face of an exogenous increase in an input price. The older results were based on a distinction between 'normal' and 'inferior' (or 'regressive') inputs: in the former case, the marginal cost curve would shift upwards, thus leading to a reduction in the equilibrium output *at a constant output price*; in the latter case, counter-intuitively, marginal cost would diminish and output increase. The new theory extended the analysis to the *average cost curve* and proved that the minimum average cost always increases when an input price increases: if the firm was initially breaking even at the bottom of its average cost curve, then the shock would drive it out of business, unless the output price increased. A new permanent equilibrium is therefore at the bottom of the *new* average cost curve, at a correspondingly higher output price. But does this involve an increase or a diminution of the equilibrium output? It was proved that everything depends on the output elasticity of the input in question, not on its being normal or inferior (see Chapter 2 for details). This result became very valuable for the contestability theory (as far as single-output firms were concerned) because it provided a link between input prices and market structure (see Baumol *et al.*, 1988 [1982], chapter 6). It should be stressed that the endogenous adjustment in the output price is the *only* modification that the new theory introduced; the other assumptions, such as differentiability everywhere of the production (or cost) function, were borrowed from the older theory, the analysis being inherently local.

The long-run scale adjustment has an obvious effect on the 'absolute' input use and it has been proved that an increasing scale may ultimately lead to an increase in the use of the input whose price had increased. Such a positive relationship was initially presented as a 'curiosum' by Ferguson and Saving (1969, p. 782), but further reflection revealed that it is not a fluke (Silberberg, 1974, p. 735). This possibility *never* arose in the older theory, not even in the case of an inferior input (in which output increases): it requires that the new equilibrium be characterized by both a higher scale and a higher price. Ultimately, then, the failure in the predictive power of the 'law of demand' for inputs is due to the collateral increase in the product price. Likewise, by multiple price changes, the symmetry of the cross-price effects (the so-called reciprocity condition) also no longer holds.

In sharp contrast, with respect to 'relative' input use, i.e. *per unit of output*, the traditional relationships between input use and input price were confirmed: input use per unit of output was proved to be inversely related to its own price and the cross-price effects to be symmetrical. More formally, the Hessian of the indirect *average* cost function (whose terms are completely independent of the output price) was proved to have exactly the same properties as the ordinary cost function Hessian (again, see Chapter 2 for details). Assuming identical firms in a certain industry, the regularities in 'relative' input use were apt to characterize the industry itself and this was taken to be the important 'positive' result of the new theory: a rigorous zero-net-profits comparative statics gave the same qualitative results as the simpler partial-equilibrium comparative statics as far as the proportions of inputs to output (and to one another) were concerned. In this respect, the new theory strengthened the old one. (However, apart from the constant returns to scale case, one might wonder how often it is recalled that the traditional price–quantity relations for input use can be referred to the long run only in relative terms.)

It would be a mistake, however, to consider the new comparative statics merely as a refinement of the older one, because it completely recast the relationship between the firm and its economic environment and adopted a wider conception of competition, stressing a *mutual* dependence between each firm and the industry as a whole. 'Price-taking behaviour' lost its practical meaning because input and output prices were not all parameters and notably the output price was determined endogenously. The presence of many firms, very small relative to the industry, did not eliminate the necessity of examining such mutual relationships. The equilibrium of the firm depended on that of the industry no less than the latter depended on the former. It is not coincidental, therefore, that the long-run theory of the firm avoided the term 'perfect competition', but used rather the more neutral phrase 'free competition' or even the simple term 'competition'; this wider conception of competition reflected the reduced importance of the number of the firms forming the industry.

A second wave of studies in the 1980s and 1990s (Heiner, 1982; Braulke, 1984, 1987, Chavas and Cox, 1997) went further, by taking into account some relationships between the individual industry and the rest of the economy and by introducing market-clearing conditions in both output and input markets. Of course, in so doing it leaned towards general equilibrium analysis, even though the main focus remained on the regularities in the comparative statics of the individual firm and industry in the face of a parametric change; specifically, it identified restrictions which are sufficient for the traditional 'laws' of input demand and output supply to be confirmed in the wider framework.

Surprisingly, some direct linkages among industries, such as the use of common inputs and input–output relations, received far less attention. It is an obvious observation that one can find in practice no 'isolated industry' supplying to consumers a product which is made from 'labour and land' that are completely specific to that industry: primary factors can normally move from one industry to another and over half of the cost of production normally derives from the use of produced means of production. These are sufficient reasons for any shock to reverberate beyond the boundaries of a particular industry. By the tendency to uniform input prices across industries, an input price change originating in one industry is bound to affect all the industries using the same input (or inputs that are perfect substitutes for that input) and this determines a change in many output prices; a tax or technical progress in an input-*producing* industry naturally affects equilibrium in input-*using* industries; a change in the terms of trade (from the standpoint of a small open economy) often affects many industries at once; and so on. The sole tendency to vanishing net profits in all industries, in the presence of common and produced inputs, has a remarkable influence on the comparative statics of the firm and the industry. Do the results referred to above (and notably those concerning relative input use) still hold in this wider framework? When can we still count on the predictive power of the 'laws' of input demand and output supply? We aim in this book to answer such questions in the spirit of taking seriously the existence of mutual relations among the firm, the industry and the economy, under the forces of competition.

1.2 The long-period theory of production, the industry and the firm

The 1960s and 1970s also saw the development of a vast literature originated by the publication of Sraffa's *Production of Commodities by Means of Commodities* (1960), which formulated a rational long-period theory of production relating to the economy as a whole, based on the fundamental premise that competition tends to eliminate any divergence of profitability in the various industries. (An excellent technical and historical account is given in Kurz and Salvadori, 1995; a classical textbook is Pasinetti, 1977 [1975].) This literature, too, reached the general conclusion that different zero-extra-profit positions generally differ in a variety of input and output prices and that this leads to comparative statics results different from those implied by traditional partial equilibrium analysis.

The marginalist long-run theory of the firm and the Sraffian long-period theory of production were apparently developed in parallel, never crossing or even recognizing each other. Of course, this might be explained by the fact that they belonged to different and even opposing wider traditions. Nonetheless, we argue in this book that a cross-fertilization can be fruitful for both of them.

As the reader may recall, the aim of the Sraffian long-period theory of production was to reformulate and revive with modern emphases and tools the old classical and early neoclassical conception of an 'economic system characterized by a uniform rate of profit and uniform rates of remuneration for each particular kind of "primary" input in

the production process, such as different kinds of labor and natural resources' (Kurz and Salvadori, 1995, p. 1). Its primary object was
therefore the whole set of existing industries, not any individual firm: in
this perspective, the Sraffian literature analysed the attaining of upper
bounds in real wage, real rent, rate of profit combinations in the economic system as a whole, rather than decentralized profit-maximizing
behaviour; it determined the long-period structure of relative prices 'at
once', as a solution of a system of equations, rather than relying on
any average-cost pricing principle in each individual industry. Albeit
Sraffa's book generally makes no explicit assumption on the regime of
returns to scale, the literature that followed normally assumed strictly
constant returns (similarly to the 'activity analysis' approach of the
1950s), not firm-level U-shaped average cost curves.

Even on matters of terminology the two approaches diverged. The
long-period theory of production calls 'extra profit' what is called
'profit' by the long-run theory of the firm; and it calls 'profit' what
is called 'interest' in the neoclassical tradition; it also tends to avoid
the term 'equilibrium', in favour of the term 'position', thus stressing
its rejection of a 'market-clearing' view of the economy; a 'technique'
means a *combination* of economic activities used by *all industries taken
together* and not a single activity of an individual firm or industry; the
time in which free competition exerts its full effect is called the 'long
period', not the 'long run'; and so on.

Yet, these differences notwithstanding, the two theories share significant common ground.

To begin with a simple terminological issue, 'since the rate of interest
is assumed to be uniform throughout the economy, no profit (in the
Marshallian sense) means, in the language of the classicals [. . .], that
the rate of profit is uniform' (Kurz and Salvadori, 1995, p. 29). There
is no harm, then, in saying that in a Sraffian economy the firms earn
zero (net) profits and pay a uniform rate of interest on capital (and in
fact we find this terminology even in some contributions to the Sraffian tradition). Second, and more importantly, in a given long-period
position of the economic system, cost minimization by each firm is
implied by wage maximization at any given rate of profit (interest)
(cf. Kurz and Salvadori, 1995, theorem 5.5, pp. 145–46): to say that
in a long-period position the economy is always on its real wage–rate
of profit/interest frontier is just another way of saying that the firms
in all industries minimize average cost and are led by competition to

average cost pricing. Of course, these average costs are interdependent and no one of them can be determined without reference to the others; nonetheless, it remains true that in a long-period position the *maximum* (net) profit in each industry is equal to zero. *This* is the critical condition to be satisfied both in a Sraffian long-period position and in a marginalist long-run equilibrium of the firm. It should be stressed that this condition alone is responsible for the unconventional comparative statics both of the long-run theory of the firm and of the Sraffian theory.

Market clearing would involve other aspects, such as the *number* of firms in the industry, which we need not consider in the comparative statics of the firm and in that of the industry as expressed in per unit of output terms. We may even, if we wish, clothe the Sraffian arguments in full marginalist dress assuming smooth, conventional microeconomic production functions, such as those of the constant elasticity of substitution (CES) variety and still reproduce some unconventional results (see Steedman, 2013 and Section 4.9 for details). Or we may with little consequence assume firm-level U-shaped average cost curves rather than strictly constant returns to scale.

The Sraffian analysis of the inverse relationship between real wages and the rate of interest (profit) and of the dependence of the long-run relative prices on the rate of interest *enriches* the long-run theory of the firm by developing it further. It makes it clear that the zero-net-profit condition inherently concerns the entire economy and not an individual industry in isolation; that many inputs of one industry are the outputs of others; that the same input (primary or produced) is normally employed in a variety of industries at a uniform price – all this provides a sufficient reason for the establishment of some fundamental linkages among prices, quite independently of consumer preferences and market-clearing conditions. (The multi-sector view of competition is certainly *not* an idiosyncratic aspect of the Sraffian literature, of course.) Another and somewhat symmetrical question is whether a fuller consideration of long-run (long-period) *microeconomic* equilibrium can also throw some further light on the Sraffian comparative statics and offer some new results.

The long-period theory of production often finds it useful to replace the set of actual industries with an equivalent set of hypothetical vertically integrated sectors, whose outputs are the net outputs of the various commodities (e.g. Kurz and Salvadori, 1995, p. 169). Because all the relevant relations among prices, wages and the interest rate can always be expressed more simply in terms of vertically integrated sectors, it is indeed quite natural to consider them as a reduced-form, 'as if' transformation of the actual industries. For instance, if the rate of interest is null, the input–output relations cancel each other out in vertically integrated sectors and the argument may run 'as if' only primary inputs were used. From a formal point of view, the minimum average costs in vertically integrated sectors can then be expressed as functions of primary input prices alone.

Such a reduced form of the equality between prices and minimum average costs, useful as it may be on analytical grounds, nonetheless conceals some relevant aspects of reality, because actual choices are made in actual industries, not in vertically integrated sectors: in order to know the reason *why* a certain shock provokes effects in vertically integrated sectors, one has to trace back these effects from this 'semi-aggregated' level to the proper microeconomic level. Think, for instance, of an excise tax on a polluting material, or of a productivity increase in the production of ICT tools: they will naturally affect actual industries by modifying (directly and indirectly) some produced input prices and we may examine, by applying microeconomic reasoning, how this change affects industrial choices. By contrast, with reference to a vertically integrated sector, in which the prices of produced inputs do not appear explicitly, microeconomic theory would give us no guidance as to the reason why some changes originating in actual industries have taken place.

Similar reasoning can be referred to a change in the rate of interest, which features prominently in the Sraffian literature. Denoting by i the rate of interest and by f_j the profit function of firms belonging to industry j, the null-profit condition can be expressed, in obvious notation, by the equation $f_j(\mathbf{p}, \mathbf{w}, i) = 0$. Solving for $\mathbf{p}$, we have $f_j(\mathbf{p}\,(\mathbf{w}, i),\ \mathbf{w}, i) = 0$: using some well-known properties of profit functions, we can examine in detail the chain of causation from the rate of interest to industry-level choices. Using vertically integrated sectors, we immediately express the null-profit condition with $g_j(\mathbf{w}, i) = 0$ and go straight to the real wage–rate of interest frontier (in terms of commodity j), which is no doubt a highly important construction; however, we lose sight of the precise *microeconomic* reactions leading to certain changes in the *total* use of primary and produced inputs. In synthesis, by replacing the actual industries with vertically integrated sectors we lose some information: *both* points of view should therefore be taken into account.

A nuanced comparative statics of actual industries, therefore, helps to explain the microeconomic rationale of the Sraffian unconventional results, thus bridging a gap between the long-run theory of the firm and the long-period theory of production. However, it can go even further: there might be unconventional industrial phenomena which escaped the attention of the long-period theory of production because they are consistent with perfectly conventional outcomes at the level of the vertically integrated sectors: Chapter 5 shows that this is indeed the case.

1.3 Full industry equilibrium

The common ground of the long-run theory of the firm and the long-period theory of production – that firms make zero net profits in equilibrium – is also shared by a variety of other approaches, as we have seen at the beginning of the chapter. However, it was mainly these two theories that, each in its own way, worked out a proper null-profits comparative statics analysis stressing the differences from conventional partial equilibrium; taken together, they therefore constitute the natural theoretical background of the present book. We aim to shed more light on the microeconomics of industry equilibrium when there is an economy-wide tendency to vanishing net profits, claiming that this tendency alone provides a sufficient reason for a series of results (of either a positive or a negative nature) to hold. This may be a useful building block common to many overall theories.

The distinction between a short-run and a long-run industry equilibrium, the latter being characterized by zero net profits, is of course a *locus classicus* of many textbooks; comparisons between distinct long-run equilibria are typically focused on a change in the number of firms brought about by a change in output demand, in a regime of free entry and exit (e.g. Mas-Colell *et al.*, 1995, pp. 340–41); far less attention, if any, is devoted to other shocks, which modify the long-run equilibrium of the individual firm, independently of any effect on the number of the firms. It is with just such other shocks that we shall be particularly concerned.

The concept of a full industry equilibrium which will be developed in this book needs some preliminary discussion.

Knut Wicksell, in his *Lectures on Political Economy*, called 'Full Equilibrium' for a firm a situation in which the firm operates at an optimum scale minimizing its average cost and selling its output at a price equal to this minimum average and to marginal cost (Wicksell, 1934 [1901], p. 130). In his understanding, equilibrium is 'full' when not only does each firm attain the maximum possible profit in given market circumstances, but also such circumstances have been shaped by the forces of competition and this maximum profit is equal to zero. Wicksell had in mind a firm which is very small relative to the industry, so that his conception of a 'Full Equilibrium' in fact is in harmony with the long-run theory of Flux, Edgeworth, Pigou and Viner.

We borrow Wicksell's terminology, but widen its scope. As already said, a null-profit equilibrium can be attained in industries formed by a small number of firms and not even freedom of entry and exit is necessary. We also emphasize the presence of multiple industries.

By 'full industry equilibrium' we mean *any situation in which the firms forming a particular industry make maximum net profits of zero. When there is more than one industry, all firms must be in this situation.*

We assume that all firms belonging to an industry are identical, as in a symmetrical Bertrand equilibrium. This is not to deny that firm heterogeneity is an important aspect of reality, of course; we simply concentrate on other aspects, in the spirit of what Spence once wrote about contestability theory: 'It is neither fair nor reasonable to require microeconomic models to capture all relevant aspects of reality. No model that is tractable and informative does' (Spence, 1983, p. 982). In the same spirit, we ignore any possible external economies or diseconomies. We are *not* concerned, therefore, with the equilibrium *number* of firms forming the industry or with the industry-level absolute output and absolute input use: all this depends in a complex way on the formation of output demand, which we do not seek to analyse. In our study, 'industry equilibrium' is by no means a synonym of 'market clearing' and we concentrate on the properties of equilibrium which are independent of the size of the market. Our analysis of the firm, therefore, immediately involves some conclusions on the *proportions* among inputs and output in the industry.

1.4 Comparing full industry equilibria

Paul Samuelson, in his 1970 Nobel Laureate Memorial Lecture, regarded a partial equilibrium downward-sloping input demand curve as an example of the 'maximum principles of analytical economics' in which 'commonsense and advanced mathematics happen to agree' (Samuelson, 1972, p. 253). Both in that lecture and in his *Foundations* he stressed that this crucial property can be established very generally for either infinitesimal or discrete parametric changes in prices and quite independently of the specific technology characterizing the firm. For example, let A and B denote two distinct equilibria having the same output level; it is assumed that at prices A the choices B are available and conversely. The sole assumption of cost minimization involves

$$\sum w_i^A X_i^A \leq \sum w_i^A X_i^B \tag{1.1}$$

$$\sum w_i^B X_i^B \leq \sum w_i^B X_i^A \tag{1.2}$$

where w_i is an input price and X_i is an input quantity.

If we define $\Delta w_i = (w_i^B - w_i^A)$, $\Delta X_i = (X_i^B - X_i^A)$, it follows from (1.1) and (1.2) that

$$\sum \Delta w_i \Delta X_i \leq 0 \tag{1.3}$$

which is Samuelson's 'generalized substitution theorem'. No theory of the cost-minimizing firm can ever violate this theorem. Accordingly, no comparison of FIE can contradict (1.3); all of our results are therefore perfectly consistent with it. At the same time, a downward-sloping input demand curve (conditional on a given output and all other prices) is no doubt a logical consequence of (1.3): if an input price changes, *all others remaining constant*, we know for sure that $\Delta w_i \Delta X_i \leq 0$.

Allowing for output to differ as between equilibria, inequalities (1.1) and (1.2) can be further generalized. The sole assumption of profit maximization implies

$$p^A Q^A - \sum w_i^A X_i^A \geq p^A Q^B - \sum w_i^A X_i^B \tag{1.1$'$}$$

$$p^B Q^B - \sum w_i^B X_i^B \geq p^B Q^A - \sum w_i^B X_i^A \tag{1.2$'$}$$

where (p, Q) are the output price and quantity (assuming a single output, for simplicity), which implies

$$\Delta p \Delta Q - \sum \Delta w_i \Delta X_i \geq 0 \tag{1.3$'$}$$

A strict partial equilibrium interpretation of (1.3′), in which *only one price changes at a time*, provides the familiar qualitative restrictions on the output supply curve and the input demand curves: $\Delta p \Delta Q \geq 0$, $\Delta w_i \Delta X_i \leq 0$.

Yet, is this a significant inference from the theorem? Does an increase, say, in one input price not also trigger an increase in the output price to keep profit equal to zero? The long-run theory of the firm argued that it does. Taking this adjustment into account, inequality (1.3′) still holds, of course, but determines the sign of neither $\Delta p \Delta Q$ nor $\Delta w_i \Delta X_i$. Further analysis is required.

In fact we can say very little, in general, even about input use *per unit of output*. To see this, let us first notice that no choice concerning input use can ever depend on the mere metric of input and output prices; thus, we may sensibly set $p^A = p^B = 1$ and define w_i as an 'output-deflated' or 'real' input price. Moreover, setting $x_i^{A,B} = (X_i^{A,B}/Q^{A,B})$ we can re-write (1.1′) and (1.2′) as

$$\sum w_i^A x_i^A \leq \sum w_i^A x_i^B \tag{1.1''}$$

$$\sum w_i^B x_i^B \leq \sum w_i^B x_i^A \tag{1.2''}$$

yielding, of course

$$\sum \Delta w_i \Delta x_i \leq 0 \tag{1.3''}$$

Now, if profits are null in both equilibria, we must impose the further condition

$$\sum w_i^A x_i^A = 1 = \sum w_i^B x_i^B \tag{1.4}$$

Setting only one non-null Δw_i in (1.3″) involves *ipso facto* violating (1.4); for if $w_i^B > w_i^A$, then $\sum w_i^B x_i^B > \sum w_i^A x_i^A$, by (1.1″); conversely, if $w_i^B < w_i^A$, then $\sum w_i^B x_i^B < \sum w_i^A x_i^A$, by (1.2″). The only way to use (1.3″) when (1.4) holds is to include both a positive Δw_i and a negative Δw_j, but then no general rule for signing $\Delta w_i \Delta x_i$ is available.

The same kind of problem arises, of course, when we limit our attention to infinitesimal changes and to the local properties of equilibrium. Let us assume for simplicity strictly constant returns to scale and let $c(\mathbf{w})$ be the unit cost function of a certain firm, homogeneous of degree one and twice-differentiable. The cost function Hessian, $\mathbf{H}$, is negative semidefinite, thus yielding $(\mathbf{dw} \cdot \mathbf{H} \cdot \mathbf{dw}^T) \leq 0$. However, by

Shephard's lemma $\mathbf{H} \cdot \mathbf{dw}^T = \mathbf{dx}$; hence

$$\mathbf{dw} \cdot \mathbf{dx} \leq 0 \qquad\qquad (1.3''')$$

Under FIE, however, we also have $c(\mathbf{w}) = 1$ and hence

$$\mathbf{dw} \cdot \mathbf{x} = 0 \qquad\qquad (1.5)$$

If only one input price could change, then we would have $(dx_i/dw_i) = (\partial^2 c/\partial x_i^2) \leq 0$, but this assumption violates (1.5): under FIE (dx_i/dw_i) is in fact a weighted sum of terms in the Hessian, using the (dw_j/dw_i) ratios as weights.

It should be noted, however, that, with only two inputs, if w_1 rises then $x_1/x_2 = X_1/X_2$ will certainly fall. Less-conventional conclusions will only begin to emerge with at least three inputs, as will be seen in the rest of the book. It hardly needs to be added that the case of three or more inputs is the only one that really matters.

The FIE comparative statics is therefore more 'inclusive' – and yields less definite results – than a strict partial equilibrium comparative statics. Many things, including the price ratios, depend on the characteristics of the overall economic system within which an individual firm and industry operates, as well as on the specific shock which is examined. In this book we present an orderly sequence of different specifications of the economic system and of different shocks, aiming both to coordinate previous knowledge and to offer new results.

1.5 Concluding remarks

Samuelson's 'generalized substitution theorem' offers no guide to the comparative statics of firms which earn zero net profits both before and after a shock: albeit perfectly correct, it is, alas, of little use in a long-run competitive context. The familiar inference from the theorem – that an input use is inversely related to its price – has in fact been proved to be violated both by the long-run theory of the firm and by the Sraffian long-period theory of production (as considered from the standpoint of an individual industry). A serious long-run analysis of the input price–input use relationship should both be consistent with the theorem and seek regularities (if any) other than the conventional 'law of demand'. Such an analysis can and should draw on a series of elements consistently (although independently) developed by both strands of literature.

2 | An isolated industry

The tendency to zero net profits under free competition affects industry equilibrium through a variety of channels which normally involve many industries. It is convenient, however, to study these various channels initially within the context of an individual industry, as if just one good were produced in the economy. In fact, the modern studies of the firm in long-run equilibrium began with what we may call an 'isolated industry', ignoring all the potential linkages among industries, while preserving, of course, the economy's fundamental competitive properties.

We, too, start from this simple case, along the lines of Ferguson and Saving (1969), Bassett and Borcherding (1970a, 1970b, 1970c), Silberberg (1974) and Panzar and Willig (1978). We first formulate their approach making use of duality theory, which simplifies matters and makes the underlying structure of relative prices more transparent: after characterizing full industry equilibrium (Section 2.1), we provide an illustration by means of a simple example (Section 2.2) and then discuss the FIE comparative statics (Section 2.3). We confirm, of course, the main findings concerning input use in relation to input price, when the output price adjusts in order to restore zero-net-profit conditions. However, the output price is not the only possible compensating variable in the long-run adjustment and we extend the analysis to all possible relative price changes.

In Sections 2.4 and 2.5, we provide a link between the structure of relative prices and each price expressed in a general numéraire and clarify the meaning of an FIE relation between input use and the input's own price (or between output and price), comparing it to a conventional input demand (or output supply) curve.

In these preliminary sections we make no distinction between primary and produced inputs.

The next two sections concern some significant economic circumstances in which the change in the price structure is not of the simple kind considered by the above-mentioned literature and we do now distinguish between primary and produced inputs. As a prelude to Chapter 4, Section 2.6 focuses on an industry whose inputs include its own product along with labour and land. Section 2.7 presents an application concerning the effects of a parametric fall in the real price of a produced input (say, computing power), accompanied by a change in relative wages (as in the 'Job Polarization' literature); in this section we assume Hicksian complementarity between two inputs.

In Section 2.8 we drop the conventional assumption that the cost function is twice-differentiable everywhere and admit that a small change in prices may determine a qualitative change in the input mix, in which certain produced inputs completely replace others; we refer to such inputs as 'on/off inputs'. Section 2.9 concludes.

Our main argument assumes that all inputs are substitutes for one another (with the exception of Section 2.7). We initially adopt the familiar definition of Hicksian substitution subject to a constant output and then switch to a variable-output definition, which fits our FIE context better. A mathematical and historical coordination of alternative definitions of substitution is presented in Appendix 1. In a second appendix we note that the central theorems of the Heckscher–Ohlin–Samuelson (HOS) theory of international trade are in fact well worked-out cases of FIE analysis.

2.1 Full industry equilibrium

Let $C(Q, \mathbf{w})$ be the cost function, which is increasing and linear homogeneous in the input prices, $\mathbf{w}$ (no matter at this stage whether they are primary or produced) and increasing in the output, Q, displaying U-shaped average cost curves. Until Section 2.8, it is also assumed to be twice-differentiable everywhere in all variables. All firms, both incumbents and potential entrants, are identical. The useful property of C – Shephard's lemma – is that its partial derivative with respect to an input price gives the cost minimizing use of that input (X_i):

$$\frac{\partial C}{\partial w_i} = X_i(Q, \mathbf{w}) \tag{2.1}$$

The second-order partial derivatives $\partial C^2 / \partial w_i \partial Q$ and $\partial C^2 / \partial w_i \partial w_j$ $i \neq j$ are all assumed to be positive, so that all inputs are 'normal' and Hicksian substitutes (in the familiar constant-output definition; more on this in Appendix 1). It goes without saying that $\partial C^2/\partial w_i^2 \leq 0$ and that, under profit maximization, $\partial^2 C/\partial Q^2 > 0$.

It is important to note from the outset that the firm unambiguously has U-shaped average cost curves only when this is so *at all possible* vectors of input prices, as we assume to be the case. Otherwise some vectors **w** may be unable to sustain an FIE: in the absence of external diseconomies (or economies), there could be a continuing incentive for new firms to enter the industry (or for incumbents to leave it). In order to avoid this complication, it might seem tempting to assume a homothetic cost function, $g(Q)\gamma(\mathbf{w})$, as in Shephard (1970, p. 93). However, this would exclude any dependence of the optimum scale on relative input prices, which is an important aspect of reality. A cost function of the kind $a(\mathbf{w})Q^{1/2} + b(\mathbf{w})Q + c(\mathbf{w})Q^{3/2}$ always has the desired properties, like the more familiar cubic $a(\mathbf{w})Q - b(\mathbf{w})Q^2 + c(\mathbf{w})Q^3$, provided that the three functions of **w** satisfy some restrictions (see the example below).

Under the present assumptions, at given input prices, there exists one and only one point of minimum average cost. Its coordinates are determined by the usual condition of equality between marginal and average cost:

$$\frac{\partial C(Q, \mathbf{w})}{\partial Q} = \frac{C(Q, \mathbf{w})}{Q}, \quad Q > 0 \tag{2.2}$$

or

$$Q\left(\frac{\partial C(Q, \mathbf{w})}{\partial Q}\right) = C(Q, \mathbf{w}) \tag{2.2'}$$

which we may interpret as displaying 'local constant returns to scale'.

We can solve (2.2) for Q, obtaining a function of input prices, $Q(\mathbf{w})$. This function is homogeneous of degree zero, because both marginal and average costs are homogeneous of degree 1 in input prices.

Substituting $Q(\mathbf{w})$ into the average cost function, one obtains the so-called indirect average cost function (cf. Silberberg, 1974, p. 735):

$$c(\mathbf{w}) = \frac{C(Q(\mathbf{w}), \mathbf{w})}{Q(\mathbf{w})} \tag{2.3}$$

It will be immediately clear that $c(\mathbf{w})$ is homogeneous of degree 1 'as if' it were an ordinary unit cost function for firms characterized by strict constant returns to scale. Most importantly, Shephard's lemma still holds, as is readily found by differentiating (2.3), so that

$$\frac{\partial c(\mathbf{w})}{\partial w_i} = \frac{X_i}{Q}$$

In order to simplify notation, let $(X_i / Q) \equiv x_i$. If one is interested *only* in the relationship between input prices and input use per unit of output – which is certainly a very interesting and sufficiently complex topic apt to characterize the industry as a whole – then the 'indirect average cost function' can be a very convenient starting point. However, a complete description of the equilibrium of the firm naturally requires an explicit consideration of the output level and of 'absolute' input use.

Denoting by p the output price, competition implies:

$$p = c(\mathbf{w}) \tag{2.4}$$

Equations (2.1)–(2.4) are a formulation of the 1970s long-run theory of the firm. They define what we call an FIE of the firm and the isolated industry.

Because only relative prices matter, we may divide both sides of (2.4) by p, for instance, to obtain

$$1 = c\left(\frac{1}{p}\mathbf{w}\right) \tag{2.4'}$$

where $(1/p)\mathbf{w}$ is the vector of 'real' input prices, in terms of the industrial output. Equation (2.4') defines a 'real input price surface' which shows, by definition, all the real input prices consistent with zero net profits. This makes it completely transparent that in an FIE an input price can increase in real terms only if at least one other real input price decreases: a shock which is not merely 'nominal' always involves a change in two or more real input prices and can be expressed as a movement across the real input price surface. A level set of a cost function is sometimes called a 'factor price frontier'. However, because this term has been used with several different meanings (e.g. Samuelson, 1962, p. 195; Diewert, 1971, p. 495; McFadden, 1978, p. 89), we prefer, in the interest of clarity, to use our own terminology.

We may note finally that dividing both sides of (2.4) by w_i the 'real' price of input i, (w_i/p), can also be expressed as a parametric function of the $(n-1)$ *relative* input prices. We shall return to this in Sections 2.4 and 2.5.

2.2 An example

Let us consider a simple example of firms employing only two inputs. Let their common cost function be

$$C(Q, w_1, w_2) = \left(aw_1^t w_2^{1-t}\right) Q - 2b\sqrt{w_1 w_2}\, Q^2 + \left(dw_1^{1-t} w_2^t\right) Q^3$$

It will be clear that with $0 < t < 1$ and $4b^2 < 3ad$, there are U-shaped average cost curves for all input prices. Moreover, it is easily shown that the inputs are normal if $b^2 < 3adt(1-t)$. (The two restrictions on b^2 coincide when $2t = 1$ and $C(\ )$ is thus homothetic.)

At the point of minimum average cost, we have

$$Q = \frac{b}{d} \left(\frac{w_1}{w_2}\right)^{t-0.5} \tag{2.5}$$

Substituting Q into C/Q gives

$$c(w_1, w_2) = \left(\frac{ad - b^2}{d}\right) w_1^t w_2^{1-t} \tag{2.6}$$

which is the 'indirect average cost function'.

The *maximum* profit of the firm is thus null when

$$p = \left(\frac{ad - b^2}{d}\right) w_1^t w_2^{1-t} \tag{2.7}$$

All potential long-run prices are constrained to satisfy (2.7). The obvious observation is that, by homogeneity of degree 1 of both sides, the zero-net-profit condition is never affected by a mere change in the metric of prices; nor is the critical output in (2.5). Everything depends on relative prices, as in any genuine microeconomic argument. Now we see at once that in the long run no pair of relative prices can be arbitrary. In fact, dividing both sides of (2.7) by p, we get

$$1 = \left(\frac{ad - b^2}{d}\right) \left(\frac{w_1}{p}\right)^t \left(\frac{w_2}{p}\right)^{1-t} \tag{2.8}$$

the real input price surface, which is here simply a curve. For given technical conditions, there cannot be a long-run increase in, say, (w_1/p) without a fall in (w_2/p) and, as we said above, an exogenous change which has real effects on the industry involves either a movement along the curve or a shift of the curve itself (as in the case of a reduction in the values of *a* and/or *d* due to technical progress). By (2.5) and (2.8), then, everything is determined on the basis of one relative price only, say (w_1/w_2), which (in the absence of any definite context) we may treat as a parameter. Each point on the curve and the chosen $(X_1, X_2; Q)$ combination can therefore be expressed in relation to (w_1/w_2). As a prelude to Section 2.5, it may also be noted that if one takes $(p/w_1^{\alpha_1} w_2^{\alpha_2})$ as the 'input price deflated' (Shephard, 1970, p. 95) price of the output (with $\alpha_1 + \alpha_2 = 1$) then, from (2.5) and (2.7), whether Q is positively or negatively related to this real output price depends on the sign of $(t - \alpha_1)(t - 0.5)$. It thus depends on both technical conditions (t) and the arbitrary choice of the output price deflator (α_1).

By (2.5), the output level rises or falls as (w_1/w_2) rises according to whether $t > 0.5$ or $t < 0.5$. The case in which $t = 0.5$ is worth noting: as mentioned above, the cost function is now *homothetic* and output at the point of minimum average cost is determined by Shephard's input price deflated curve $aQ - 2bQ^2 + dQ^3$, quite independently of input prices. In this case, the turning point from increasing to diminishing returns corresponds to a specific isoquant and the relative input price simply affects the position on that isoquant. Homotheticity simplifies matters very much, by separating, so to speak, the choice concerning the scale of output from that concerning the method of production, and this explains why it recurs so often in applications. However, it is certainly a very special case, which should only be used with full awareness of the real complexities which are hidden by it.

It may be helpful to represent the above argument diagrammatically. Figure 2.1 shows the real input price curve (2.8). Figure 2.2 (which supposes $t > 0.5$) shows the curves of average cost, relative to the FIE product price, corresponding to the points A and B in Figure 2.1. These curves are drawn in dotted lines to emphasize that only the points marked A and B – the minimum average cost points – are genuine FIE points. (At all other points on the curves the firms would make a loss.)

Turning now to input use, one has to differentiate the cost function with respect to input prices, thus obtaining, in the case of input 1

$$X_1 = \frac{\partial C}{\partial w_1} = ta \left(\frac{w_1}{w_2}\right)^{t-1} Q - b \left(\frac{w_1}{w_2}\right)^{-0.5} Q^2 + (1-t)d \left(\frac{w_1}{w_2}\right)^{-t} Q^3$$

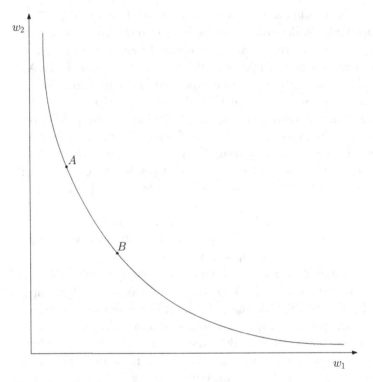

Figure 2.1 The real input price curve.

Substituting for Q from (2.5), one obtains

$$X_1 = bt\frac{(ad - b^2)}{d^2}\left(\frac{w_1}{w_2}\right)^{2t-1.5}$$

The use of input 1 is *positively* related to (w_1/w_2) when $t > 0.75$, because in this case the chosen output increases sufficiently to outweigh the effect of input substitution. This is an example of the 'curiosum' found by Ferguson and Saving (1969). The interested reader may verify that, likewise, the use of input 2 is positively related to (w_2/w_1) if $t < 0.25$: only within the range of ±0.25 around the homothetic value of 0.5 is t such that both inputs react to the relative input price in the conventional way.

The reader may find it instructive to consider how FIE varies with (w_1/w_2) in a figure with X_2 on the vertical axis and X_1 on the

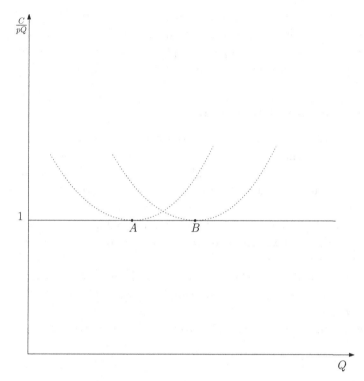

Figure 2.2 Two alternative FIE outputs.

horizontal one. It is easy to show that

$$\left(\frac{X_1}{t}\right)^{(0.25-t)} \left(\frac{X_2}{1-t}\right)^{(t-0.75)} = \frac{d}{\sqrt{b(ad-b^2)}}$$

It follows that

(a) if $0 < t < 0.25$ then Q, X_1 and X_2 all fall as (w_1/w_2) rises; moreover, $(d^2 X_2/d X_1^2) < 0$
(b) if $0.75 < t < 1$ then Q, X_1 and X_2 all increase as (w_1/w_2) rises; and $(d^2 X_2/d X_1^2) > 0$
(c) if $0.25 < t < 0.75$ then X_1 falls and X_2 increases as (w_1/w_2) rises; also $(d^2 X_2/d X_1^2) > 0$. The $X_2(X_1)$ curve thus looks like an isoquant but is, of course, no such thing, because Q is varying $(t \neq 0.5)$. If $0.25 < t < 0.50$ the $X_2(X_1)$ curve cuts each genuine isoquant from above to below as X_1 increases; if $0.50 < t < 0.75$ it cuts each genuine isoquant from below to above as X_1 increases.

After completing the story with the cases $t = 0.25$, $t = 0.5$ and $t = 0.75$, the reader will be well aware that many possibilities are open in FIE, even in the context of a simple example, and that they do not all match the patterns suggested by the usual partial analysis.

2.3 The comparative statics of FIE

The main message of the example just considered is that, in a generic industrial context where competition eliminates positive, or negative, net profits, the relative prices, although 'given' to the firm, can by no means all be arbitrary. In the example only one relative price was free to change without destroying long-run equilibrium altogether and this generally had consequences for the comparative statics. We should now examine those consequences more generally in the presence of m inputs (and a single output).

It should be noted from the outset that our FIE comparative statics results are always expressed by differential quotients, not by simple 'curly derivatives'.

Differentiating (2.1), (2.2) and (2.4) totally, we obtain, respectively

$$dX_i = \sum_{j=1}^{m} \frac{\partial X_i}{\partial w_j} dw_j + \frac{\partial X_i}{\partial Q} dQ \qquad (2.9)$$

$$\frac{\partial^2 C}{\partial Q^2} dQ = \sum_{j=1}^{m} \left(1 - \frac{\partial X_i}{\partial Q} \frac{Q}{X_i}\right) x_i dw_i \qquad (2.10)$$

$$dp = \sum_{j=1}^{m} x_j dw_j \qquad (2.11)$$

Let w_i change and let the output price adjust to this change to keep profits equal to zero, all other input prices remaining constant. Equations (2.10) and (2.11) become, respectively

$$\frac{\partial^2 C}{\partial Q^2} dQ = \left(1 - \frac{\partial X_i}{\partial Q} \frac{Q}{X_i}\right) x_i dw_i$$
$$dp = x_i dw_i$$

We see at once that (dQ/dw_i) can be of either sign, depending on the output-elasticity of input i (cf. Silberberg, 1974, p. 738, theorem 4; see also Ferguson and Saving, 1969, p. 777, and Baumol *et al.*, 1988, pp. 154–55). Moreover, (dQ/dp), too, can be of either sign. This contrasts sharply with some conventional partial equilibrium results, involving a negative $(\partial Q/\partial w_i)$ (so long as input i is normal) and a positive $(\partial Q/\partial p)$ (cf. Mosak, 1938; Hicks, 1939; Samuelson, 1947).

Turning to the input response, we have from (2.9) and (2.10) that

$$\frac{dX_i}{dw_i} = \frac{\partial X_i}{\partial w_i} + \frac{1}{\partial^2 C/\partial Q^2} \frac{\partial X_i}{\partial Q} \left(1 - \frac{\partial X_i}{\partial Q} \frac{Q}{X_i}\right) x_i \qquad (2.12)$$

Once again, no general qualitative restrictions are available: the first addend on the right-hand side (rhs) is always negative but the second can easily be positive, depending on the output-elasticity of input i, and can outweigh the first term (cf. Ferguson and Saving, 1969, p. 782; and Silberberg, 1974, p. 737). It will be noted that in the case of a homothetic cost function, (2.12) reduces to $(dX_i/dw_i) = (\partial X_i/\partial w_i) < 0$ for every input. In general, however, the second term is negative for some inputs and positive for others, because $\sum(\partial X_i/\partial Q)w_i = \sum(X_i/Q)w_i$.

To effect a comparison with conventional partial equilibrium results, the overall effect (dX_i/dw_i) can be broken down into three parts: a negative own-price effect conditional on a constant output $(\partial X_i/\partial w_i)$; a negative output effect conditional on a constant output price, $-(\partial X_i/\partial Q)^2/(\partial^2 C/\partial Q^2)$; and a positive output effect associated with the adjustment of the output price to the new minimum average cost, $(\partial X_i/\partial Q)x_i/(\partial^2 C/\partial Q^2)$. Conventional partial equilibrium analysis concerns only the first and the second effects, which are always negative, irrespective of whether input i is normal or inferior (cf. Bear, 1965; more on this in Chapter 9).

When an increase in w_i is compensated, not by an increase in p, but by a fall in another input price, w_j, with $dw_j = -(x_i/x_j)dw_i$, (2.10) becomes

$$\frac{\partial^2 C}{\partial Q^2} dQ = \left(\frac{\partial X_j}{\partial Q} \frac{Q}{X_j} - \frac{\partial X_i}{\partial Q} \frac{Q}{X_i}\right) x_i dw_i$$

The qualitative change in the profit-maximizing output depends now on the difference between the output-elasticities of inputs j and i.

Substituting this dQ into (2.9) we obtain

$$\frac{dX_i}{dw_i} = \left(\frac{\partial X_i}{\partial w_i} - \frac{\partial X_i}{\partial w_j} \frac{x_i}{x_j}\right) + \frac{1}{\partial^2 C/\partial Q^2} \frac{\partial X_i}{\partial Q} \left(\frac{\partial X_j}{\partial Q} \frac{Q}{X_j} - \frac{\partial X_i}{\partial Q} \frac{Q}{X_i}\right) x_i$$

The own-price effect is now reinforced by the cross-price variation (so long as all inputs are Hicksian substitutes in the familiar definition), but we are still uncertain about the sign of (dX_i/dw_i): when the output-elasticity of input j is greater than that of input i, the use of input i can be positively related to its own price.

The qualitative difference between the case with a compensating change in the output price and the case with a compensating change in another input price vanishes when there are only two inputs, as the interested reader can easily confirm.

More generally, we can relate dQ and dX_i to any change in the structure of relative prices. Denoting by a 'hat' a proportional rate of change and making use of homogeneity properties, we can re-write (2.9) and (2.10) as

$$dX_i = -\sum_{j\neq i} \frac{\partial X_i}{\partial w_j} w_j(\hat{w}_i - \hat{w}_j) + \frac{\partial X_i}{\partial Q} dQ \qquad (2.9')$$

$$dQ = \frac{1}{\partial^2 C/\partial Q^2} \sum_{j\neq i} \left(\frac{\partial X_j}{\partial Q}\frac{Q}{X_j} - 1\right) w_j x_j(\hat{w}_i - \hat{w}_j) \qquad (2.10')$$

Substituting dQ into (2.9') we finally get

$$dX_i = -\sum_{j\neq i} \frac{\partial X_i}{\partial w_j} w_j(\hat{w}_i - \hat{w}_j) + \frac{\partial X_i/\partial Q}{\partial^2 C/\partial Q^2}$$

$$\times \sum_{j\neq i} \left(\frac{\partial X_j}{\partial Q}\frac{Q}{X_j} - 1\right) w_j x_j(\hat{w}_i - \hat{w}_j) \qquad (2.13)$$

It is left to the interested reader to verify how the two cases discussed above fit into (2.9'), (2.10') and (2.13) as special cases. The qualitative results concerning input use become more definite if the focus is shifted from 'absolute' inputs to inputs per unit of output. Differentiating the indirect average cost function (2.3) twice, we get

$$dx_i = \sum_{j=1}^{m} \frac{\partial x_i}{\partial w_j} dw_j \qquad (2.14)$$

Now everything is determined by the indirect-average-cost-function Hessian. By negative semi-definiteness, we immediately see that, if $dw_{j\neq i} = 0$ (and $dp = x_i dw_i$), then $(dx_i/dw_i) = (\partial x_i/\partial w_i) < 0$ (cf. Silberberg, 1974, corollary 2, p. 736). On the other hand, if $dp = 0 = dw_{s\neq i,j}$ and $dw_j = -(x_i/x_j)dw_i$, then $(dx_i/dw_i) = (\partial x_i/\partial w_i) - (\partial x_i/\partial w_j)(x_i/x_j)$. In order to reach definite results, it is convenient here to define substitution between inputs i and j as involving a positive sign of $(\partial x_i/\partial w_j)$, not of $(\partial X_i/\partial w_j)$. We see from (2.14) that input substitutability under such a definition ensures $(dx_i/dw_i) < 0$. The two definitions (in terms of 'absolute' or 'per unit of output' input levels) are clearly not independent of one another and their relationship is explored towards the end of Appendix 1.

An explicit consideration of relative prices provides a more general rule for signing dx_i. It is easy to see from (2.14) that

$$dx_i = -\sum_{j \neq i} \frac{\partial x_i}{\partial w_j} w_j (\hat{w}_i - \hat{w}_j) \tag{2.15}$$

Let $(\hat{w}_i - \hat{w}_j) > 0$ for all j, so that we can unambiguously say that the price of input i rises. If $(\hat{w}_i - \hat{w}_j)$ is uniform for all j then (2.15) reduces to $dx_i = (\partial x_i/\partial w_i)w_i(\hat{w}_i - \hat{w}_j)$, which indeed has a negative sign, whether or not i is a Hicksian substitute for every other input. If $(\hat{w}_i - \hat{w}_j)$, albeit always positive, is *not* uniform, then dx_i in (2.15) can be positive provided that there are complementarities defined in terms of some negative off-diagonal elements of the indirect-average-cost-function Hessian (see Section 2.7). Finally, it need hardly be added that in economic contexts in which the $(\hat{w}_i - \hat{w}_j)$ do not all have the same sign, dx_i cannot be signed a priori (see Section 2.6).

2.4 On the relationship between input use and input price

The above analysis suggests that there are three different kinds of relationship between input use by the individual firm and the input's own-price: (i) the proper partial equilibrium 'input demand curve', conditional on both a constant output price and a constant output level; (ii) a relationship conditional on a constant output price but allowing for profit-maximizing changes in the output level; and (iii) a relationship allowing for changes in both the output price and the output level, under the assumption of zero maximum profits. These successive relationships are characterized by an increasing inclusiveness and a diminishing determinateness, in the sense that fewer qualitative restrictions are available as one passes to 'less partial' contexts. The fact that they have all been called an 'input demand curve (or function)' (see, in order, Samuelson, 1947, p. 74; Mosak, 1938, p. 777; and Ferguson and Saving, 1969, p. 782; for further historical details the reader is referred to Chapter 9) does not aid clarity and we propose to limit that terminology to the first conception.

What is then the nature and significance of a $X_i(w_i)$ relationship under FIE?

Let us first remark that X_i depends on relative, not nominal, prices, as in Equation (2.13). It is regrettable that the received long-run theory of the firm formulated the input use–input price relationship in 'money' units (e.g. Ferguson and Saving, 1969, p. 779). Such a convention can be safely adopted with reference to a partial equilibrium 'input demand curve', where an input price changes at a given proportional rate relative to all other things (be it the output, other inputs or even 'money'). However, under FIE the modification in the structure of relative prices is rather complex and an input price change has no precise meaning unless the change in the whole structure of relative prices is explicated. Behind each of our equations displaying dw_i there were specific assumptions concerning other price changes. In order to clarify the significance of a $X_i(w_i)$ relationship we must always make fully transparent the connection between w_i, as expressed in a real numéraire, and the vector of relative prices.

In this and the next section we depart from our usual convention of expressing all prices in terms of the output and introduce a general numéraire formed by the m inputs and the product, $(\sigma_1, \ldots, \sigma_m, \sigma_0)$. The 'real' prices must now satisfy

$$1 = \sigma_1 w_1 + \cdots + \sigma_m w_m + \sigma_0 p \tag{2.16}$$

from which we obtain the 'real' w_i as a function of relative prices

$$w_i = \left(\sigma_1 \frac{w_1}{w_i} + \cdots + \sigma_i + \ldots + \sigma_m \frac{w_m}{w_i} + \sigma_0 \frac{p}{w_i} \right)^{-1} \tag{2.17}$$

Now a $X_i(w_i)$ curve (be it positively or negatively sloped) is meaningful *only if* all price ratios in (2.17) change in the same direction; otherwise one could manipulate the sign of dw_i (and of dX_i/dw_i) by mere choice of numéraire, thus making $X_i(w_i)$ a chimera, with properties entirely dependent on the theorist's whim. In Section 2.6 (and again in later chapters), we shall see that the price ratios in (2.17) may change in *opposite directions* when 'input i' is a produced input and that in this important case the economic theorist should attach no importance to the implied $X_i(w_i)$ relationships and should, rather, lay full stress on relations like (2.13) and (2.15). For a fuller discussion of numéraire problems concerning long-run input use–input price relations, the reader is referred to Opocher and Steedman (2009).

2.5 On a supposed relationship between long-run output and price

A change in the relative input prices determines both a change in the firm's long-run output, in accordance with (2.10), and a change in the output price, expressed in a numéraire, and one might see in this a significant long-run $Q(p)$ relationship. Unfortunately, the very slope of this curve in output-price space always depends on the choice of numéraire and is thus devoid of any theoretical substance. Manipulating (2.16) we obtain

$$p = \left(\sigma_1 \frac{w_1}{p} + \cdots + \frac{w_m}{p} \sigma_m + \sigma_0 \right)^{-1} \tag{2.18}$$

Between two distinct FIE, (w_i/p) increases for some i and falls for others, as can be seen from (2.4′) above; hence, we can always manipulate the sign of dp by mere choice of numéraire, while dQ remains determined by the change in relative input prices. The very sign of (dQ/dp) is thus arbitrary.

Notice that the same kind of problem can also be referred to an industry-level long-run $Q(p)$ relationship: FIE comparative statics presents no analogue to the partial equilibrium supply curve. In Section 9.6 we shall see that such a 'numéraire problem' surfaced in the literature on the long-run industry supply curve but never received proper attention; see also Opocher and Steedman (2008a).

2.6 Produced input use. A very simple case

The cost of production normally incorporates a substantial share of intermediate inputs. As a prelude to a more comprehensive analysis with many industries, it seems quite natural to introduce this fact by assuming that the industry's own product is used as an input, along with labour and land. The input prices are now (p, w, r), respectively; for simplicity, no interest is paid over and above the replacement price of the produced input.

If the indirect average cost function is $c(p, w, r)$ then FIE is here defined by

$$p = c(p, w, r)$$

The produced input use per unit of output, k, say, is of course given by

$$k = \frac{\partial c(p, w, r)}{\partial p}$$

We now ask how k changes as we move around the real wage–real rent frontier defined here by

$$1 = c(1, w/p, r/p)$$

(see Section 4.2 for more general discussion). Setting $p = 1$ for simplicity and denoting by (l, t), respectively, labour and land use per unit of output, we have

$$0 = l\,dw + t\,dr$$

and

$$dk = \frac{\partial^2 c}{\partial w\,\partial p}dw + \frac{\partial^2 c}{\partial r\,\partial p}dr$$

or

$$dk = \frac{\partial l}{\partial p}dw + \frac{\partial t}{\partial p}dr$$

It follows at once that

$$\frac{dk}{dr} = t\left(\frac{1}{t}\frac{\partial t}{\partial p} - \frac{1}{l}\frac{\partial l}{\partial p}\right)$$

The assumption that the produced input is a Hicksian substitute (using the definition based on the indirect-average-cost-function Hessian) for both labour and land does not enable one to determine the sign of (dk/dr). (Ironically, taking the produced input to be a substitute for one of the primary inputs but a complement to the other one would allow us to sign (dk/dr)). Nor does it establish whether $k(r)$ is monotonic or non-monotonic. To consider these matters further we consider two different forms of $c(p, w, r)$.

If the indirect average cost function is of the CES form *and* $p = c(p,w,r)$ always – that is we consider only FIE – then k is simply a constant, taking exactly the same value at every point on the real wage-real rent frontier, despite the changes in the three input-price ratios.

There is more to be said, however, when such a function is of the quadratic square root (QSR) form (as in Diewert, 1971) and

$$p = c() = \kappa p + \lambda w + \tau r + 2\alpha\sqrt{pw} + 2\beta\sqrt{pr} + 2\gamma\sqrt{wr}$$

(We take (α, β, γ) to be positive, so that all three pairs of inputs are Hicksian substitutes. We also take (κ, λ, τ) to be non-negative and, of course, $\kappa < 1$.) Here

$$k = \kappa + \alpha\sqrt{w} + \beta\sqrt{r} \quad \text{if } p = 1$$

It can now be shown that

$$A(k - \kappa)^2 + 2(k - \kappa) - (1 - \kappa) = 0$$

where

$$A \equiv \frac{(\lambda + 2\gamma\sqrt{z} + \tau z)}{(\alpha + \beta\sqrt{z})^2} \quad \text{and} \quad z \equiv \frac{r}{w}$$

It is obvious that k is inversely related to A, so that everything now turns on how A is related to z, the rent–wage ratio. A little investigation leads to the result that (dk/dz) has the same sign as

$$\alpha\sqrt{w}((\lambda/\alpha^2) - (\gamma/\alpha\beta)) + \beta\sqrt{r}((\gamma/\alpha\beta) - (\tau/\beta^2))$$

Note first that, while the coefficients of our QSR function (other than κ) are not pure numbers, the three magnitudes (λ/α^2), $(\gamma/\alpha\beta)$ and (τ/β^2) are pure numbers and are thus entirely independent of the units in which we measure output, labour and land. The same is true of both $\alpha\sqrt{w}$ and $\beta\sqrt{r}$.

What, then, is the sign of (dk/dz)?

(i) If $(\lambda/\alpha^2) = (\gamma/\alpha\beta) = (\tau/\beta^2)$ then k is completely independent of z.

(ii) If $(\lambda/\alpha^2) < (\gamma/\alpha\beta) < (\tau/\beta^2)$, or vice versa, then $k(z)$ is a monotonic relation, with $(dk/dz) < 0$ in the first case and $(dk/dz) > 0$ in the second.

(iii) If $(\gamma/\alpha\beta) > \max[(\lambda/\alpha^2), (\tau/\beta^2)]$ then $(dk/dz) < 0$ for 'low' r but $(dk/dz) > 0$ for 'low' w.

(iv) If $(\gamma/\alpha\beta) < \min[(\lambda/\alpha^2), (\tau/\beta^2)]$ then $(dk/dz) > 0$ for 'low' r but $(dk/dz) < 0$ for 'low' w.

In both cases (iii) and (iv), the turning point in $k(z)$ occurs at $(\alpha\tau - \beta\gamma)\sqrt{r} = (\beta\lambda - \alpha\gamma)\sqrt{w}$.

Various types of $k(z)$ relation are thus possible. However, if we ignore fluke equalities between any two of our three crucial magnitudes, we can say that there are *six* possible orderings of them and that *four* of those orderings imply non-monotonicity of $k(z)$. The reader may wish to envisage (or even to sketch) a three-dimensional diagram with (λ/α^2), $(\gamma/\alpha\beta)$ and (τ/β^2) on the three axes. A 'random' choice of a ray entering the positive orthant in this diagram will imply non-monotonicity in 2 cases out of every 3 and monotonicity in 1 case out of every 3.

In the non-monotonic case, of course, there are infinitely many values of k that are adopted for two distinct values of (r/w), while never being adopted for intermediate (r/w) values. That is, we have recurrence of the capital–output ratio. (Although not, of course, reswitching, because l always rises – and t always falls – as (r/w) increases.) In particular, if $(\lambda/\alpha^2) = (\tau/\beta^2)$ then $k(r = 0) = k(w = 0)$ so that, if k is varying with z, every adopted value of k recurs (other than the unique maximum or minimum value). A more general analysis of this phenomenon of capital–output ratio recurrence, with any input–output structure, is presented in Section 5.6.

The above considerations should suffice to support the general conclusion that one cannot have any useful a priori expectation about how produced input use will differ as between alternative FIE, not even in a one-commodity model with a zero rate of interest, in which the produced input is taken to be a Hicksian substitute (in the definition based on the indirect average cost function) for each of the two primary inputs.

Notice, too, that we can always express the commodity price in terms of a general numéraire, setting $1 = \sigma_l w + \sigma_t r + \sigma_0 p$. However, because (p/w) rises *and* (p/r) falls as (r/w) increases, the qualitative slope of the implied $k(p)$ relationship could be manipulated by mere choice of numéraire and would be devoid of any true economic substance: there is no possible analogy here with a conventional partial equilibrium input demand curve.

Turning to primary input use, it may be noted that, by (2.15), the change in land use per unit of output due to an increase in the rent/wage ratio is

$$dt = -\frac{\partial^2 c}{\partial r \partial w} w(\hat{r} - \hat{w}) - \frac{\partial^2 c}{\partial r \partial p} p(\hat{r} - \hat{p}), \quad \text{with } (\hat{r} - \hat{w}) > (\hat{r} - \hat{p}) > 0$$

(A similar relation holds for labour.) Thus, if land is a substitute (in the above definition) for both labour and the produced input and the indirect cost function is twice-differentiable, then $(dt/dr) < 0$. Therefore, under FIE there is a striking difference between the reaction of primary inputs to a price change and that of produced inputs.

2.7 A falling real price of computing power. The role of complementarity

The preceding arguments assumed input substitution, however defined. But it is clear from (2.13) and (2.15) that input complementarity may have a specific role in the comparative statics of FIE. We consider in this section a case borrowed from the 'Job Polarization' literature (see Autor, Katz and Kearney, 2006 (AKK); Goos and Manning, 2007), in which such a role may contradict the predictions of the conventional 'law of demand' as expressed in terms of input per unit of output.

We assume in this section strictly constant returns to scale, so that $c(\ )$ below denotes a *unit* cost function.

Let us then consider an industry which uses skilled labour, unskilled labour, middle-skilled routine labour and computers. Keeping to our 'isolated industry' framework, let computers be imported at a parametric price, ρ, expressed in terms of the industrial output. Middle-skilled labour is a perfect substitute for computers (see AKK, p. 192), so that its real wage is equal to ρ, by appropriate choice of measurement units (and assuming that positive amounts of both routine labour and computers are used), while the real wages of skilled and unskilled labour, denoted by (w_s, w_u), respectively, are determined by labour market mechanisms. Skilled labour has a high degree of complementarity with computers (see AKK, p. 193). The Job Polarization literature is based on the assumption of 'a precipitous decline in the price of computing power', accompanied by an increase in the real wages of both skilled and unskilled labour, with $\hat{w}_s > \hat{w}_u$ (AKK, p. 192).

It is taken for granted that, 'Since own-factor demand curves are downward sloping, a decline in ρ raises demand for routine tasks [that is, routine labour and computers taken together]' (AKK, p. 192). Now, this would no doubt be true if w_s, w_u remained constant, or even increased at the same proportional rate, but need not be so when $\hat{w}_s > \hat{w}_u > 0$.

By perfect substitutability, routine labour and computers can be treated as a single aggregate, 'routine task'. Denoting by r_t its use per unit of output, we have by (2.15)

$$dr_t = \frac{\partial^2 c}{\partial \rho \partial w_s} w_s(\hat{w}_s - \hat{\rho}) + \frac{\partial^2 c}{\partial \rho \partial w_u} w_u(\hat{w}_u - \hat{\rho}) \text{ with } \hat{\rho} < 0 < \hat{w}_u < \hat{w}_s$$

By complementarity between skilled labour and the routine task $(\partial^2 c/\partial \rho \partial w_s < 0)$, there may be, locally at least, a positive relation between r_t and ρ, contrary to the above-mentioned presumption.

Our argument does not show, of course, that the Job Polarization theory is incorrect: it shows that in significant contexts, in which the economic theorist compares long-run equilibria which are different in more than one input price, the conventional wisdom concerning downward-sloping input demand curves (per unit of output) should not be accepted as a sound guide to the comparative statics, but should be explicitly tested case by case.

2.8 Beyond twice-differentiable average cost functions. On/off inputs

The assumption of twice-differentiability that we have made so far allows one to study the reaction of input use to a given change in the structure of input prices in a relatively simple way, making extensive use of the properties of the cost function Hessian. When a small change in input prices prompts 'small' modifications in the proportions within a given list of inputs, twice-differentiability is a highly convenient assumption which can approximate discrete changes.

The very list of inputs used might change, however. For instance, in the electricity industry, a change in the trend price of oil relative to coal from below to above a critical value may prompt a change from oil- to coal-fuelled plants; or a change in the trend price of wind turbines relative to that of photovoltaic panels may determine a radical switch in the input structure of 'green' electricity production.

The analysis of 'corner solutions' on an isoquant is, of course, well developed in microeconomic theory and Samuelson (1947, p. 69) already regarded it as an 'interesting case', but the possible properties of a 'jump' from one corner (or an edge) to another have received far less attention than the case of continuous substitutability, apart from the obvious case in which *all* inputs are perfect substitutes for one another. (A notable exception, however, is Samuelson's famous 'Surrogate Production Function' (Samuelson, 1962) in which the smallest change in the rate of interest determines, in the consumer good industry, the substitution of one kind of machine for another.)

There can be no presumption that the qualitative results derived from the cost function Hessian remain valid also when there are discontinuous jumps. In this book we shall analyse such cases (including Samuelson's construction: see Section 5.5) in some detail and denote by 'on/off inputs' the inputs which are used for some relative input prices but are completely replaced by qualitatively different inputs at other relative input prices (see also Opocher and Steedman, 2011). In other words, we consider that a certain firm can use different 'technologies', characterized by qualitatively different lists of inputs: there may be smooth substitutability within each technology, but normally not across technologies.

It will be assumed in this section that commodity inputs are of the on/off kind and that they are imported from foreign countries at constant prices, in terms of the industrial output; two primary inputs, land and labour, are common to both technologies. As in the previous section, we also assume strictly constant returns to scale.

Let two technologies be known, each associated with a specific commodity input. Within each technology there is substitutability, as fine as we like, between labour, land and the technology-specific input. The firm's unit cost function can therefore be expressed as

$$c(p_1, p_2, w, r) = \min[c^1(p_1, w, r), c^2(p_2, w, r)] \qquad (2.19)$$

with p_1, p_2 both constant. Let $p = c(\ ) = 1$. The unit level set satisfying (2.19) is our real rent–real wage frontier, except that there is now a kink. Unless one technology dominates at the given commodity prices, there will be one or more (r/w) ratios which make the two technologies equally profitable. For simplicity, let there be only one such ratio, z' and suppose that commodity 1 is used as an input when $z \leq z'$, while commodity 2 is used when $z > z'$. The effect of a small increase in z within the former or the latter range can be studied using the cost function Hessian as in the previous sections: by the logic of (2.15), if the three inputs in use are Hicksian substitutes (in the constant-output definition), then the use of land per unit of output falls and that of labour rises. However, when there is a small increase in z across the critical value, (2.15) is of no help. Denoting by (t^i, l^i), respectively, the per-unit-of-output uses of land and of labour when commodity i is in use and by k_i the amount of that commodity, it is easy to see that, at z', $(t^1/l^1) > (t^2/l^2)$. (Measuring w on the vertical axis, the geometrical idea is that at the switch point the frontier has a kink and it is steeper with commodity-input 1 than it is with commodity-input 2.) In the neighbourhood of z', therefore, an increase in z certainly determines a reduction in the land/labour ratio. However, this says nothing definite about the behaviour of land and labour use per unit of output and we are left without qualitative restrictions. A simple example proves, in fact, that the use of one primary input may increase (per unit of output) when its relative price (in terms of every other input) increases. (Note that the example involves two switching values of z.)

Let the two technologies be characterized, respectively, by the following cost functions à la Diewert (cf. Diewert, 1971):

$$c^1 = 0.5(\sqrt{w\,p_1} + \sqrt{wr} + \sqrt{r\,p_1})$$

$$c^2 = 0.6\sqrt{w\,p_2} + 0.3\sqrt{wr} + 0.55\sqrt{r\,p_2}$$

We take the prices of the two commodity inputs, in terms of the industrial output, as constant and equal to 1. The real wage–real rent curves for the two technologies are, respectively

$$\sqrt{w_{(1)}(r)} = \frac{1 - 0.5\sqrt{r}}{0.5 + 0.5\sqrt{r}}$$

$$\sqrt{w_{(2)}(r)} = \frac{1 - 0.55\sqrt{r}}{0.6 + 0.3\sqrt{r}}$$

The frontier for the industry is, of course, $w(r) = \max\{w_{(1)}(r), w_{(2)}(r)\}$. A little calculation shows that there are two switch points, one at $r \cong 0.64$, and the other at $r = 1$. In the interval of the real rent $(0, 0.64)$ commodity 1 is used, then in the interval $(0.64, 1)$ the industry switches to commodity 2 and for real rents above 1, the use of commodity 1 recurs. There is thus recurrence of the type of produced input used. Within each interval, the land use per unit of output is inversely related to r, but this need not be so as between intervals. In fact, when $r = 1$ (and $w = 0.25$) input use with the two technologies is, respectively, $(t_{(1)} = 0.375;\ l_{(1)} = 1;\ k_1 = 0.375)$ and $(t_{(2)} = 0.35;\ l_{(2)} = 0.9;\ k_2 = 0.425)$: increasing the real rent from below to above 1 we have, at $r = 1$, a sudden increase in the use of land per unit of output, due to the shift from technology 2 to technology 1.

In the presence of on/off produced inputs, the use of a primary input per unit of output can be positively related to its real price. (And note that no reswitching is involved here.)

2.9 Concluding remarks

The long-run theory of the firm developed in the 1970s introduced an innovative way of thinking about microeconomic equilibrium, aware of the effects of free entry and exit. Such an approach provided the basis for further studies concerning the relations between the firm, the industry and the economic system, as we have seen in Chapter 1 (and shall see in more detail in Chapter 9). Yet this long-run theory of the firm did not go far enough, even in the narrow framework of an isolated industry. Using the properties of cost functions, we have formulated in this chapter a more explicit and general relation between the structure of relative prices and long-run choices. Such a relation can be viewed, of course, from the standpoint of $X(w)$, $x(w)$ and $Q(p)$ curves, but these curves have little (if anything) to do with the conventional, partial equilibrium, input demand and output supply curves. They do not share the same properties and in some cases they are even completely insignificant, because their properties depend on the mere choice of numéraire. Thus, the microeconomist should never lose sight of the entire structure of relative prices and of the complex way in which it affects choices. As a prelude to further developments in this book, we have found some simple cases of 'unexpected' results concerning the use of a produced input, or the presence of complementarities, or the use of on/off inputs. Thus we have seen, for example, that a physical capital–output ratio can change non-monotonically as the rent–wage ratio increases; that the type of produced input in use can exhibit recurrence as the rent–wage ratio changes; and that land use per unit of output can increase with the real rent, even in the absence of reswitching.

APPENDIX 1 ON HICKSIAN SUBSTITUTION

A1.1 Input substitution in *Value and Capital* and beyond

The customary concept of input substitutability (complementarity) consists of a positive (negative) effect of a change in one input price on the use of another input, when output is held constant (see Allen, 1938, p. 509; Hicks, 1939, p. 92). This can be expressed by the sign of the off-diagonal elements of the cost function Hessian (see McFadden, 1978, p. 48). In order to distinguish such a definition from the earlier Edgeworth–Pareto criterion, the above definition is normally called 'Hicksian'.

Yet *Value and Capital* itself also provides an alternative definition in which output is variable. Whereas the definition based on a constant output was preferred in the case of constant returns to scale (because of the firm-level output indeterminateness), Hicks thought that a definition allowing for output effects was generally 'better' (see Hicks, 1939, pp. 95–96, n. 2). Because his arguments concerning the likelihood of 'input complementarity' oscillated from one definition to the other, an explicit coordination may be useful.

Let us consider Hicks's variable-output definition, based on the sign of dX_i/dw_j when output adjusts to an isolated change in w_j and let us mark all differential quotients by a subscript indicating $dw_{s \neq j} = 0 = dp$. (Note that these quotients with subscripts are *not* the same as those without subscripts which appear so frequently in our FIE comparative statics.) Profit maximization (with positive inputs and output) implies

$$X_i = \frac{\partial C}{\partial w_i}(Q, \mathbf{w})$$

$$p = \frac{\partial C}{\partial Q}(Q, \mathbf{w}), \quad \frac{\partial^2 C}{\partial Q^2} > 0$$

Now let w_j change, all other prices remaining constant. Differentiating with respect to w_j we obtain, respectively

$$\frac{dX_i}{dw_j}_{dw_{s \neq j}=0=dp} = \frac{\partial^2 C}{\partial w_i \partial w_j} + \frac{\partial^2 C}{\partial w_i \partial Q} \frac{dQ}{dw_j}_{dw_{s \neq j}=0=dp}$$

$$\frac{dQ}{dw_j}_{dw_{s \neq j}=0=dp} = -\frac{1}{\partial^2 C/\partial Q^2} \frac{\partial^2 C}{\partial Q \partial w_j}$$

It follows that

$$\frac{dX_i}{dw_j}_{dw_{s \neq j}=0=dp} = \frac{\partial^2 C}{\partial w_i \partial w_j} - \frac{1}{\partial^2 C/\partial Q^2} \left(\frac{\partial^2 C}{\partial Q \partial w_i} \frac{\partial^2 C}{\partial Q \partial w_j} \right)$$

If both inputs are either 'normal' or 'regressive' ('inferior', in later terminology), then

$$\frac{dX_i}{dw_j}_{\,dw_{s\neq j}=0=dp} < \frac{\partial^2 C}{\partial w_i \partial w_j}$$

Conversely, if one input is 'normal' and the other is 'regressive', then

$$\frac{dX_i}{dw_j}_{\,dw_{s\neq j}=0=dp} > \frac{\partial^2 C}{\partial w_i \partial w_j}$$

Excluding regressiveness, the cross-price effect under the variable-output definition is definitely smaller than that under the constant-output definition; the former may even be negative when the latter is positive.

The above inequalities may offer a justification for two propositions which in *Value and Capital* were rather conjectural. The first concerns Hicks's emphasis on input complementarity in the variable-output definition, notwithstanding substitution in the constant-output definition; as he put it, 'a pair of factors employed by a single firm *ordinarily tend to be complementary*'; 'the *typical* result of a fall in the price of a factor is [...] that [...] the demand for other factors will expand too' (Hicks, 1939, p. 96, n. 2 and p. 97, respectively; emphases added). We see from the above inequalities that this possibility is intimately related to the sign of $(\partial^2 C/\partial w_i \partial Q)$ relating to each input; considering regressiveness as 'grossly improbable' or as an 'exception' (see Hicks, 1939, pp. 94 and 97, respectively), we have complementarity provided that the marginal cost curve is not too steep ('fixed resources are not influential enough' in Hicks's understanding: see p. 97) and substitution under the constant-output definition is not too big. On this interpretation, his position was indeed quite justified. The second proposition, which prompted a debate with Morishima, concerns the dominance of complementarity (in the variable-output definition) under nearly constant returns to scale (Hicks, 1939, p. 95, n. 2; Hicks, 1953–4; Morishima, 1953–4a and 1953–4b). If both inputs are normal, then it is certain that $(dX_i/dw_j)_{dw_{s\neq j}=0=dp} < 0$, as can be seen by setting $(\partial^2 C/\partial Q^2)$ positive but nearly zero. (For more on the Hicks–Morishima debate, see Section 9.2.1.)

It should be noted that $(dX_i/dw_j)_{dw_{s \neq i}=0=dp}$ is equal to $(dX_j/dw_i)_{dw_{s \neq i}=0=dp}$ which is of course a desirable symmetry (reciprocity) property. To see this, we may consider the profit function:

$$P(p, \mathbf{w}) = pQ(p, \mathbf{w}) - C(Q(p, \mathbf{w}), \mathbf{w})$$

We know that Shephard's lemma applies to both the profit function and the cost function and specifically that

$$\frac{\partial P}{\partial w_i}(p, \mathbf{w}) = -X_i(p, \mathbf{w}) = -\frac{\partial C}{\partial w_i}(Q(p, \mathbf{w}), \mathbf{w})$$

Hence

$$\frac{\partial^2 P}{\partial w_i \partial w_j} = -\frac{\partial^2 C}{\partial w_i \partial w_j} - \frac{\partial^2 C}{\partial w_i \partial Q}\frac{dQ}{dw_j}_{dw_{s \neq j}=0=dp}$$

$$= -\frac{\partial^2 C}{\partial w_i \partial w_j} + \frac{1}{\partial^2 C/\partial Q^2}\left(\frac{\partial^2 C}{\partial Q \partial w_i}\frac{\partial^2 C}{\partial Q \partial w_j}\right)$$

Input substitutability (complementarity) under the variable-output definition can therefore be expressed by a negative (positive) sign of the off-diagonal terms of the profit function Hessian.

It should be noted that we also have

$$\frac{\partial^2 P}{\partial w_i \partial p} = \frac{dQ}{dw_i}_{dw_{s \neq i}=0=dp} = -\frac{1}{\partial^2 C/\partial Q^2}\frac{\partial^2 C}{\partial Q \partial w_i}$$

It follows that input normality or regressiveness, too, can be defined in terms of the profit function Hessian, with $(\partial^2 P/\partial w_i \partial p)$ negative (positive) if input i is normal (regressive).

Finally, we may consider input use per unit of output under FIE and say that inputs i and j are substitutes when $(\partial^2 c/\partial w_i \partial w_j)$ is positive. The connection with the two definitions above can easily be derived by differentiating $(C(Q(\mathbf{w}), \mathbf{w})/Q(\mathbf{w}))$ twice, obtaining

$$Q\frac{\partial^2 c}{\partial w_i \partial w_j} = \frac{\partial^2 C}{\partial w_i \partial w_j} - \frac{1}{\partial^2 C/\partial Q^2}\left(\frac{\partial X_i}{\partial Q} - \frac{X_i}{Q}\right)\left(\frac{\partial X_j}{\partial Q} - \frac{X_j}{Q}\right)$$

It will be noted that, unless the cost function is homothetic, the sign of $(\partial^2 c/\partial w_i \partial w_j)$ may well differ from the sign of $(\partial^2 C/\partial w_i \partial w_j)$ and/or from the sign of $-(\partial^2 P/\partial w_i \partial w_j)$.

In conclusion, Hicks's conception of input substitution/complementarity as a 'cross-price' response can be defined in (at least) three different ways (all having the symmetry or reciprocity properties):

(i) by the sign of $\partial^2 C(Q, \mathbf{w})/\partial w_i \partial w_j$, where the output is constant;

(ii) by the sign of $\partial^2 P(p, \mathbf{w})/\partial w_i \partial w_j$, where the output price is constant but the output is variable;

(iii) by the sign of $\partial^2 c(\mathbf{w})/\partial w_i \partial w_j$, where the output price is variable and inputs are measured relative to output.

Because in a given firm a pair of inputs may be defined as 'substitutes' in one definition and 'complements' in another, one must be very clear as to the reason why a specific definition is chosen. The first definition fits the case of strictly constant returns to scale (if inputs are expressed in absolute terms) but is generally inconsistent with profit maximization, unless a very short-run view is taken; the second and third definitions have the advantage of being consistent with profit maximization and of being based on the 'true' long-run data of the firm; only the third definition, however, is consistent with *zero* maximum profits and it should be preferred in FIE comparative statics, so long as single-output firms are concerned. (Definitions proper to multiproduct firms are discussed in Section 3.5.)

A1.2 Hicksian substitution and on/off inputs

The different 'cross price' effects at the basis of the alternative Hicksian definitions are calculated for infinitesimal changes. Is their sign pattern robust to discrete changes? That is, is the sign of dX_i/dw_j, in any of the three definitions, always the same as the sign of $\Delta X_i/\Delta w_j$ in the same definition? We do not question that, when the cost function is twice-differentiable everywhere, it is. However, the presence of on/off inputs (see Section 2.8) may undermine this desirable property, at least as far as definition (iii) is concerned, as proved by the following example. It should be stressed that we continue here to adopt a strict partial equilibrium logic.

Let the two average cost functions constrained on the use of a certain commodity input (see Equation (2.19)) be

$$c^1(w, r, p_1) = \sqrt{w p_1} + \sqrt{wr} + \sqrt{r p_1}$$
$$c^2(w, r, p_2) = 2.1\sqrt{w p_2} + 0.7\sqrt{wr} + 2.2\sqrt{r p_2}$$

Commodity inputs 1 or 2 are in use according to whether $(c^1 - c^2)$ is negative or positive, with

$$c^1 - c^2 = \left(\sqrt{p_1} - 2.1\sqrt{p_2}\right)\sqrt{w} + 0.3\sqrt{wr} + \left(\sqrt{p_1} - 2.2\sqrt{p_2}\right)\sqrt{r}$$

Table 2.1 *Input use per unit of output with on/off inputs.*

	$c^1 \leq c^2$	$c^2 < c^1$
Labour	$0.5\sqrt{\dfrac{p_1}{w}} + 0.5\sqrt{\dfrac{r}{w}}$	$1.05\sqrt{\dfrac{p_2}{w}} + 0.35\sqrt{\dfrac{r}{w}}$
Land	$0.5\sqrt{\dfrac{p_1}{r}} + 0.5\sqrt{\dfrac{w}{r}}$	$1.1\sqrt{\dfrac{p_2}{r}} + 0.35\sqrt{\dfrac{w}{r}}$
Commodity 1	$0.5\sqrt{\dfrac{w}{p_1}} + 0.5\sqrt{\dfrac{r}{p_1}}$	0
Commodity 2	0	$1.05\sqrt{\dfrac{w}{p_2}} + 1.1\sqrt{\dfrac{r}{p_2}}$

For simplicity, we assume that commodity 1 (and not commodity 2) is used when $c^1 = c^2$.

The cost minimizing use of the various inputs per unit of output is specified in Table 2.1.

When one calculates the 'marginal' cross-price effects, it turns out that the reciprocity conditions hold and we obtain the following sign structure

$$\frac{\partial l}{\partial r} > 0, \ \frac{\partial l}{\partial p_1} \geq 0, \ \frac{\partial t}{\partial p_1} \geq 0, \ \frac{\partial l}{\partial p_2} \geq 0, \ \frac{\partial t}{\partial p_2} \geq 0, \ \frac{\partial x_1}{\partial p_2} = 0$$

By symmetry of the cross-price effects we need not state explicitly the remaining partial derivatives. According to the Hicksian definition (iii), land and labour are substitutes for one another, land (labour) and either commodity input are substitutes in a weak sense, but the two commodity inputs are neither substitutes nor complements. Yet for a discrete change we may obtain different signs. Initially, let $w = r = p_2 = 1$, $p_1 = 4$. We see at once that $c^1 = c^2$; because we are assuming that in such a case commodity input 1 is used, we have

$$l = t = 1.5; \quad x_1 = 0.5, \ x_2 = 0$$

Now let the rent rate increase to $r' = 1.21$, while all other prices remain constant. There will be a switch from the use of commodity 1 to the use of commodity 2. The new vector of input use per unit of output is

$$l' = 1.435, \ t' = 1.318, \ x_1' = 0, \ x_2' = 2.26$$

We see at once that

$$\frac{\Delta l}{\Delta r} = -\frac{0.065}{0.21}, \quad \frac{\Delta x_1}{\Delta r} = -\frac{0.5}{0.21}, \quad \frac{\Delta x_2}{\Delta r} = \frac{2.26}{0.21}$$

Land and labour behave now as complements, like land and commodity input 1. The interested reader may easily verify that the only pair of inputs that behave like substitutes across the switch are the two commodity inputs.

The Hicksian concept of substitute inputs, as referred to the case of constant returns to scale, is therefore not robust to 'jumps' in input use: it should therefore be adopted with care in empirical applications!

APPENDIX 2 A SMALL OPEN ECONOMY

Sections 2.7 and 2.8 dealt with an industry which used a commodity input, imported at an exogenous price. This Appendix departs from our main line of reasoning by focusing on foreign trade as such. To this end, we introduce a second industry, assuming that the relative output prices are given internationally. In such a setting, we can see that some long-established results of trade theory are in fact examples of FIE analysis.

A2.1 The standard HOS model as an example of FIE

Let us first assume that the two industries use the same inputs – homogeneous labour and land – and that their indirect average cost functions are $c_1(w,r)$, $c_2(w,r)$, respectively.

In an open economy, we have FIE when

$$\begin{aligned} p_1 &\leq c_1(w,r) \\ p_2 &\leq c_2(w,r) \end{aligned} \tag{2.20}$$

with at least one strict equality. A commodity is (is not) produced domestically if the corresponding minimum average cost is equal to (exceeds) the output price.

By the homogeneity properties of $c_1(\ )$ and $c_2(\ )$, we may divide both inequalities by, say, p_1, obtaining

$$\begin{aligned} 1 &\leq c_1\left(\frac{w}{p_1}, \frac{r}{p_1}\right) \\ \frac{p_2}{p_1} &\leq c_2\left(\frac{w}{p_1}, \frac{r}{p_1}\right) \end{aligned} \tag{2.21}$$

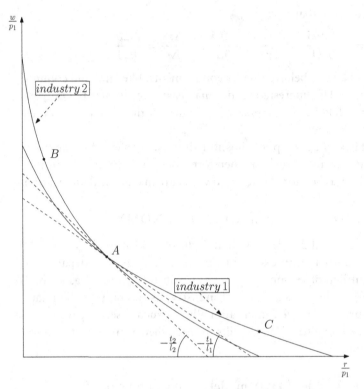

Figure 2.3 The real wage–real rent frontier in an open economy.

By our choice of numéraire, the first inequality in (2.21) is satisfied by the real wage–real rent frontier for industry 1 and by the area above it. The same can be said of the second inequality with reference to industry 2, under the proviso that the real wage and rent are still in terms of commodity 1. Because at least one inequality must be satisfied as a strict equation, the w–r frontier for the economy is the outer envelope of the two industrial frontiers, as in Figure 2.3.

At point B industry 2 makes profits of zero, while industry 1 is not active; the reverse is true at point C. At point A both industries make profits of zero and are active; now we can compare their respective 'factor intensities' t_i/l_i, which are expressed by the absolute slopes of the two curves.

It should be stressed that the position of the frontier for industry 2 critically depends on the terms of trade: the higher is p_2/p_1 the 'further

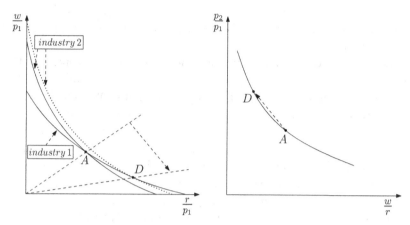

Figure 2.4 The real wage–real rent frontier and the Stolper–Samuelson theorem.

up' is its w–r frontier. It follows that there exist upper and lower bounds of p_2/p_1 beyond which industry 2 or industry 1, respectively, dominates. Within these bounds there can be either diversification or specialization, depending on the value of w/r.

If there is diversification, how does a small increase in p_2/p_1 affect the real wage and the real rent? This is precisely the question addressed by Stolper and Samuelson (1941). As we know, all depends on relative 'factor intensities'. If in the neighbourhood of the initial diversification point, industry 2 is relatively land-intensive, then the real rent increases and the real wage falls. In terms of Figure 2.3, this happens if the frontier for industry 2 cuts that for industry 1 'from above'.

This change is represented geometrically in Figure 2.4, where the dotted line on the left-hand side (lhs) represents the frontier for industry 2 *after* the increase in p_2/p_1. On the rhs we have a familiar representation of the Stolper–Samuelson theorem, in the version concerning relative input prices.

We could also easily deal with Stolper–Samuelson's 'index number problem' (see Stolper and Samuelson, 1941, pp. 64–66) consisting in the determination of the change in input prices expressed in any numéraire. Suppose that we were to draw the industrial w–r frontiers with commodity 2 as numéraire, their relative slopes being still dictated by relative factor intensities. Now the above change would be mirrored by a downward shift of the frontier for industry 1, thus leading to a decrease in w/p_2 and an increase in r/p_2: the qualitative changes in the 'real' input prices are indeed the same in terms of both commodities.

Let us now consider two trading countries, both diversified and sharing the same industrial technologies. By means of Figures 2.3 and 2.4, we may express two other famous theorems of HOS trade theory. First, by the mere fact that the relative commodity price is the same in the two countries, the real input prices are also necessarily the same (the so-called Factor Price Equalization Theorem). Second, let the input prices (in terms of commodity 1) under autarky be at A in country 2 and at D in country 1 (because country 2 is relatively abundant in land); it follows that, under autarky, p_2/p_1 will be higher in country 1 than in country 2 and that, under trade, commodity 1 (2) would be exported by country 1 (2) (the Heckscher–Ohlin theorem in its price version).

Needless to say, the above results are subject to the absence of 'factor intensity reversals'; these could be dealt with in terms of w–r frontiers intersecting more than once, as the interested reader may easily see.

The traditional HOS theory of trade assumes that diversification prevails; however, we can also deal with specialization, as in the original contribution of Stolper and Samuelson and in the classical theory of trade. For instance, if p_2/p_1 is higher than a critical value, then industry 2 dominates: a further improvement in the terms of trade would shift the frontier in terms of the imported commodity 1 upwards. This could determine an increase in both real factor prices in terms of this commodity, but the precise outcome cannot be determined on this basis alone.

The practical importance of the case in which international prices dictate unique real input prices may be and has been doubted (e.g. Bhagwati, 1994, pp. 241–42): we stress, however, that our analysis includes such a case (in the original version with two primary inputs), but is not confined to it.

A2.2 Trade and industry-specific factors

An interesting case in which the terms of trade do not uniquely determine the domestic input prices under diversification is when a factor is 'industry-specific'. So now let each of the two industries use the same kind of labour and an industry-specific kind of 'land'.

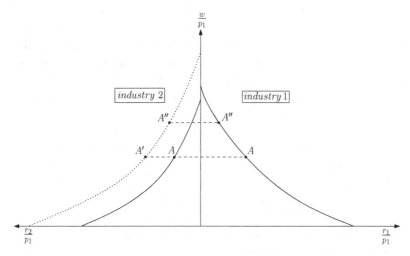

Figure 2.5 The real wage–real rent frontier with industry-specific kinds of land.

Denoting by r_i, $i = 1, 2$, the rent of the kind of land which is specific to industry i, the (indirect) average cost function in industry i will be $c_i(w, r_i)$. Inequalities (2.21) should now be replaced by

$$1 \le c_1\left(\frac{w}{p_1}, \frac{r_1}{p_1}\right)$$
$$\frac{p_2}{p_1} \le c_2\left(\frac{w}{p_1}, \frac{r_2}{p_1}\right) \tag{2.22}$$

These weak inequalities are represented by the solid curves in Figure 2.5 and the areas above them.

The frontier on the rhs represents the real input price frontier for industry 1 in terms of its own product, while the solid curve on the lhs represents an initial real input price frontier for industry 2 in terms of commodity 1.

It is clear that knowledge of the relative commodity price alone is not sufficient to fix unique real input prices even under diversification. Assume an initial equilibrium with two strict equations as at points A. Now let p_2/p_1 increase exogenously. Graphically, this amounts to a radial outward shift of the frontier for industry 2 as shown by the dotted line. (If we express both frontiers in terms of commodity 2, the same parametric change will determine an inward shift of the frontier for industry 1.) The immediate effect of the change is clearly that industry 2 can make positive profits. This may be simply compensated by an increase in the real rent of land 2, r_2/p_1, to point A'. Note that, in terms of commodity 2, the wage and the rent of land 1 would fall, while the rent of land 2 would rise. A change in the terms of trade in favour of commodity 2 would benefit only the owners of the land used in industry 2. Notice that this qualitative outcome may hold for any increase in p_2/p_1, however big.

Other outcomes are possible, however. It may happen, for instance, that the wage remains constant in terms of commodity 2, thus involving an increase in w/p_1, as at points A'': in this case, the workers would also benefit from the change in p_2/p_1 and the only loss would be suffered by the owners of land 1, both in terms of commodity 1 and a fortiori in terms of commodity 2. Interpreting the two kinds of 'land' as a metaphor for two non-competing groups of workers each specialized in one industry, this confirms that the removal of a tariff, say, may have an adverse effect on the wage of the group of workers employed in the industry producing the commodity whose relative price falls (e.g. Haberler, 1936, p. 195).

If the increase in p_2/p_1 is big enough, no diminution of rent 1, not even a free use of land 1, would prevent industry 1 from making losses and the economy would specialize in the production of commodity 2. In this latter case, a further improvement in the terms of trade can be beneficial, again, to the workers and to the owners of land 2.

More formally, let the proportional rate of increase in p_2/p_1 be τ. Differentiating Equations (2.22) totally, we have

$$0 = l_1 \frac{w}{p_1} (\hat{w} - \hat{p}_1) + t_1 \frac{r_1}{p_1} (\hat{r}_1 - \hat{p}_1)$$

$$\tau = l_2 \frac{w}{p_2} (\hat{w} - \hat{p}_1) + t_2 \frac{r_2}{p_2} (\hat{r}_2 - \hat{p}_1) \tag{2.23}$$

Making alternative assumptions about $(\hat{w} - \hat{p}_1)$ (and implicitly about $(\hat{w} - \hat{p}_2)$), one may solve for $(\hat{r}_1 - \hat{p}_1)$, $(\hat{r}_2 - \hat{p}_1)$ (and implicitly for $(\hat{r}_1 - \hat{p}_2)$, $(\hat{r}_2 - \hat{p}_2)$).

A2.3 The HOS model with intermediate products

Let us revert now to the common factors context of the HOS theory. An obvious extension towards realism is to include trade in intermediate commodities, which is a sizeable fraction of total trade (McKinnon,

1966, p. 584, claimed that 'at least 60 to 70 per cent of world trade [was in the 1960s] in intermediate products'. Still today such trade is estimated to constitute about 60% of world trade: cf. Gamberoni *et al.*, 2010, p. 2).

We have known ever since Vanek (1963) that, under conventional assumptions, intermediate inputs do not upset the logic of the above-mentioned theorems of trade. Yet it is still useful to consider here in some detail the modifications that must be made.

Let us assume that both commodities are used as inputs in both industries. The two indirect average cost functions are now $c_1(w, r, p_1, p_2)$, $c_2(w, r, p_1, p_2)$ and FIE requires

$$
1 \le c_1 \left(\frac{w}{p_1}, \frac{r}{p_1}, 1, \frac{p_2}{p_1} \right)
$$
$$
\frac{p_2}{p_1} \le c_2 \left(\frac{w}{p_1}, \frac{r}{p_1}, 1, \frac{p_2}{p_1} \right)
$$

(2.24)

If p_2/p_1 is a given constant, (2.24) determines industrial real wage–real rent frontiers which are similar in many respects to those determined by (2.21), except that we now have four inputs in each industry. Because p_2/p_1 is a parameter, the absolute slope of each frontier is still equal to the ratio of land use to labour use per unit of (gross) output when cost is minimized. Accordingly, all the theorems still hold. The effect of an increase in p_2/p_1 on the real wage and real rent is even 'reinforced' by the fact that the two commodities are used as inputs, as shown in Figure 2.6: the upward shift in the real wage–real rent frontier for industry 2 is reinforced by the fact that value added is only a share of total cost; the downward shift of the frontier for industry 1 is reinforced by the fact that the real cost of commodity input 2 increases.

Taking (2.24) as equalities and differentiating totally, the interested reader may easily calculate the proportional changes in the real rent and wage rates associated with an increase in p_2/p_1 at a proportional rate τ.

The comparative statics of input *use* is far less definite. Let us first compare the relative input prices at points A and B (the latter being characterized by a higher p_2/p_1 ratio). A little reflection shows that the proportional changes in prices are ranked as follows:

$$
\hat{w} < \hat{p}_1 = 0 < \hat{p}_2 < \hat{r}
$$

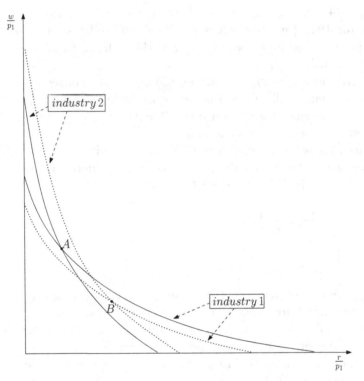

Figure 2.6 The real wage–real rent frontier and the Stolper–Samuelson theorem with intermediate inputs.

The wage falls and the rent rises in any standard. If all inputs are Hicksian substitutes (in definition (iii) of Appendix 1) and can be marginally substituted for one another, we can be sure that labour use per unit of output increases in both industries and land use per unit of output falls, as in the absence of intermediates. By contrast, p_2 increases relative to p_1 and w but decreases relative to r; conversely, p_1 decreases relative to p_2 and r but increases relative to w: it can by no means be taken for granted that commodity 2 is used less (per unit of output) and commodity 1 is used more. Even assuming highly conventional cost functions, in the familiar framework of the HOS theory, the comparative statics of *produced* input use per unit of output obeys no general 'law' and should be examined case by case. (For further discussion, see Steedman, 2005.)

A2.4 Conclusion

The HOS theory of trade can be considered as a familiar, well worked-out case of FIE analysis, assuming as it does that competition leads active industries to earn zero net profits. Accordingly, any change from one equilibrium to another within the HOS theory involves multiple price changes. This has important consequences for the comparative statics of produced input use. Of course, the FIE analysis of trade is wider than the HOS theory and may include other aspects, such as specialization and the presence of industry-specific factors, but this Appendix may nevertheless have served to show that FIE analysis is far from being a new-fangled idiosyncracy.

3* Multiproduct firms

Although we concentrate in this book on the single-product firm, we should at least indicate how the analysis of FIE can be extended to – or is modified by – the case of the firm producing joint products. It can hardly be denied that most, if not all, actual firms in fact produce a variety of outputs.

The microeconomic theory of the multiproduct, competitive firm based on Hicks's *Value and Capital* and reshaped in terms of duality theory by modern literature (e.g. McFadden, 1978; Diewert, 1982; Chambers, 1988, chapter 7; Cornes, 1992, pp. 155–60) offered only few insights on *long-run* equilibrium, characterized by zero net profits. Conversely, the 1970s long-run theory of the firm focused only on the single-output case. Multiproduct firms under conditions of free entry and exit did receive proper attention in the contestable markets literature of the 1980s. However, that literature, concerned as it was with industrial organization, did not thoroughly investigate the implied comparative statics at the level of the firm.

An independent tradition, based on von Neumann (1945–46) and Sraffa (1960), analysed zero-net-profit positions in the economy as a whole when firms can produce different output combinations in fixed proportions. (A valuable survey is in Kurz and Salvadori, 1995, chapter 8.) However, it did not explicitly consider the industry-level comparative statics.

An extension of our FIE analysis to the case of joint production requires, therefore, some new analysis. For simplicity, we shall suppose that while producers are multiproduct firms, we may still refer to industries, because products fall into disjoint groups such that no product is produced in more than one industry.

In Sections 3.1 and 3.2 we consider firms which produce many outputs by means of only *one* input and stress a fundamental symmetry with the one-output, many-input case discussed so far: making use of the revenue function, we shall derive some relations between outputs and prices that mirror those discussed in the previous chapter. Sections 3.3 and 3.4 generalize our analysis to *m* inputs and *n* outputs, on the basis of the firm's profit function. We shall see that all the results of the long-run theory of the firm do generalize (in their positive aspects as well as in their negative ones) to multiproduct firms. As in the previous chapter, we shall take care to emphasize the role of relative prices and provide rules for signing dQ_i, dX_j and ratios between these quantities for any possible variation in the structure of prices. In Section 3.5, we also generalize the definition of 'substitution' relating to both inputs and outputs along Hicksian lines. Section 3.6 concludes.

This starred chapter is a digression from our main line of argument and can perhaps be skipped on a first reading, without prejudice to the reading of the following chapters.

3.1 FIE with many outputs and one input

The simplest context in which we can analyse the zero-net-profit equilibrium in firms with multiple outputs is when only one input is used. In such a case there is a neat symmetry with the one-output, multiple-input case discussed so far.

Let us describe the firm in terms of its revenue function, $R(\mathbf{p}; X)$, which is increasing and linear homogeneous in the output prices, $\mathbf{p}$, increasing and S-shaped in the single-input quantity, X, and twice-differentiable in all variables. Unless otherwise stated, we assume $\partial^2 R / \partial p_i \partial X > 0$ and $\partial^2 R / \partial p_i \partial p_j < 0$. It goes without saying that, under profit maximization, $\partial^2 R / \partial X^2 < 0$ and $\partial^2 R / \partial p_i^2 > 0$.

At given product prices, the firm has curves of revenue per unit of input and of 'marginal revenue' (as calculated for small variations in input use) which first rise and then fall, as in Figure 3.1. At the top of the (R/X) curve, we have local constant returns to scale. We take this to apply for all $\mathbf{p}$.

The firm seeks to maximize

$$R(\mathbf{p}, X) - wX$$

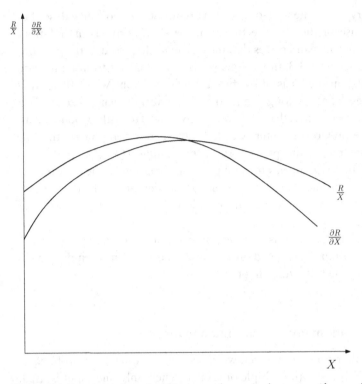

Figure 3.1 Revenue per unit of input and marginal revenue (for small variations in input use).

in the face of given prices $(w, \mathbf{p})$. We have, for a solution with positive (X, Q_i):

$$\frac{\partial R}{\partial X}(\mathbf{p}, X) = w \qquad\qquad (3.1)$$

$$\frac{\partial R}{\partial p_i}(\mathbf{p}, X) = Q_i, \quad i = 1, 2, \ldots, n \qquad\qquad (3.2)$$

If the firm is always in FIE, then we also have

$$\frac{R}{X}(\mathbf{p}, X) = \frac{\partial R}{\partial X}(\mathbf{p}, X) \qquad\qquad (3.3)$$

Solving (3.3) for X and then inserting in $R(\mathbf{p}, X)/X$, we define an 'indirect revenue per unit of input' function, $\rho(\mathbf{p})$, which is increasing and linear homogeneous, and which is the multiple-output, single-input counterpart of the 'indirect average cost function' of Chapter 2. The interesting property of $\rho(\mathbf{p})$ is that Shephard's lemma still holds in relative, 'per unit of input' terms, that is

$$\frac{\partial \rho}{\partial p_j} = \frac{Q_j}{X} \equiv q_j$$

By (3.1) and (3.3) we have

$$1 = \rho\left(\frac{1}{w}\mathbf{p}\right) \tag{3.4}$$

as the analogue to Equation (2.4′) in Chapter 2. Here we have a 'real output price surface' which shows by definition the 'input-commanded' product prices consistent with FIE.

Let us pause to remark that nothing guarantees that, at all possible output prices, the FIE output levels will all be strictly positive. We need to assume economies of scope for this to be so, as in the contestable markets literature. This condition corresponds to $(\partial \rho(\mathbf{p})/\partial p_j) > 0$ for all j and all vectors $\mathbf{p}$ (which is indeed a formulation of the economies of scope assumption).

A graphical argument with two outputs will be useful to illustrate this point. Equation (3.4) describes now a real output price curve, decreasing and convex from below. A possible case is illustrated in Figure 3.2. The absolute slope of the curve is the ratio of revenue maximizing outputs per unit of input q_1/q_2 and the tangent line cuts the axes at $1/q_2$ and $1/q_1$.

In the case described by the figure both outputs are positive at all the relevant price ratios including the extremes A and B. In order to understand when this happens, we should map A and B onto a different diagram.

Because we can associate an FIE input use to each point on the output price curve, we can also draw output possibility curves, conditional on FIE input use, like curves a and b in Figure 3.3. If p_1/w is null (and p_2/w has its maximum value), we have a certain profit-maximizing input level, $X^{(a)}$, and an output possibility curve, a. Revenue maximization occurs at point A. Conversely, if p_2/w drops to zero (and p_1/w reaches its maximum value), then input use normally changes

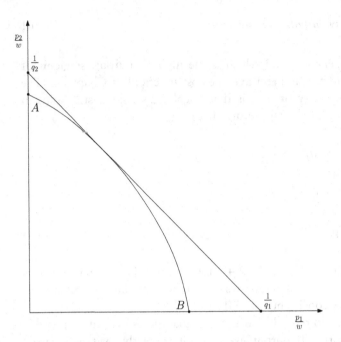

Figure 3.2 The real output price curve; first case.

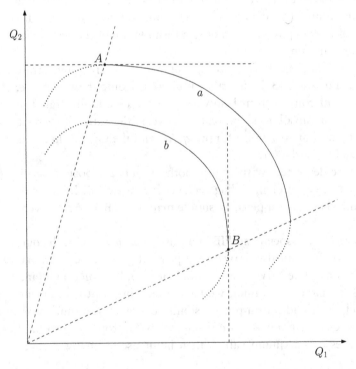

Figure 3.3 Output possibility curves conditional on FIE input use; first case.

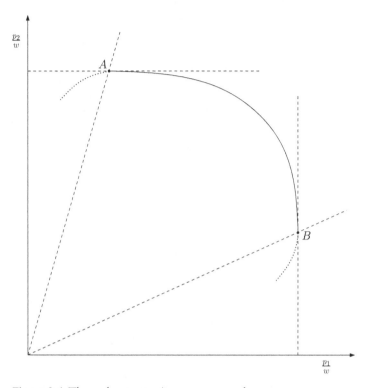

Figure 3.4 The real output price curve; second case.

and we assume here that it falls. It should be noted, however, that, in the movement from A to B, input use may first rise and then fall: nothing guarantees a monotonic relation between the FIE input use and relative commodity prices. The conditional output frontier shifts downwards to *b* and the new FIE equilibrium is at point B. Diversification at both A and B is assured by the fact that the output possibility curves 'bend backward' when one output is lower than a critical value: both outputs are positive even though one price is null, so that it pays to produce (jointly) a free good rather than to specialize in the production of the good with a positive price. Under such an assumption, there is a cone within which the output pairs must lie.

This is not the only possible case, however. A symmetrical case is when the firm specializes in one output, even though both prices are strictly positive: under such an assumption, diversification occurs only when the relative output prices lie within a certain cone. In Figure 3.4,

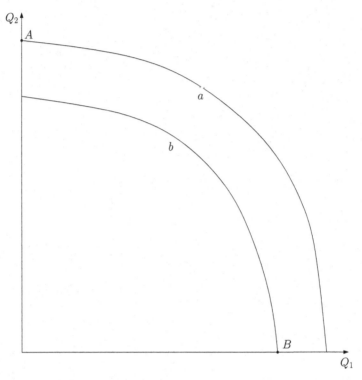

Figure 3.5 Output possibility curves conditional on FIE input use; second case.

output prices at point A determine $Q_1 = 0$ even though $p_1/w > 0$. A reduction in p_1/w, at a constant p_2/w would be completely irrelevant. Conversely, output prices at B determine $Q_2 = 0$ even though $p_2/w > 0$ and a further reduction in p_2/w, at a constant p_1/w, would be completely irrelevant. These two equilibria are mirrored in Figure 3.5, where it is assumed that $X^{(a)} > X^{(b)}$.

These two symmetrical cases include two opposite extreme possibilities, of course. In order, the first is when the output cone collapses to a ray: the firm is then characterized by fixed output proportions (similarly to the von Neumann and Sraffa models), the FIE output levels are rigidly determined and the output price curve is a straight line. The second is when the output price cone collapses to a ray and the prices consistent with multiple outputs are rigidly determined; the output possibility curves conditional on FIE input use are now straight lines.

3.2 The comparative statics of FIE

What are the comparative statics of (3.1)–(3.4)? Let us first consider the partial equilibrium comparative statics.

Differentiating (3.1) and (3.2) totally, we have, respectively,

$$\sum_{j=1}^{n} \frac{\partial Q_j}{\partial X} dp_j + \frac{\partial^2 R}{\partial X^2} dX = dw \tag{3.1'}$$

$$\sum_{j=1}^{n} \frac{\partial Q_i}{\partial p_j} dp_j + \frac{\partial Q_i}{\partial X} dX = dQ_i, \quad i = 1, 2, \ldots, n \tag{3.2'}$$

Let an output price, p_i, change, while $dw = 0 = dp_j$, $j \neq i$. We obtain

$$\frac{dX}{dp_i} = -\frac{1}{\partial R^2 / \partial X^2} \frac{\partial Q_i}{\partial X}$$

$$\frac{dQ_i}{dp_i} = \frac{\partial Q_i}{\partial p_i} - \frac{1}{\partial R^2 / \partial X^2} \left(\frac{\partial Q_i}{\partial X} \right)^2 > 0$$

In this conventional partial equilibrium setting, an output is positively related to its own price, while dX/dp_i has the same sign as dQ_i/dX. We should normally expect a positive sign, but the opposite is also possible (in the case of Hicksian regressiveness; more on this in Chapter 9).

Now, symmetrically, change the input price w, while each $dp_j = 0$. We have

$$\frac{dX}{dw} = \frac{1}{\partial^2 R / \partial X^2} < 0$$

$$\frac{dQ_i}{dw} = \frac{1}{\partial^2 R / \partial X^2} \frac{\partial Q_i}{\partial X}$$

Not surprisingly, the own price effect now is negative, while the sign of the cross-price effect again depends on the sign of dQ_i/dX. Of course, this comparative statics corresponds to that of conventional theory.

Changing only one price at a time, however, certainly violates (3.3) and (3.4) and would drive the firm out of FIE. Similarly to the single-output, multi-input case, a compensating change in at least one other price must be considered. Differentiating (3.3), we get

$$\sum_{j=1}^{n} \left(\frac{\partial Q_j}{\partial X} - \frac{Q_j}{X} \right) dp_j + \frac{\partial^2 R}{\partial X^2} dX = 0 \tag{3.3'}$$

(3.1′) and (3.3′) cannot both be satisfied unless at least two prices change. Let these prices be p_i and w. It is easily found that

$$dw = q_i dp_i$$

$$\frac{\partial^2 R}{\partial X^2} dX = -\left(\frac{\partial Q_i}{\partial X} \frac{X}{Q_i} - 1\right) q_i dp_i$$

$$dQ_i = \left[\frac{\partial Q_i}{\partial p_i} - \frac{1}{\partial^2 R/\partial X^2} \frac{\partial Q_i}{\partial X}\left(\frac{\partial Q_i}{\partial X} \frac{X}{Q_i} - 1\right) q_i\right] dp_i$$

If, by free competition, an initial increase in a product price determines an increase in the input price in such a measure as to restore zero net profits, then input use increases or falls according to whether the elasticity $(\partial Q_i/\partial X)(X/Q_i)$ is greater or lower than 1. This effect is generally different from the standard partial equilibrium effect referred to above. Likewise, the effect of the change in price on the output of commodity i is also different from a conventional partial equilibrium effect. The sum in the square brackets can be broken down into three components: in order, a positive component conditional on a constant input level and input price; a second positive component due to the change in the input level at a constant input price; and a third component due to the change in the input price. This last component is normally negative (that is, excluding regressiveness) and can outweigh the former two. Under FIE, nothing guarantees, therefore, that $dQ_i/dp_i > 0$. It will be noted that, if the output i elasticity with respect to input use is equal to one, then the two latter effects cancel each other out, so that the FIE response dQ_i/dp_i is equal to the partial equilibrium response $\partial Q_i/\partial p_i$. A little reflection shows that a sufficient condition for this to happen is that the revenue function be homothetic.

The differential equations above can also be referred, of course, to an 'original' change in w which is 'compensated' by a change in an output price. It is easily seen that, contrary to simple partial equilibrium analysis, the sign of dX/dw critically depends on the output i elasticity with respect to input use. The close analogy with symmetrical results obtained for firms with one output and many inputs will not have escaped the reader's attention: see, in particular Equations (2.9)–(2.12).

The original change in p_i may be compensated, not by a change of the same sign in w, but by a change of opposite sign in some other output price p_j. In this case we have

$$dp_j = -\frac{q_i}{q_j}dp_i$$

$$\frac{\partial^2 R}{\partial X^2}dX = -\left(\frac{\partial Q_i}{\partial X}\frac{X}{Q_i} - \frac{\partial Q_j}{\partial X}\frac{X}{Q_j}\right)q_i dp_i$$

$$dQ_i = \left[\frac{\partial Q_i}{\partial p_i} - \frac{\partial Q_i}{\partial p_j}\frac{q_i}{q_j} - \frac{1}{\partial^2 R/\partial X^2}\frac{\partial Q_i}{\partial X}\left(\frac{\partial Q_i}{\partial X}\frac{X}{Q_i} - \frac{\partial Q_j}{\partial X}\frac{X}{Q_j}\right)q_i\right]dp_i$$

Let us assume that outputs i and j are Hicksian substitutes (in the definition conditional on a constant input; see Section 3.5), so that $\partial Q_i/\partial p_j < 0$. Yet the FIE comparative statics still differ from those of partial equilibrium. Specifically, $dQ_i/dp_i < 0$ is possible provided that (a necessary condition) the input-elasticity of output j is greater than that of output i.

The above FIE relations, with $dw = 0$, can be easily generalized to any change in relative prices. From $(3.1')$ to $(3.3')$ and by the homogeneity properties of the revenue function, we obtain

$$\frac{\partial^2 R}{\partial X^2}dX = -\sum_{j\neq i}\left(1 - \frac{\partial Q_j}{\partial X}\frac{X}{Q_j}\right)p_j q_j(\hat{p}_i - \hat{p}_j)$$

$$dQ_i = \left[\sum_{j\neq i}\frac{\partial Q_i}{\partial p_j}p_j - \frac{\partial Q_i}{\partial X}\frac{1}{\partial^2 R/\partial X^2}\sum_{j\neq i}\left(1 - \frac{\partial Q_j}{\partial X}\right)p_j q_j\right](\hat{p}_i - \hat{p}_j)$$

In Chapter 2 we have insisted on the fact that an input use per unit of output is inversely related to the own input price even when there is a compensating change in the output price. We expect, then, that the same is true, *mutatis mutandis*, of the output per unit of input. In fact, differentiating $\rho(\mathbf{p})$ twice we have, by Shephard's lemma,

$$dq_i = -\sum_{j\neq i}\frac{\partial q_i}{\partial p_j}p_i(\hat{p}_i - \hat{p}_j)$$

If $(\hat{p}_i - \hat{p}_j)$ has a uniform sign and $\partial q_i/\partial p_j < 0$ for all $j \neq i$, then we have a positive relation between a FIE output and its relative price. The same is true, irrespective of the signs of $\partial q_i/\partial p_j$, if $(\hat{p}_i - \hat{p}_j)$ is equal for all j.

3.3 FIE with many outputs and many inputs

Now we turn to the more general case in which n outputs are produced by means of m inputs. A firm can still be characterized by its revenue function $R(X, p)$, with the proviso that X is now an m vector; alternatively, it can be characterized by its cost function $C(Q, w)$, with the proviso that Q is an n vector. The latter alternative has been followed in the contestable markets literature, which introduced the notions of 'ray average cost' and 'trans-ray convexity' (see Baumol *et al.*, 1988, chapters 3 and 4). More generally, the condition of (local) constant returns to scale can be expressed by (local) homogeneity of degree one of $R(X, p)$ with respect to X and of $C(Q, w)$ with respect to Q, that is

$$XR_X = R(X, p) \quad \text{and} \quad QC_Q = C(Q, w)$$

where R_X and C_Q denote vectors of partial derivatives. This pair of equations extends to higher dimensionality our former assumptions that revenue per unit of input had a maximum and that cost per unit of output had a minimum.

It will be assumed throughout that at any output prices there exists a vector of input use such that the former equation is satisfied; and that at any input prices there exists a vector of outputs such that the latter equation is satisfied. Only in this case is the firm unambiguously characterized by 'local constant returns'. The important consequence of this assumption is that a null maximum profit is always possible at significant prices, by the first-order condition for profit maximization, $R_X \leq w$ and $C_Q \geq p$, with strict equalities for positive inputs and outputs.

However, the revenue and cost functions, useful as they are for a characterization of the firm, remain nonetheless 'half-way houses' which need further elaboration. For this reason, in this and the following sections, we prefer to build immediately on the firm's profit function, $P(p_1, \ldots, p_n; w_1, \ldots, w_m)$, the comparative statics of which are more elegant.

As is well known, $P(p, w)$ is defined for prices such that profits are bounded from above, it is linear homogeneous in (p, w), increasing in p and decreasing in w. We also assume $P(p, w)$ to be twice-differentiable. The profit function Hessian, H, is positive semidefinite and we assume unless otherwise stated that the off-diagonal terms h_{ij} are all negative and that the diagonal terms h_{ii} are strictly positive. Further details on this assumption are given in Section 3.5.

Shephard's lemma still holds, so that

$$\frac{\partial P}{\partial p_j}(\mathbf{p}, \mathbf{w}) = Q_j(\mathbf{p}, \mathbf{w}) \quad j = 1, \dots, n \tag{3.5}$$

$$\frac{\partial P}{\partial w_i}(\mathbf{p}, \mathbf{w}) = -X_i(\mathbf{p}, \mathbf{w}) \quad i = 1, \dots, m \tag{3.6}$$

Now FIE requires that

$$P(\mathbf{p}, \mathbf{w}) = 0 \tag{3.7}$$

Our assumption on returns guarantees that the level set defined by (3.7) contains significant price combinations. Condition (3.7) makes it very clear that two alternative equilibria under FIE can never differ in just one price: the comparative statics of FIE is therefore inherently different from the familiar partial equilibrium analysis, whatever the number of goods and factors.

3.4 The comparative statics of FIE. The general case

Even though the comparative statics of (3.5), (3.6) and (3.7) depend on relative prices, it helps intuition to present first an argument in terms of combined 'absolute' price variations; after that we can, of course, present succinct conclusions in the proper relative prices terms.

Differentiating (3.5) and (3.6) totally we obtain

$$(dQ_1, \dots, dQ_n; -dX_1, \dots, -dX_m)$$
$$= (dp_1, \dots, dp_n; dw_1, \dots, dw_m)\mathbf{H} \tag{3.8}$$

It follows at once that $(\partial Q_j / \partial p_j) > 0 > (\partial X_i / \partial w_i)$. However, these simple and elegant conclusions cannot tell us how the firm in FIE reacts to price changes. For such a firm, the only permissible changes in $\mathbf{p}$ and $\mathbf{w}$ are those satisfying $P = 0$ always and hence

$$Q_1 dp_1 + \cdots + Q_n dp_n = X_1 dw_1 + \cdots + X_m dw_m \tag{3.9}$$

We see from (3.9) that it is quite impossible for only one (product or input) price to change; at least two must do so.

Our FIE comparative statics are thus implicit in (3.8) and (3.9) taken together and certainly cannot be derived from the (positive) diagonal elements of **H** alone, even when we consider 'own-price' effects. For example, if $n = m = 2$, we have

$$\frac{dQ_1}{dp_1} = h_{11} + h_{21}\frac{dp_2}{dp_1} + h_{31}\frac{dw_1}{dp_1} + h_{41}\frac{dw_2}{dp_1}$$

$$Q_1 + Q_2\frac{dp_2}{dp_1} = X_1\frac{dw_1}{dp_1} + X_2\frac{dw_2}{dp_1} \tag{3.10}$$

Consequently, the magnitude and even the sign of dQ_1/dp_1 may depend both on (i) the magnitudes and signs of (h_{21}, h_{31}, h_{41}) and (ii) the changes in (p_2, w_1, w_2) which are assumed to compensate the change in p_1. As to (i), we know from the linear homogeneity property of $P(\ )$ that

$$p_1h_{11} + p_2h_{21} + w_1h_{31} + w_2h_{41} \equiv 0$$

and hence that, h_{11} being positive, at least one of (h_{21}, h_{31}, h_{41}) must be negative; we make the strong assumption that all three are in fact negative. As to (ii), suppose first that $dw_1 = dw_2 = 0$, so that if $dp_1 > 0$ then $dp_2 < 0$. In this case, from (3.10), $dQ_1/dp_1 > 0$, just like $(\partial Q_1/\partial p_1)$. Suppose now, however, that $dp_2 = dw_2 = 0$, so that, if $dp_1 > 0$ then $dw_1 > 0$ (from (3.9)). Now (3.10) tells us that

$$\frac{dQ_1}{dp_1} = h_{11} - \frac{Q_1}{X_1}|h_{31}| \tag{3.10'}$$

and it is not clear from (3.10') that dQ_1/dp_1 can be signed a priori.

Similarly, consider

$$-\frac{dX_1}{dw_1} = h_{13}\frac{dp_1}{dw_1} + h_{23}\frac{dp_2}{dw_1} + h_{33} + h_{43}\frac{dw_2}{dw_1}$$

$$\text{where} \quad Q_1\frac{dp_1}{dw_1} + Q_2\frac{dp_2}{dw_1} = X_1 + X_2\frac{dw_2}{dw_1} \tag{3.11}$$

and suppose that (h_{13}, h_{23}, h_{43}) are all negative. If $dw_1 > 0 = dp_1 = dp_2$ then $dw_2 < 0$ (from (3.9)) and thus (3.11) implies that $(dX_1/dw_1) < 0$, just like $(\partial X_1/\partial w_1)$. But if $dw_1 > 0 = dp_2 = dw_2$ then (3.11) tells us that

$$\frac{dX_1}{dw_1} = -h_{33} + \frac{X_1}{Q_1}|h_{13}| \tag{3.11'}$$

and it is not obvious from (3.11') that even the sign of (dX_1/dw_1) is known a priori.

Because both (3.10') and (3.11') suppose $dp_2 = dw_2 = 0$, it is worth comparing them. Since $h_{11}h_{33} > h_{13}^2$ (because **H** is positive semidefinite) we can see that $(dQ_1/dp_1) < 0 < (dX_1/dw_1)$ is not possible and that if

$$\frac{|h_{13}|}{h_{33}} < \frac{Q_1}{X_1} < \frac{h_{11}}{|h_{31}|} \tag{3.12}$$

then, indeed, $(dQ_1/dp_1) > 0 > (dX_1/dw_1)$. However, if (Q_1/X_1) lies outside the range specified in (3.12), then *either* $(dQ_1/dp_1) < 0$ *or* $(dX_1/dw_1) > 0$.

What then of cross-price effects in FIE with joint production? (We appreciate that to speak of own-price or of cross-price effects when more than one price is changing is to engage in terminological licence, but we beg the reader's indulgence.) Reasoning in the same way as before we see, for example, that if $dw_1 = dw_2 = 0$, then

$$\begin{aligned}
\frac{dQ_1}{dp_2} &= h_{21} - \frac{Q_2}{Q_1}h_{11} \\
\frac{dQ_2}{dp_1} &= h_{12} - \frac{Q_1}{Q_2}h_{22}
\end{aligned} \tag{3.13}$$

From (3.13), $(dQ_1/dp_2) = (dQ_2/dp_1)$ now holds iff $h_{11}Q_2^2 = h_{22}Q_1^2$, a fluke which can in effect be ignored, so that we can say that symmetry does not hold here. If $h_{12} = h_{21}$ is taken to be negative, as above, then at least we can conclude that $(dQ_1/dp_2) < 0 > (dQ_2/dp_1)$. Even if we allow $h_{12} = h_{21}$ to be positive it is not possible to have $(dQ_1/dp_2) > 0 < (dQ_2/dp_1)$, because $h_{11}h_{22} > h_{12}^2$. The two (dQ_i/dp_j) in (3.13) will both be negative (with positive h_{12}) if

$$\frac{h_{12}}{h_{22}} < \frac{Q_1}{Q_2} < \frac{h_{11}}{h_{21}}$$

but if (Q_1/Q_2) lies outside this range then one will be positive and the other negative.

The analysis of (dX_1/dw_2) and (dX_2/dw_1) with $dp_1 = dp_2 = 0$, would be very similar to that of (3.13), so we move on to set $dp_2 = dw_2 = 0$ and to consider

$$\begin{aligned}
\frac{dQ_1}{dw_1} &= h_{31} + \frac{X_1}{Q_1}h_{11} \\
\frac{dX_1}{dp_1} &= h_{13} + \frac{Q_1}{X_1}h_{33}
\end{aligned} \tag{3.14}$$

These two cross-price effects will be equal iff $h_{33}Q_1^2 = h_{11}X_1^2$; flukes apart, they are unequal. By contrast with (3.13), (3.14) gives the simplest results when $h_{13} = h_{31}$ is positive (contrary to our previous assumption) for then $(dQ_1/dw_1) > 0 < (dX_1/dp_1)$. If $h_{13} = h_{31}$ is negative then it is impossible that dQ_1/dw_1 and dX_1/dp_1 should both be negative, because $h_{11}h_{33} > h_{13}^2$. They will both be positive if

$$\frac{|h_{31}|}{h_{11}} < \frac{X_1}{Q_1} < \frac{h_{33}}{|h_{13}|}$$

and they will be of opposite signs if X_1/Q_1 lies outside this range.

It might be thought intuitive that both $dQ_1/dw_1 < 0$ and $dX_1/dp_1 > 0$. However, this would in fact hold iff $h_{13} = h_{31} < 0$ *and* $h_{11}X_1 < |h_{13}|Q_1$; in words, if not only X_1 but also X_1/Q_1 is increasing with p_1.

The above comparative statics can easily be generalized to any pattern of change in relative prices, reformulating (3.8) and (3.9) in terms of proportional price changes. The change in, say, the nth output and the mth input is given by

$$dQ_n = -\left[\sum_{j \neq n} h_{jn} p_j(\hat{p}_n - \hat{p}_j) + \sum_i h_{(n+i)n} w_i(\hat{p}_n - \hat{w}_i)\right] \qquad (3.15)$$

$$dX_m = \sum_j h_{j(n+m)} p_j(\hat{w}_m - \hat{p}_j) + \sum_{i \neq m} h_{(n+i)(n+m)} w_i(\hat{w}_m - \hat{w}_i) \qquad (3.16)$$

It will be noted that (3.15) and (3.16) involve only off-diagonal terms of $\mathbf{H}$, which are assumed to be negative.

Now (3.15) and (3.16) give the same qualitative results as conventional comparative statics when the relative price changes in the round brackets have a uniform sign. A little reflection makes it clear that this happens when either a change in p_n is compensated by an opposite change in p_j, or a change in w_m is compensated by an opposite change in w_i. However, if a change in p_n is compensated by a change in w_m, then we have $p_n Q_n \hat{p}_n = w_m X_m \hat{w}_m$ and the sign of $(\hat{p}_n - \hat{w}_m)$ turns out to depend upon the sign of $(w_m X_m - p_n Q_n)$, which is not known a priori.

This generalizes a result obtained by the long-run theory of the firm in the special case with $n = 1$ (Silberberg, 1974; discussed earlier in Section 2.3); it also generalizes our result of Section 3.2 with $m = 1$. In such cases, however, input use per unit of output and output per unit of input, respectively, behaved conventionally and one may wonder whether these results can be generalized to the $n \times m$ case. It is easily shown that they can. Let dp_n and dw_m be the only non-zero price changes. Equations (3.8) and (3.9) become

$$dQ_n = h_{nn}dp_n + h_{(n+m)n}dw_m$$

$$-dX_m = h_{n(n+m)}dp_n + h_{(n+m)(n+m)}dw_m \tag{3.8'}$$

$$Q_n dp_n = X_m dw_m \tag{3.9'}$$

We can deduce from (3.8') and (3.9') that

$$X_m Q_n^2 \left(\frac{1}{X_m}\frac{dX_m}{dw_m} - \frac{1}{Q_n}\frac{dQ_n}{dw_m} \right)$$
$$= - \left(h_{nn}X_m^2 + 2h_{(n+m)n}X_m Q_n + h_{(n+m)(n+m)}Q_n^2 \right) \tag{3.17}$$

Because **H** is positive semidefinite, the rhs of (3.17) is always negative. Hence

$$\frac{d(X_m/Q_n)}{dw_m} < 0$$

This is Silberberg's result (1974, corollary 2), albeit in a multiproduct setting.

Now let the price change dw_m be compensated not by dp_n, but by dw_1, where

$$X_1 dw_1 + X_m dw_m = 0$$

and all other prices are constant. An exactly analogous argument to that above leads to the conclusion that

$$\frac{d(X_m/X_1)}{dw_m} < 0$$

Finally, let dp_1 and dp_n be the only non-zero price changes, where

$$Q_1 dp_1 + Q_n dp_n = 0$$

to keep $P(\ )$ constant. Analogously to the previous cases, we find that

$$\frac{d(Q_n/Q_1)}{dp_n} > 0$$

It perhaps bears repetition that in long-run comparative statics, one must change at least two prices (not just one) and that – if one wishes to reach constructive conclusions – one must focus on ratios of quantities (not on absolute quantities). On this understanding Silberberg's result can be generalized to encompass the multiproduct firm and to apply not only to X_i/Q_j ratios, but also to X_i/X_k and Q_j/Q_h ratios. In each case the result is 'intuitive'. (Because these ratios are also the absolute slopes of the price surface, as we have seen, the results above provide some qualitative restrictions on the possible curvature of such a surface.)

3.5 Alternative concepts of substitution. A general formulation

It was seen in Chapter 2 and its first appendix that it is valuable to distinguish between various alternative concepts of substitution. We now consider how such concepts are to be defined in a multi-input, multi-output context.

By Shephard's lemma, it is clear that negative off-diagonal terms of the profit function Hessian imply

(i) $\partial Q_i(\mathbf{p}, \mathbf{w})/\partial p_j = \partial Q_j(\mathbf{p}, \mathbf{w})/\partial p_i < 0$ when i and j indicate two outputs;

(ii) $\partial X_i(\mathbf{p}, \mathbf{w})/\partial w_j = \partial X_j(\mathbf{p}, \mathbf{w})/\partial w_i > 0$ when they indicate two inputs;

(iii) $-\partial X_j(\mathbf{p}, \mathbf{w})/\partial p_i = \partial Q_i(\mathbf{p}, \mathbf{w})/\partial w_j < 0$ when they indicate an output and an input.

Conditions (i) and (ii) provide a general definition of substitution among outputs and among inputs; condition (iii) defines a pair of one input and one output as 'normal'.

Such definitions starting from the profit function are more appropriate for long-run analysis than the definitions based on the sign structure of the cost function (or the revenue function) Hessian, because the long-run data for the firm are the long-run prices and not any given levels of outputs (or inputs). It is not difficult to relate such different definitions to one another, however, extending to multiproduct firms our analysis in Chapter 2, Appendix 1.

The second-order partial derivatives of the profit function, $\partial^2 P/\partial w_i \partial w_j$ and $\partial^2 P/\partial p_i \partial p_j$ can be expressed, respectively, as

$$\frac{\partial X_i(\mathbf{p}, \mathbf{w})}{\partial w_j} = \frac{\partial X_i(\mathbf{Q}; \mathbf{w})}{\partial w_j} + \sum_{k=1}^{n} \left(\frac{\partial X_i(\mathbf{Q}; \mathbf{w})}{\partial Q_k} \frac{\partial Q_k(\mathbf{p}, \mathbf{w})}{\partial w_j} \right) \tag{3.18}$$

$$\frac{\partial Q_i(\mathbf{p}, \mathbf{w})}{\partial p_j} = \frac{\partial Q_i(\mathbf{X}; \mathbf{p})}{\partial p_j} - \sum_{k=1}^{m} \left(\frac{\partial Q_i(\mathbf{X}; \mathbf{p})}{\partial X_k} \frac{\partial X_k(\mathbf{p}, \mathbf{w})}{\partial p_j} \right) \tag{3.19}$$

As far as the partial derivatives $\partial^2 P/\partial w_i \partial p_j$ and $\partial^2 P/\partial p_i \partial w_j$ are concerned, they can be expressed as

$$\frac{\partial Q_j(\mathbf{p}, \mathbf{w})}{\partial w_i} = -\frac{1}{\partial^2 C(\mathbf{Q}; \mathbf{w})/\partial Q_j^2} \frac{\partial X_i(\mathbf{Q}; \mathbf{w})}{\partial Q_j} \tag{3.20}$$

$$\frac{\partial X_j(\mathbf{p}, \mathbf{w})}{\partial p_i} = -\frac{1}{\partial^2 R(\mathbf{X}; \mathbf{p})/\partial X_j^2} \frac{\partial Q_i(\mathbf{X}; \mathbf{p})}{\partial X_j} \tag{3.21}$$

It is clear from (3.20) and (3.21) that

$\partial Q_j(\mathbf{p}, \mathbf{w})/\partial w_i < 0$ when $\partial X_i(\mathbf{Q}; \mathbf{w})/\partial Q_j > 0$ and
$\partial X_j(\mathbf{p}, \mathbf{w})/\partial p_i > 0$ when $\partial Q_i(\mathbf{X}; \mathbf{p})/\partial X_j > 0$

'Normality' can be defined indifferently using profit-function, cost-function, or revenue-function second-order partial derivatives.

By contrast, whether inputs or outputs are substitutes does generally depend on the definition adopted. Let us eliminate $\partial Q_k(\mathbf{p}, \mathbf{w})/\partial w_j$ in (3.18) and $\partial X_k(\mathbf{p}, \mathbf{w})/\partial p_j$ in (3.19), obtaining

$$\frac{\partial X_i(\mathbf{p}, \mathbf{w})}{\partial w_j} = \frac{\partial X_i(\mathbf{Q}; \mathbf{w})}{\partial w_j} - \sum_{k=1}^{n} \left(\frac{1}{\left(\partial^2 C/\partial Q_k^2 \right)} \frac{\partial X_i(\mathbf{Q}; \mathbf{w})}{\partial Q_k} \frac{\partial X_j(\mathbf{Q}; \mathbf{w})}{\partial Q_k} \right)$$

$$\frac{\partial Q_i(\mathbf{p}, \mathbf{w})}{\partial p_j} = \frac{\partial Q_i(\mathbf{X}; \mathbf{p})}{\partial p_j} + \sum_{k=1}^{n} \left(\frac{1}{\left(\partial^2 R/\partial X_k^2 \right)} \frac{\partial Q_i(\mathbf{X}; \mathbf{p})}{\partial X_k} \frac{\partial Q_j(\mathbf{X}; \mathbf{p})}{\partial X_k} \right)$$

If inputs i and j are normal with respect to every output, then

$\partial X_i(\mathbf{p}, \mathbf{w})/\partial w_j < \partial X_i(\mathbf{Q}; \mathbf{w})/\partial w_j$
$\partial Q_i(\mathbf{p}, \mathbf{w})/\partial p_j > \partial Q_i(\mathbf{X}; \mathbf{p})/\partial p_j$

We see at once that

$\partial X_i(\mathbf{Q}; \mathbf{w})/\partial w_j > 0$ does not ensure $(\partial X_i(\mathbf{p}, \mathbf{w})/\partial w_j) > 0$ and
$\partial Q_i(\mathbf{X}; \mathbf{p})/\partial p_j < 0$ does not ensure $(\partial Q_i(\mathbf{p}, \mathbf{w})/\partial p_j) < 0$.

Thus there can be substitution in the 'partial' definition and complementarity in the more general definition (but *not* vice versa). Hicks's argument for the prevalence of complementarity both between inputs and between outputs (see Chapter 2, Appendix 1) has firm foundations if referred to the general profit-function definition; such a tendency is more pronounced the flatter are the marginal cost curves relating to each output.

3.6 Concluding remarks

When just one input produces a variety of outputs, the results of the long-run theory of the firm derived for the single-output, multi-input case are mirrored by equivalent results: under FIE an absolute output may decrease when both its price and the input price increase, whereas an output per unit of input is always positively related to the output's price. Using the firm's revenue function, we have derived in the first part of this chapter a complete comparative statics in relation to any change in the structure of prices.

More generally, a multiproduct, multi-input firm can best be analysed using the firm's profit function and imposing the condition $P(\mathbf{p}, \mathbf{w}) = 0$ (which makes it very immediate and clear that the comparative statics of FIE inherently considers multiple price variations). In this framework both the results of the 1970's long-run theory of the firm and their symmetrical counterparts are obtained as special cases. Moreover, we have shown that they generalize to the case of any number of inputs and outputs and we have provided rules for signing dQ_i, dX_j and $d(Q_i/X_j)$ in correspondence to any potential change in the structure of relative prices.

We did not place our firm within any specific economic context and in this respect our analysis should be considered only as a first step. One might wish to remove the assumption that products fall into disjoint groups and to admit that the different sets of outputs which characterize different firms may have elements in common, or to introduce input–output relations among firms. While allowing for input–output relationships, for example, may well lead to rather less conventional results than those set out above, such complications are already developed at some length in our single-product chapters and the interested reader can no doubt bring them into the joint-products analysis of this chapter, not least when that analysis is adapted to deal with the case of fixed capital à la Sraffa. We therefore end our brief excursion into the territory of joint production at this point and return to our main line of argument.

4 | *Interdependent industries*

We must now put an individual industry into its multi-industry context. There are many direct linkages among industries, such as input–output relations or the presence of common factors in scarce supply. The indirect linkages are, of course, countless, because a change originating in one industry may determine a change in the composition of demand, in real incomes and so on.

We shall focus here on input–output relations. Despite a certain degree of vertical integration, the value of intermediate inputs is a sizeable fraction of the value of industrial gross output. According to Jorgenson *et al.* (2005, p. xix), 'intermediate inputs predominate in gross output for about 70 per cent of the industries' in the US. In a produced-input-intensive sector such as 'Motor Vehicles' the share of intermediate inputs in gross output is nearly 80% and even in a value-added-intensive sector like 'Finance', it is no less than 40% (cf. Jorgenson *et al.*, 2005, pp. 91–92; similar data can be found for Europe in the Euklems database: www.euklems.net). It can hardly be denied, then, that the presence of input–output relations is a salient feature of production and that the fiction of full vertical integration hides some important aspects of choice in actual industries.

We have already considered (in Section 2.6) a prototype in which the output of an industry is itself an input of the same industry and all the analysis presented in this chapter provides extensions and generalizations to multiple industries. We shall start with a pure consumer good industry which uses, along with land and labour, an input produced by another industry, and illustrate the main results by means of a numerical example (Sections 4.2–4.4); then we extend this kind of analysis to the case of any number of commodity inputs and industries producing them (Section 4.5*). Thus far no interest is assumed to be paid on the use of produced inputs and the equilibria to be compared differ in the ratios of primary input prices. We shall then introduce (Section 4.6) a positive and variable rate of interest, reverting initially to our 'prototype' with one industry (Section 4.7) and then extending the analysis to input–output systems with homogeneous labour and two industries (Section 4.8) or many industries (Section 4.9*). Section 4.10 concludes.

A common feature of the various analyses in this chapter is that we retain the assumption of twice-differentiable cost functions, as we did in much of Chapters 2 and 3*. This simplifying assumption will be dropped in Chapter 5. We also assume, unless otherwise stated, that the off-diagonal elements of the average-cost-function Hessian are all positive, thus implying Hicksian input substitution, in the sense clarified in Appendix 1 to Chapter 2.

In this and the following chapters, therefore, we recognize that the equilibrium of firms in one industry is truly permanent only if all firms in the other industries are also in such an FIE: all firms must make zero net profits both before and after the shock whose permanent effect on a certain industry is to be established. It will be clear that such an analysis of interdependent industries is 'less partial' than the analysis of the isolated industry proposed in the previous chapters, which in turn was less partial than the 1970s long-run theory of the firm, which was itself less partial than the conventional partial equilibrium analysis of the industry. We are thus following a path of steadily increasing inclusiveness. Of course, this does not imply that we are moving towards comparing 'general equilibria': we shall see that one can go quite far without making any reference to so-called general equilibrium. (Besides, to take resources, ownership, preferences and technical knowledge as given is hardly to engage in the most general possible form of analysis; economic activity is sometimes directed precisely to changing such 'data' and there are, indeed, specialized branches of economic theory that study such changes.) It should also be remarked that the object of our analysis remains the individual industry, even though we are placing the latter in the wider context of a series of industries having mutual relations.

4.1 The FIE input prices with interdependent industries: an introduction

When all industries are assumed to be in a long-run equilibrium, most input prices which are on our particular industry's real input price surface (see Section 2.1) cease to have any economic relevance. This is particularly evident in the special case of the famous non-substitution theorem concerning a set of industries which use a series of produced inputs, together with a single common primary input (homogeneous labour), their use yielding no interest. In this case, the real input price surface of an individual industry (suffix omitted) is defined by

$$1 = c(w, \mathbf{p})$$

where $\mathbf{p}$ denotes the vector of produced input prices. As will be recalled from classical works of the 1950s (e.g. Dorfman *et al.*, 1958), the real input prices are completely 'frozen'. In that particular context, the input price surface discussed in Chapter 2 above would be almost entirely irrelevant: indeed, only one point would be relevant, no matter how fine input substitutability in an industry might be. For, away from that point, we are certain that some other related industries would be out of long-run equilibrium. Hence the non-substitution result.

Let us consider, for example, a consumer good industry (labelled 2) which uses labour and a produced input (labelled 1); the latter is produced by labour alone (of course, the price 'surface' is now in fact a curve). If industry 2 were taken in isolation, then the zero-net-profit condition would be consistent with the entire curve drawn in Figure 4.1. However, net profits are null also in industry 1 only at a determinate w/p_1 ratio: hence only point E is consistent with FIE.

As soon as we introduce other primary inputs (be they land or different kinds of labour), the non-substitution theorem ceases to hold, but this does not mean that full input price variability is restored, because produced input prices are still tied together by relative costs of production, which are almost never independent of one another.

It may hardly be presumed, for instance, that a general fall in engineers' earnings (say, due to selective immigration or to regulatory changes) will not reduce, in the long run, the price of sophisticated alarm systems for house protection relative to the price of window bars.

The theoretical representation of this kind of interdependence, as seen from the point of view of the individual industry, we call the 'FIE input price frontier'. Its formal properties and the effects of moving along this frontier are the subjects of the next sections.

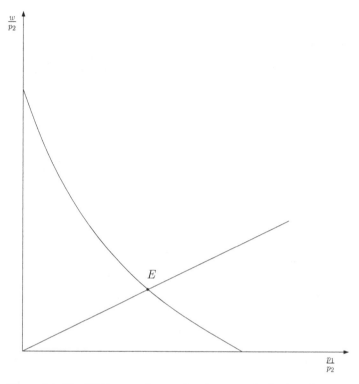

Figure 4.1 The FIE input prices under the non-substitution theorem.

4.2 The FIE input price frontier

Let us consider again a two-sector model with one pure consumption good and an intermediate commodity; but now both industries use two primary inputs, labour and land. No interest is charged on the use of the commodity input. In obvious notation, long-run equilibrium requires

$$p_1 = c_1(w, r, p_1) \tag{4.1}$$

$$p_2 = c_2(w, r, p_1) \tag{4.2}$$

Let us pause for a moment to recall that we are not assuming strictly constant returns to scale, but only 'locally' constant returns, at the bottom of U-shaped average cost curves. To any point of long-run equilibrium in each industry, then, we implicitly associate a critical long-run output level in each firm, which is a certain function of

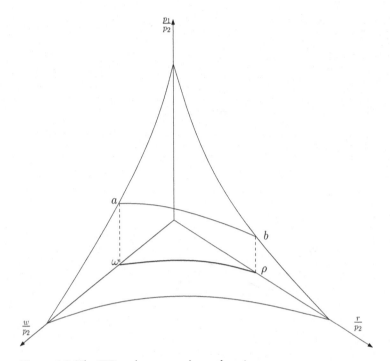

Figure 4.2 The FIE real wage–real rent frontier, $\omega\rho$.

relative input prices. We concentrate, however, on intensive variables 'per unit of output'. Nevertheless, readers should not forget that in our comparative static analysis the equilibrium output of the individual firm is variable and they are invited to work out the precise effect of a movement across the real input price surface on the long-run output, on the basis of Equations (2.9) to (2.11) of Chapter 2.

Dividing (4.2) by p_2, we obtain the equation of industry 2's real input price surface:

$$1 = c_2\left(\frac{w}{p_2}, \frac{r}{p_2}, \frac{p_1}{p_2}\right) \tag{4.3}$$

At any point on the surface defined by (4.3) (drawn in Figure 4.2) the consumer good industry is in long-run equilibrium, but this equilibrium is not 'truly' permanent unless the input-providing industry 1 is also in long-run equilibrium and we cannot presume that all relative input prices on the surface satisfy this condition. Let us divide (4.1) by p_2, obtaining

$$\left(\frac{p_1}{p_2}\right) = c_1\left(\frac{w}{p_2}, \frac{r}{p_2}, \frac{p_1}{p_2}\right) \tag{4.4}$$

We have in (4.4) a cone which crosses industry 2's input price surface: at the intersection (a curve in the space) we have a line in three-dimensional space, like line ab in Figure 4.2, which we call the FIE input price frontier. The vertical projection of ab, referred to as $\omega\rho$ in the figure, we call the real wage–real rent frontier.

Similarly to the non-substitution case, the real input price surface is almost entirely irrelevant, only a curve is significant, but now there is the possibility of some change in real input prices. We now turn to the examination of such changes.

4.3 The comparative statics of FIE

For ease of notation, let us now explicitly assume $p_2 = 1$, so that $w/p_2 = w$ and $r/p_2 = r$; moreover, let $p_1/p_2 \equiv p$.

Differentiating (4.3) and (4.4) totally, we can obtain, say, (dw, dp) as functions of dr (alternatively, one may express each price as a parametric function of the rent/wage ratio: see Equation (2.17) in Chapter 2):

$$dw = -\frac{t_2(1 - k_1) + t_1k_2}{l_2(1 - k_1) + l_1k_2}dr \tag{4.5}$$

$$dp = \frac{(t_1l_2 - t_2l_1)}{l_2(1 - k_1) + l_1k_2}dr \tag{4.6}$$

where t_j, l_j, k_j, $j = 1, 2$, denote, respectively, land, labour and commodity input use per unit of output in industry j. Moreover, we have

$$dl_2 = \frac{\partial l_2}{\partial w}dw + \frac{\partial l_2}{\partial r}dr + \frac{\partial l_2}{\partial p}dp \tag{4.7}$$

$$dt_2 = \frac{\partial t_2}{\partial w}dw + \frac{\partial t_2}{\partial r}dr + \frac{\partial t_2}{\partial p}dp \tag{4.8}$$

$$dk_2 = \frac{\partial k_2}{\partial w}dw + \frac{\partial k_2}{\partial r}dr + \frac{\partial k_2}{\partial p}dp \tag{4.9}$$

It may be helpful to consider first a special case. If the land/labour proportions in a particular FIE are the same in the two industries,

(4.5) and (4.6) become $dw = -(t_2/l_2)dr$ and $dp = 0$, respectively; if this always happens, then the ab curve of Figure 4.2 lies on a plane parallel to the $w - r$ plane. From a purely formal point of view, we are back to the case of own-product use, discussed in Section 2.6 and all conclusions reached there can be referred also to the present case. The FIE differential quotients can now be obtained by dividing (4.7) to (4.9), in turn, by dw and dr (needless to say, no differential quotient having dp in the denominator is possible). Specifically, the own-price differential ratio concerning labour use is

$$\frac{dl_2}{dw} = \frac{\partial l_2}{\partial w} - \frac{l_2}{t_2}\frac{\partial l_2}{\partial r}$$

If land and labour are Hicksian substitutes, then the partial equilibrium own-price effect is reinforced under FIE. The same is obviously true of the own-price differential quotient concerning land. Similar conclusions are reached for the cross-price differential quotients concerning primary inputs, which turn out to be

$$\frac{dl_2}{dr} = \frac{\partial l_2}{\partial r} - \frac{t_2}{l_2}\frac{\partial l_2}{\partial w} \quad \text{and} \quad \frac{dt_2}{dw} = \frac{\partial t_2}{\partial w} - \frac{l_2}{t_2}\frac{\partial t_2}{\partial r}$$

We notice, however, that the reciprocity condition need not hold under FIE.

By contrast, the reaction of k_2 to a movement along the FIE frontier recalls no properties of the partial equilibrium analysis. For instance, the quotient having dr in the denominator is

$$\frac{dk_2}{dr} = \frac{\partial k_2}{\partial w} - \frac{l_2}{t_2}\frac{\partial k_2}{\partial r}$$

Ironically, it is only possible to sign dk_2/dr if we assume that the produced input is a Hicksian complement of either labour *or* land: in both cases, however, the sign of dk_2/dr is opposite to the sign of $\partial k_2/\partial r$. Excluding complementarity, we cannot even presume that k_2 is a monotonic function of r.

The far more general case of unequal proportions introduces some further aspects. For simplicity, we take industry 1 to be always intensive in labour (there being no factor intensity reversals) so that $t_1 l_2 < t_2 l_1$ and $dp/dr < 0$. Using (4.5) and (4.6), we can calculate all the differential quotients dividing through (4.7)–(4.9) by dw, dr and

dp, in turn. Let us consider dl_2/dw and dk_2/dp. A little calculation shows that

$$\frac{dl_2}{dw} = -\frac{1}{w[t_2(1-k_1)+t_1k_2]}\left[\frac{\partial l_2}{\partial r}(1-k_1)+\frac{\partial l_2}{\partial p}t_1\right]$$

$$\frac{dk_2}{dp} = \frac{1}{p(t_1l_2-t_2l_1)}\left(\frac{\partial k_2}{\partial r}l_1-\frac{\partial k_2}{\partial w}t_1\right)$$

If $\partial l_2/\partial r > 0 < \partial l_2/\partial p$ (which is our definition of substitution between labour and both land and the produced input) then $dl_2/dw < 0$, like $\partial l_2/\partial w$. Once again, however, things are completely different for the commodity input: the own-price differential quotient dk_2/dp is of undetermined sign, unless we admit input complementarities.

Turning to the cross-price quotient, dl_2/dp, we find that it is negative, contrary to $\partial l_2/\partial p$ and specifically

$$\frac{dl_2}{dp} = \frac{1}{w(t_1l_2-t_2l_1)}\left[\frac{\partial l_2}{\partial r}(1-k_1)+\frac{\partial l_2}{\partial p}t_1\right]$$

The negative sign rests on our assumption on factor intensities and therefore dl_2/dp reflects no particular property concerning input substitution or complementarity in industry 2. (It can be easily shown that, conversely, the cross-price quotient dt_2/dp is positive, like $\partial t_2/\partial p$.)

The multi-industry framework thus widens the fundamental difference between primary and produced inputs in FIE comparative statics. First, the differential quotients having either dk_2 in the numerator or dp in the denominator do not have a definite sign, differently from the other quotients. Second, it is questionable whether the frequently discussed quotients with dp in the denominator really have any meaning. Let us consider a movement on the FIE frontier with $dr > 0$. It can be easily seen that $(dw/w) < (dp/p) < 0 < (dr/r)$: the rent increases and the wage falls relative to everything; however, the price of the commodity input falls relative to the consumer good and relative to the rent but rises relative to the wage. It is then impossible to build an unambiguous scalar index of the relative price of the commodity input: the very signs of the differential quotients having dp in the denominator depend on the specific weights used and can be made positive or negative at the theorist's whim. (We have taken the consumer good to be the numéraire; a composite numéraire would make it transparent how dp depends on the weight of each component of the numéraire, as we have seen in Sections 2.4 and 2.5.) An observed change in the commodity input price, expressed in a chosen numéraire, is thus a decidedly uninformative 'price signal'!

4.4 An example

The practical significance of representing a shock as a movement on the FIE frontier can be further illustrated by means of the following example (see Steedman, 1998, pp. 197–98), where commodity 2 is the numéraire. Let

$$c_1(w, r, p) = 0.56\sqrt{wp} + 0.02\sqrt{rp} + 0.2\sqrt{wr}$$

$$c_2(w, r, p) = 0.15r + 0.06\sqrt{wp} + 0.02\sqrt{rp} + 0.15\sqrt{wr}$$

These two minimum (indirect) average cost functions à la Diewert both have negative semidefinite Hessians for all positive (w, r, p). In addition, they have the further property that all pairs of inputs are substitutes for one another. It may also be noted that industry 1 is always relatively labour-intensive. Industry 2 is on its FIE frontier when both $c_1(\ ) = p$ and $c_2(\ ) = 1$. Let the initial FIE be $(w, r, p) = (1, 4, 1)$. In industry 2, the cost-minimizing input uses per unit of output will be $100l_2 = 18$, $100t_2 = 19.25$, $100k_2 = 5$.

Let us assume that a permanent shock has the immediate effect of raising the wage, in terms of the consumer good, to $w = 1.37$. The effect of this change alone would be to reduce industry 2's use of labour per unit of output by some 14.6%, to increase its use of land per unit of output by some 3.3% and to increase its use of the commodity input per unit of output by some 10.3%. While reacting 'optimally' to the shock, however, industry 2 would make losses (of about 6.2% of its revenues; and industry 1 would be in even worse condition, making losses of about 16.4% of its revenues). All the firms in the economy would be driven out of business, because they would be committed to distributing more output than they have produced; it follows that necessarily some further change occurs and, excluding a return of w to the previous value, one must calculate the compensating changes in the other real input prices. In particular, the rent must fall to $r = 3.64$ and the commodity input price must rise to $p = 1.21$: only then can firms in both industries make neither losses nor profits. However, in this new situation the optimal reactions to the initial shock are not those given at the beginning of this paragraph. In industry 2 the use of labour per unit of output would decrease more, by some 16.5%, to $100l_2 = 15.03$. Likewise, the use of land would increase more, by some 4.8%, to $100t_2 = 20.18$. In contrast, the use of the commodity input, far from increasing, would fall, by 1.4%, to $100k_2 = 4.93$.

The reader will have noted that the use of each input is here inversely related to its own price, but we cannot count on this qualitative result. Assume a great jump is made in the same direction, until $w = 9, r = 1$, $p = 4$: the use of the two primary inputs keeps on changing in the same direction as before, whereas the use of the commodity input reverts to $100k_2 = 5$. Thus the FIE commodity input use per unit of output in the consumer good industry is not even a monotonic function of any price and the very same use recurs at different points of the FIE input price frontier.

4.5* More general

The above results generalize to the case with m primary inputs and n commodities.

Let us label by n the industry under consideration and by (l_{in}, a_{hn}), respectively, the cost-minimizing use of labour of kind i and of produced input h per unit of output in industry n (which now need not be a pure consumer good industry).

In FIE we have

$$\mathbf{p} = \mathbf{c}(\mathbf{w}, \mathbf{p}), \quad \text{with } p_n = 1 \tag{4.10}$$

By the usual properties of the cost functions, we have

$$dl_{in} = \sum_{j=1}^{m} \frac{\partial l_{in}}{\partial w_j} w_j(\hat{w}_j - \hat{w}_i) + \sum_{s=1}^{n} \frac{\partial l_{in}}{\partial p_s} p_s(\hat{p}_s - \hat{w}_i), \quad i = 1, 2, \ldots, m$$

$$da_{hn} = \sum_{j=1}^{m} \frac{\partial a_{hn}}{\partial w_j} w_j(\hat{w}_j - \hat{p}_h) + \sum_{s=1}^{n} \frac{\partial a_{hn}}{\partial p_s} p_s(\hat{p}_s - \hat{p}_h), \quad h = 1, 2, \ldots, n \tag{4.11}$$

Let $\mathbf{c_w} = \mathbf{L}$ and $\mathbf{c_p} = \mathbf{A}$ denote the matrices of the cost-minimizing use of the different kinds of labour and of the various produced inputs per unit of output in the n industries (whose terms are, of course, functions of $(\mathbf{w}, \mathbf{p})$). By homogeneity of degree 1 of the cost functions, we have

$$\mathbf{p} = \mathbf{wL}(\mathbf{I} - \mathbf{A})^{-1}, \quad \text{with } 1 = \mathbf{wL}(\mathbf{I} - \mathbf{A})^{-1}\mathbf{e}_n \tag{4.12}$$

where e_n is the nth unit vector. If the input–output system is viable, $L(I - A)^{-1}$ is a non-negative matrix and for ease of notation let $L(I - A)^{-1} = \Lambda$. Differentiating (4.12) totally, we obtain

$$\hat{p}_s = \sum_{j=1}^{m} \left(\frac{w_j \lambda_{js}}{p_s} \hat{w}_j \right), \quad \text{with } \sum_{j=1}^{m} \frac{w_j \lambda_{js}}{p_s} = 1, \quad s - 1, 2, \ldots, (n-1)$$

$$0 = \sum_{j=1}^{m} (w_j \lambda_{jn} \hat{w}_j), \quad \text{with } \sum_{j=1}^{m} w_j \lambda_{jn} = 1 \tag{4.13}$$

Let us consider a shock increasing the real wage of labour 1 in terms of the output of industry n. In order to keep things as simple as possible (and as similar as possible to conventional analysis), let us suppose that the ratios between the other wages are constant, so that, by the last equation in (4.13)

$$\hat{w}_2 = \hat{w}_3 = \cdots = \hat{w}_n = -\left(\frac{w_1 \lambda_{1n}}{1 - w_1 \lambda_{1n}} \right) \hat{w}_1$$

By substitution, we have

$$\hat{p}_s = \frac{1}{1 - w_1 \lambda_{1n}} \left(\frac{w_1 \lambda_{1s}}{p_s} - w_1 \lambda_{1n} \right) \hat{w}_1, \quad s = 1, 2, \ldots, (n-1)$$

Let commodities be numbered in increasing order of $(w_1 \lambda_{1s}/p_s)$. If $dw_1 > 0$, we have therefore

$$\hat{w}_2 = \hat{w}_3 = \hat{w}_m < \hat{p}_1 < \cdots < \hat{p}_{n-1} < 0 < \hat{w}_1$$

(The reverse inequalities hold if $dw_1 < 0$.) We can at this point divide (4.11) by $dw_1, \ldots, dw_m, dp_1, \ldots, dp_{n-1}$, in turn. Because the signs of $(\hat{w}_i - \hat{w}_j)/dw_i$, etc., are fully determined, we can easily examine the sign pattern of the $(m + n) \times (m + n - 1)$ matrix of differential quotients. If all the off-diagonal terms of the indirect average cost function Hessian are positive, then

(a) the $m \times m$ block involving the primary inputs and their prices has negative diagonal terms dl_{in}/dw_i and positive off-diagonal terms dl_{in}/dw_j, $j \neq i$. The off-diagonal terms in symmetrical position, however, are not equal;

(b) the $(n-1) \times (n-1)$ block involving produced inputs and their prices (excluding commodity n) has diagonal terms da_{hn}/dp_h, $h \neq n$ and off-diagonal terms da_{hn}/dp_s, $s \neq n$ which may be of either sign. The off-diagonal terms in symmetrical position may even differ in sign;

(c) The other blocks with da_{hn}/dw_i, dl_{in}/dp_s, da_{nn}/dp_s, $s \neq n$, have both positive and negative terms: for instance, $dl_{1n}/dp_s > 0$ but $dl_{2n}/dp_s < 0$ and so on.

This confirms that, with full substitutability, twice-differentiable average cost functions, zero interest and FIE, there is a fundamental qualitative difference between the relatively simple 'laws' that govern primary input use and the rather irregular behaviour of produced input use (and their prices).

Not surprisingly, the presence of complementarities would destroy even the few existing 'laws', eliminating any systematic coincidence in the sign pattern between blocks of the differential quotients matrix and the corresponding blocks of the cost function Hessian.

4.6 Introducing a positive rate of interest

The foregoing analysis overlooked an important aspect of actual industries: the presence of a positive interest rate. Because, as we have seen, the value of intermediate inputs is a sizeable fraction of the value of gross output, the role of interest cannot be ignored.

The effects of interest rate changes on long-run real wages, relative prices and productive choices have been investigated extensively in the Sraffian literature and we certainly need not repeat here what can be found in many excellent presentations (e.g. Pasinetti, 1977 [1975]; Kurz and Salvadori, 1995). Yet, given the emphasis that that literature placed on the aggregate level of analysis, it will be useful to consider here the precise implications of interest rate variations on choices in an individual industry. It will be no surprise for some readers to see that the FIE qualitative changes can diverge from the predictions of simple partial equilibrium analysis. However, perhaps a precise explanation, in terms of microeconomic reasoning, of why this is so has not yet been explicated sufficiently. For example, we want to clarify whether a reduction, say, in the real wage compensated by an increase in the interest rate determines effects of a different nature from those of the same reduction compensated by an increase in the real rent. In order to isolate the specific role of interest, we confirm all the conventional assumptions on technology that we have made so far in this chapter (in this departing from much of the Sraffian literature, of course).

4.7 A one-industry economy once again

Let us return to the simple case, discussed in Section 2.6, of a completely isolated industry, which is the sole user of land and labour and whose output (which we now call 'corn') is used as a means of production (which we now call 'seeds').

Denoting now by i the rate of interest and by p the price of corn (and seeds), the indirect average cost function is

$$c = c(w, r, (1 + i)p) \tag{4.14}$$

The cost-minimizing use of labour, land and seeds per unit of gross output is:

$$l = \frac{\partial c}{\partial w}; \quad t = \frac{\partial c}{\partial r}; \quad k = \frac{\partial c}{\partial((1 + i)p)} \tag{4.15}$$

Expressing all rentals in terms of the output, the industry is in FIE when

$$1 = c\left(\frac{w}{p}, \frac{r}{p}, (1 + i)\right) \tag{4.16}$$

Equation (4.16) defines the real wage–real rent–rate of interest frontier (note that $(1 + i)$, a pure number, is the real rental rate of seeds), on which the FIE comparisons must be made. Let $p = 1$, for ease of notation.

By (4.15), total differentiation of (4.16) gives

$$k di = -(wl\hat{w} + rt\hat{r}) \tag{4.17}$$

On the other hand, we can also infer from (4.15) that

$$dl = \frac{\partial l}{\partial r}r(\hat{r} - \hat{w}) + \frac{\partial l}{\partial i}(1 + i)\left(\frac{di}{(1 + i)} - \hat{w}\right) \tag{4.18}$$

$$dt = \frac{\partial t}{\partial w}w(\hat{w} - \hat{r}) + \frac{\partial t}{\partial i}(1 + i)\left(\frac{di}{(1 + i)} - \hat{r}\right) \tag{4.19}$$

$$dk = \frac{\partial k}{\partial w}w\left(\hat{w} - \frac{di}{(1 + i)}\right) + \frac{\partial k}{\partial r}r\left(\hat{r} - \frac{di}{(1 + i)}\right) \tag{4.20}$$

Dividing (4.18) to (4.20) by dw, dr and di, in turn, we may obtain all the FIE differential quotients.

Let us consider the case in which a reduction in the real wage is compensated by an increase in the rate of interest, as a counterpart of the case discussed in Section 2.6. Because $\hat{w} < 0 = \hat{r} < di$, our assumption of positive cross-price partial equilibrium effects permits us to sign dl, dk from (4.18) and (4.20) and to conclude that $dl/dw < 0 > dk/di$ and $dl/di > 0 < dk/dw$. In contrast, dt in (4.19) is indeterminate; its sign may even be different in different equilibria, so that the use of land may be a non-monotonic function of w (or i). There is a strict symmetry, therefore, between this case and the case in which a reduction in the real wage was compensated by an increase in the real rent: there, the sign of dk was ambiguous; here, the sign of dt is ambiguous. The reason is the same: an input price (or rental) increases relative to another input price and falls relative to a third one.

In this simple one-industry economy, therefore, the interest rate has no special role and its 'unconventional' effects have the same explanation as the other effects under FIE. In order to have further, interest-specific effects we must consider at least two interrelated industries.

4.8 Two industries

When considering a two-industry economy it will be convenient to eliminate the complications arising from a changing wage/rent ratio and to assume henceforth that a single primary input (homogeneous labour) is used in all industries (which is equivalent to assuming that the wage/rent ratio is constant).

Each industry has three inputs: labour, the own-product and the product of the other industry. The indirect average cost functions in industry j is

$$c_j = c_j[w, (1+i)p_1, (1+i)p_2]$$

Setting $p_1 = 1$, FIE requires

$$1 = c_1[w, (1+i), (1+i)p_2] \tag{4.21}$$

$$p_2 = c_2[w, (1+i), (1+i)p_2] \tag{4.22}$$

Treating i as a parameter, (4.21) and (4.22) implicitly define a $w(i)$ relation – the real wage–rate of interest frontier – and a $p_2(i)$ relation. Both relations are well known from the Sraffian literature (e.g. Kurz and Salvadori, 1995, pp. 147–49). Here we want to clarify further the microeconomic structure of the effect that a change in the interest rate has on the industry-level use of each input per unit of output.

By comparison with the cost functions considered so far, in (4.21), (4.22) Shephard's lemma should be used with extra care, because a change in the interest rate automatically affects two real rentals at once, $(1 + i)$ and $(1 + i)p_2$. In order to derive a_{11}, say, as a partial derivative of c_1, we must assume that not only w but also $(1 + i)p_2$ remains constant; that is, we must impose an artificial compensating change in p_2. For brevity, and to clarify our precise notation, let '$\partial(1 + i)$' denote a marginal variation in $(1 + i)$ which keeps $(1 + i)p_2$ constant and, conversely, let '$\partial((1 + i)p_2)$' be a marginal variation in $(1 + i)p_2$ which keeps $(1 + i)$ constant. With this understanding, we have

$$l_j = \frac{\partial c_j}{\partial w}, \quad a_{1j} = \frac{\partial c_j}{\partial(1 + i)}, \quad a_{2j} = \frac{\partial c_j}{\partial((1 + i)p_2)}$$

The proper partial derivative of c_j with respect to the rate of interest gives the value of capital per unit of output in industry j, which we denote by k_j. Hence

$$k_j = \frac{\partial c_j}{\partial i} = a_{1j} + a_{2j}p_2$$

Differentiating (4.21) and (4.22) totally we get

$$0 = l_1 dw + k_1 di + (1 + i)a_{21}dp_2$$

$$[1 - (1 + i)a_{22}]dp_2 = l_2 dw + k_2 di$$

Needless to say, a significant equilibrium requires $[1 - (1 + i)a_{22}] > 0$. It is also well known that $dw/di < 0$ and that dp_2/di has the same sign as $(k_2 l_1 - k_1 l_2)$.

How then do the input rentals $(w, (1 + i), (1 + i)p_2)$ change as we move along the real wage–rate of interest frontier, and what change do they provoke in the input use per unit of output, say, in industry 1?

Let $di > 0$. If $(k_2 l_1 - k_1 l_2) > 0$, then the ranking of the proportional changes in the three input rentals is

$$\frac{dw}{w} < 0 < \frac{di}{1 + i} < \left(\frac{di}{1 + i} + \frac{dp_2}{p_2} \right)$$

An increase in the rate of interest always increases the rentals of the two commodity inputs relative to the wage. However, unless $(k_2 l_1 - k_1 l_2) = 0$, one commodity rental falls relative to the other. It should be stressed that this is not a possibility, it is a necessity! It follows that there is no microeconomic ground, based on Hicksian substitution, for presuming anything about the direction of change in the use of one of the two commodity inputs.

Considering input use explicitly, we obtain by our usual second-order differentiation

$$dl_1 = \frac{\partial l_1}{\partial(1+i)}(1+i)\left(\frac{di}{1+i} - \hat{w}\right)$$
$$+ \frac{\partial l_1}{\partial((1+i)p_2)}(1+i)p_2\left(\frac{di}{1+i} + \hat{p}_2 - \hat{w}\right) \tag{4.23}$$

$$da_{11} = \frac{\partial a_{11}}{\partial w}w\left(\hat{w} - \frac{di}{1+i}\right) + \frac{\partial a_{11}}{\partial((1+i)p_2)}(1+i)p_2\hat{p}_2 \tag{4.24}$$

$$da_{21} = \frac{\partial a_{21}}{\partial w}w\left(\hat{w} - \frac{di}{1+i} - \hat{p}_2\right) - \frac{\partial a_{21}}{\partial(1+i)}(1+i)\hat{p}_2 \tag{4.25}$$

Let us consider once again an increase in the rate of interest. Assuming all cross-price partial derivatives to be positive, the use of labour per unit of output increases and therefore we have an inverse $l_1(w)$ relationship. By contrast, the reaction of produced input use depends on the qualitative variation in the relative commodity price. If $dp_2 > 0$, then $da_{21} < 0$ but da_{11} is of uncertain sign; conversely, if $dp_2 < 0$, then $da_{11} < 0$ but da_{21} is of uncertain sign. No inverse relationships between a_{11}, a_{21} and their rentals can be postulated even under smooth substitutability, unless $(k_2 l_1 - k_1 l_2) = 0$ and thus $dp_2 = 0$.

It might perhaps be claimed that the changes in the two physical commodity inputs are less interesting than the changes in the overall 'capital/output' ratios, $k_1 = a_{11} + p_2 a_{21}$ and $k_2/p_2 = (1/p_2)a_{12} + a_{22}$. So let us consider this.

It is readily found that, for industry 1

$$\frac{dk_1}{di} = \frac{\partial k_1}{\partial i} + a_{21}\frac{dp_2}{di} \quad \text{and} \quad (1+i)l_1\left(\frac{\partial k_1}{\partial i}\right) = -\left(\frac{\partial a_{11}}{\partial w} + p_2\frac{\partial a_{21}}{\partial w}\right)$$

The change in the capital/output ratio has two components: in order, a 'real' component, evaluated at a constant p_2 and a 'price' component.

Authors in the marginalist tradition, like Burmeister and Turnovsky (1972, p. 842), insist that the real component is the relevant one for behaviour in the economy as a whole; and this component *is* negative, by our assumption of positive cross-price partial equilibrium effects.

Be that as it may, the price component is certainly relevant when we are interested in the individual industry for its own sake. It may obviously be of either sign (and of opposite sign in the two industries) and this makes either $dk_1/di > 0$ or $dk_2/di > 0$ possible.

It is truly ironic that many marginalist discussions of firm-level $k_j(i)$ should ignore the effect of a changing i on price ratios, for it can reasonably be said that an emphasis on the importance of changes in relative prices lies at the very heart of marginalist theory. Hence to leap from the truth that $\partial k_j/\partial i < 0$ to the assertion that $dk_j/di < 0$ is to fail to take marginalism seriously!

It should be stressed that dk_j/di may be positive even with typical marginalist cost functions such as CES functions, as will be seen in the next (starred) section. For a wider discussion of capital–output ratios at the industry level increasing with the rate of interest, the reader is referred to Steedman (2009).

4.9* Many industries with CES cost functions

Our results generalize to n industries, but rather than presenting an abstract argument, we prefer in this section, which draws on Steedman (2013), to examine in detail the specific and highly conventional case of n CES average cost functions.

For simplicity, let the constant elasticity of substitution be uniform in all industries and equal to σ, with $0 < \sigma < 1$. The following price = unit cost relationship holds for $j = 1, \ldots, n$:

$$p_j^{1-\sigma} = \varepsilon_j w^{(1-\sigma)} + \sum_{s=1}^{n} \alpha_{sj}[(1+i)p_s]^{(1-\sigma)} \tag{4.26}$$

We choose our measurement units for labour and for the n commodities so that when $i = 0$, Equation (4.26) is satisfied by $p_j = w$ for every j. Hence the non-negative coefficients ε_j and α_{sj} sum to unity for each j; that is, in obvious vector and matrix notation,

$$\boldsymbol{\varepsilon} + \mathbf{u}\tilde{\mathbf{A}} = \mathbf{u} \tag{4.27}$$

where $\mathbf{u}$ is a row vector of unit elements. Note that we have thereby ensured that the system is productive. It will be assumed throughout that the rate of interest is sufficiently low so as to ensure non-negative wages and prices.

The direct use of labour and of commodity input s per unit of output in industry j is

$$l_j = \varepsilon_j (p_j/w)^\sigma \tag{4.28}$$

$$a_{sj} = \alpha_{sj} \left[\frac{p_j}{(1+i)p_s} \right]^\sigma \tag{4.29}$$

In (4.28) and (4.29) each l_j and a_{sj} is a decreasing function of the corresponding real rental in terms of the product, along conventional marginalist lines (albeit in the case of a_{sj} this property does not generalize to other functional forms, as we showed in the previous section). However, this is not an interesting result, in the long-run context, for the off-diagonal a_{sj}. The ratio $[(1+i)p_s/p_j]$ is not something that can sensibly be treated as an exogenously given parameter – even less can all such ratios be so treated simultaneously! Under FIE, we must take either (some measure of) the real wage or the interest rate as our parameter.

Three simple and definite results emerge at once from (4.28) and (4.29) concerning the changes in input–output coefficients as the interest rate rises. First, every l_j increases; second, every a_{ss} decreases; third, every 'physical-capital–labour' ratio, $(a_{sj}/l_j) = (\alpha_{sj}/\varepsilon_j)(w/(1+i)p_s)^\sigma$, decreases.

It is less immediately obvious, however, whether the off-diagonal a_{sj} bear a simple relation to i. We may begin by noting that, from (4.29)

$$a_{sj}a_{js} = [\alpha_{sj}\alpha_{js}/(1+i)^{2\sigma}] \tag{4.30}$$

and hence that at least one of a_{sj} and a_{js} must decrease as i increases. (More generally,

$$a_{hs}a_{sj}a_{jh} = [\alpha_{hs}\alpha_{sj}\alpha_{jh}/(1+i)^{3\sigma}],$$

etc., and to this extent there is a 'prevalence' of decreasing a_{sj} as i increases.) This does not ensure that they both decrease, however. For suppose that industry j is fully automated ($\varepsilon_j = 0$) and that only α_{sj} and α_{jj} are positive. As i increases, a_{jj} will always fall and hence a_{sj} must be monotonically increasing as industry j moves around its isoquant. Thus monotonic movement of $a_{sj}(i)$ is possible in either direction. It is left to the interested reader to verify that $a_{sj}(i)$ can also move non-monotonically.

Turning now to the capital–(gross) output ratio in industry j, this can be written as either

$$k_j = \sum a_{sj} \left(\frac{p_s}{p_j}\right) = (1+i)^{-\sigma} \sum \alpha_{sj} \left(\frac{p_s}{p_j}\right)^{1-\sigma} \tag{4.31}$$

or

$$k_j = (1+i)^{-1} \left[1 - \varepsilon_j \left(\frac{w}{p_j}\right)^{1-\sigma}\right] \tag{4.32}$$

Because every (w/p_j) is a decreasing function of i, we see from (4.32) that, as i increases, k_j is subject to two opposing influences, the first term on the rhs decreasing and the second increasing (unless $(1-\sigma)\varepsilon_j = 0$). One should not be too hasty, then, to suppose that k_j must fall as i rises.

Now consider (4.31). At a generic i, there is a commodity price that is rising relative to every other such price. Clearly, k for that industry is decreasing in i (at the given value of i). At the same time, one commodity price is falling relative to every other price and for that industry we again see, now from (4.31), that k is subject to a decreasing effect, via $(1+i)^{-\sigma}$, and to $(n-1)$ increasing effects, via the $(p_s/p_j)^{1-\sigma}$ terms.

We focus now on the simple case $n = 2$. From (4.31) we have

$$\left[(1+i)^\sigma k_1 - \alpha_{11}\right]\left[(1+i)^\sigma k_2 - \alpha_{22}\right] = \alpha_{12}\alpha_{21}$$

so that at least one of k_1 and k_2 must fall as i rises. Can one of them nevertheless increase? Because k_1, say, is given by

$$k_1 = a_{11} + a_{21}(p_2/p_1) \tag{4.33}$$

it might be thought at first glance that $(da_{21}/di) > 0$ favours $(dk_1/di) > 0$. However, if we eliminate (p_2/p_1) from (4.33) and from the formula for a_{21}, we find that

$$\left[(1+i)k_1\right]^\sigma = \alpha_{11}{}^\sigma (1+i)^{\sigma-1} + \alpha_{21}a_{21}{}^{\sigma-1}$$

and thus we see that a necessary condition for k_1 to increase with i is in fact that a_{21} must fall as i rises.

To illustrate how k_1 can vary with i we present three examples, in each of which $\sigma = 1/2$ and

$$\alpha_{12} = 0.7; \quad \alpha_{22} = 0.3; \quad \varepsilon_2 = 0$$

Differences in the $(\alpha_{11}, \alpha_{21}, \varepsilon_1)$ vector are sufficient to produce qualitatively different $k_1(i)$ movements.

(i) If $\alpha_{11} = \alpha_{21} = 0.35$ and $\varepsilon_1 = 0.3$ then $k_1(i)$ is monotonically decreasing.

(ii) If $\alpha_{11} = 0.2$, $\alpha_{21} = 0.4$ and $\varepsilon_1 = 0.4$ then $k_1(i)$ falls at first as i rises from zero. However, it achieves a minimum value at i just above 11.25%; thereafter $k_1(i)$ is increasing. Clearly $k_1(0) = 0.6$ and $k_1(i)$ returns to this value at i just a little below 23.5%. Thus infinitely many values of k_1 *recur*, being adopted at two distinct rates of interest but not at any intermediate rate. (But no reswitching is involved here.)

(iii) If $7\alpha_{11} < 3\alpha_{21}$ then $k_1(i)$ is monotonically increasing.

Even for given $(\sigma, \alpha_{12}, \alpha_{22}, \varepsilon_2)$, $k_1(i)$ can exhibit three qualitatively different kinds of behaviour. (Note that no values of $(\alpha_{11}, \alpha_{21}, \varepsilon_1)$ will lead $k_1(i)$ first to increase and then to decrease.)

Thus distinctly conventional technologies, such as CES average cost functions in all industries, do not ensure that the capital–(gross) output ratios (nor the use of all physical capital items per unit of output) in the various industries are inversely related to the rate of interest under FIE.

4.10 Concluding remarks

We have examined in this chapter the FIE comparative statics of input use per unit of output in an industry engaged in input–output relations. Our focus was on actual industrial sectors, not on vertically integrated sectors. The latter are sometimes useful abstractions when referred to economy-wide phenomena, but at the same time they distract attention from the phenomena that originate in actual industries, such as a change in the methods of production brought about by price realignments.

In order to facilitate comparison of our results with those from more conventional partial equilibrium analyses, we have always assumed twice-differentiable cost functions and the absence of input complementarity.

Our analysis highlighted a fundamental difference between primary and produced inputs, under FIE. It is regrettable that quite often we find (in both textbooks and applications) treatments of long-run 'input use' in relation to 'input prices' that make no distinction whatever between these two different groups of inputs. Yet we have shown in various different contexts that produced input use reacts to a given shock in qualitatively different ways as compared to primary inputs; and we have noted that a produced-input price (rental) cannot be considered as a parameter.

The conventional assumptions guarantee that primary input use per unit of output is in fact inversely related to the own input price. This is so both when a change in one primary input price is 'compensated' by an opposite change in other primary input prices (thus confirming also the conventional positive response to these 'cross-prices') and when it is compensated by an opposite change in the rate of interest. This is a notable result, interesting in its own right. However, there is no such regularity concerning the use of commodity inputs: any movement on the FIE frontier leaves the change in each commodity input per unit of output undetermined a priori. Even with utterly conventional cost functions in all industries, such as those of the CES variety, the behaviour of commodity inputs (other than the 'own input') is undetermined a priori. Like the above-mentioned 'positive' result, this 'negative' result also holds both when the rate of interest is taken as constant (and possibly null) and when it is variable. It has therefore no essential connection with interest-rate variations, but has everything to do with the more fundamental FIE property that 'price = unit cost' always and everywhere.

Having said this, a change in the interest rate has also some specific effects, distinguished from those of primary input price variations. First, it automatically modifies the rentals of all the inputs which attract interest payments: such a simultaneous variation is a further source of inadequacy of the conventional partial equilibrium analysis (as referred to each physical input) and, under FIE, it adds to the other sources of price realignments. Second, an interest rate variation is naturally put into relation not only with the physical inputs, but also with the aggregate value of the produced inputs used in a certain industry. In fact this is commonly done in conventional theory and applications. We have proved that, even with distinctly conventional technologies such as those implied in CES cost functions, the industrial capital–output ratios need not be inversely related to the rate of interest. The phenomenon of capital reversing, which featured so prominently in the famous capital theory debates of the 1960s and 1970s, can therefore be referred to an individual industry, even when we make the standard assumptions of twice-differentiability and Hicksian substitution concerning technology.

The next chapter will continue our discussion of interdependent industries. However, we shall there drop the assumption of twice-differentiable cost functions; in this setting, after a succinct analysis of the relationship between industry-level choices and the rate of interest along Sraffian lines, we shall return to the main path of our reasoning, in which the rate of interest is identically null.

5 | Industry-level input use. Some aftershocks from capital theory

The capital theory debates of the 1960s and 1970s did not clarify whether unconventional phenomena can occur, under FIE, in a particular industry even though everything is conventional in the aggregate. Yet, as one of the present authors has argued, 'there is good reason also to focus attention explicitly on what takes place at the level of the industry, not least because that is the level of analysis at which so much microeconomic theory is presented. Moreover, most applied micro-economists are interested in specific industries and it is relationships at this level that interest them' (Steedman, 2009, p. 150).

Can unconventional results concern only one or more industries, without any echo in the economy as a whole? Perhaps more importantly, can they occur even when the rate of interest is constant and zero and under all the assumptions which ensure a conventional aggregate behaviour? Is FIE as such, rather than interest and capital, responsible for the failure of simple partial equilibrium predictions about the firm and the industry?

The aim of the present chapter is to answer these questions. Section 5.1 concerns the industry-level direct labour use per unit of output in relation to the rate of interest, as a sequel to Section 4.8. Differently from Chapter 4, however, we now restrict our attention to a limited number of alternative methods in order to facilitate a comparison with Sraffian findings. Section 5.2 argues the need for a shift in focus from the economy to the industry (under FIE) and from variations in the rate of interest to variations in relative primary input prices. We consider then a variety of cases characterized by the presence of labour, land, produced means of production and a null rate of interest – a two-period Wicksellian case (Section 5.3), a Nuti-model case (Section 5.4), a Samuelson–Surrogate case (Section 5.5) and an input–output case (Section 5.6). In all these cases everything is utterly conventional for the economy as a whole and we ask whether the same is true of every individual industry. Section 5.7 develops the input–output case somewhat further and examines the possibility that the entire material input–output matrix might recur across different FIE. We assume (strictly) constant returns to scale throughout this chapter, although we do not exclude that some arguments, at least, could also be referred to firms characterized by U-shaped average cost curves, as in the previous chapters (and indeed we encourage the interested reader to investigate this). However, because the literature in the light of which our results are discussed typically assumed strict constant returns, it is useful here to make the same assumption. Section 5.8 concludes.

5.1 Labour and capital per unit of output in a particular industry

Let us consider a stationary economy, subject to constant returns to scale, whose *net* output consists of a single good, labelled n. The aggregate economy can thus be described by the nth vertically integrated sector. In the presence of labour and circulating capital and assuming temporarily only one method of production to be known in each industry, we have under FIE (in standard notation)

$$\mathbf{p} = w\mathbf{l} + (1+i)\mathbf{p}\mathbf{A} \tag{5.1}$$

Setting $\lambda \equiv \mathbf{l}(\mathbf{I} - \mathbf{A})^{-1}\mathbf{e}_n$ and $\kappa = \mathbf{p}\mathbf{A}(\mathbf{I} - \mathbf{A})^{-1}\mathbf{e}_n/p_n$, where $\mathbf{e}_n$ is the nth unit vector, we have therefore

$$1 = \frac{w}{p_n}\lambda + i\kappa \tag{5.2}$$

It is clear that λ is the total, direct and indirect, employment per unit of net output and that κ is the corresponding capital/net-output ratio. We also know, of course, that κ generally varies with i, by the simple fact that the price ratios $\mathbf{p}/p_n$ vary with i. Taking κ as a function of i, (5.2) determines a familiar real wage–interest rate curve.

Turning to the industrial sector n, direct employment per unit of (gross) output is l_n, while the direct capital/output ratio is $k_n = \mathbf{p}\mathbf{A}\mathbf{e}_n/p_n$. We see immediately from (5.1) that

$$1 = \frac{w}{p_n}l_n + (1+i)k_n$$

In Figure 5.1, we easily read off both λ and l_n, the latter by simply extending the real wage–interest rate curve back to $i = -1$.

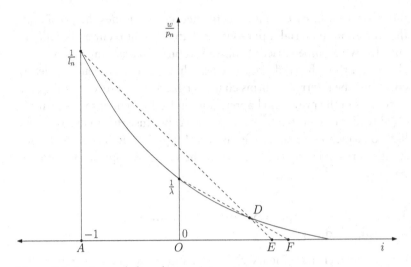

Figure 5.1 An 'extended' real wage–interest rate curve.

Now let us consider a specific real wage–rate of interest combination, at point D. For that combination, $OF = (1/\kappa)$ and $AE = (1/k_n)$. Although the (aggregate) capital/labour ratio was typically considered in the capital theory debates, we prefer to concentrate on capital/output ratios. The latter have the desirable property of being pure numbers (in a period analysis), while the former have the unfortunate characteristic of depending on the arbitrary choice of numéraire, so that as the rate of interest changes, two different measures of one and the same capital–labour ratio can move in opposite directions (see Steedman, 2009, p. 151).

In Figure 5.1, both κ and k_n are inversely related to the rate of interest. This need not be so, of course, and we know that in general they need not even be monotonic. We remark, in particular, that the main qualitative properties of $k_n(i)$ for $0 \leq i \leq \max i$ depend on the curvature of the wage–interest rate curve in the entire range $(-1 < i \leq \max i)$. (The interested reader is invited to figure out cases in which κ and k_n behave differently when only one method is known in each industry.)

If we shift our attention to capital–output ratios in the other industries, we find that they cannot all behave in the same way, excluding the fluke case in which relative prices are independent of the rate of interest. In particular, by choice of labelling let (in our usual

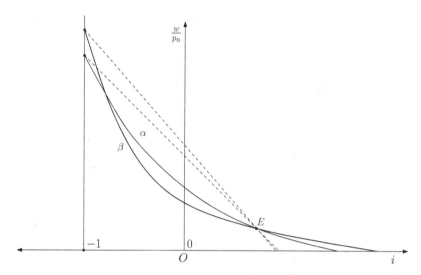

Figure 5.2 Two methods in industry n.

notation) $\hat{p}_1 < \hat{p}_2 < \cdots < \hat{p}_n$; it follows immediately that $k_n = \mathbf{p}\mathbf{A}\mathbf{e}_n/p_n$ (locally) decreases with the rate of interest (as in Figure 5.1) and $k_1 = \mathbf{p}\mathbf{A}\mathbf{e}_1/p_1$ locally increases with it (see Steedman, 2009, for further details).

Now let us suppose that industry n can choose between two methods of production, α and β, while every other industry knows only one method, and let these two 'techniques' determine the (extended) real wage–interest rate curves drawn in Figure 5.2 (thick line for method β). This diagrammatic example will suffice to present the main point. As the rate of interest increases from zero, industry n initially adopts method α and then it switches to method β until the real wage is zero. There is therefore no reswitching. Moreover, κ is inversely related to the rate of interest both within each method and across the switch point; likewise, the aggregate employment per unit of net output is inversely related to the real wage. By contrast, within industry n, the direct capital–output ratio increases with the rate of interest and direct employment per unit of output falls with the real wage, across the switch point. In the case described by Figure 5.2, the unconventional properties of the $l_n(w/p_n)$ and $k_n(i)$ relations are two sides of the same coin.

The remainder of this chapter introduces a second primary factor, homogeneous land, and presents an analysis of the direct use of primary inputs in a particular industry when the rate of interest is constant and equal to zero.

5.2 The direct use of primary inputs in a particular industry; previous literature

During the capital theory debates, many examples were provided showing how reswitching and capital reversing could occur. Various different models of production were employed, but all the examples were based on the comparison of alternative FIE (with a uniform wage and a uniform rate of interest). While the emphasis was always placed on the behaviour of the economy as a whole, it was implicit in each such example that in some industry (often the consumer good industry) the direct use of labour per unit of output was not monotonically related to the real wage rate, and hence not inversely related to it. This could be illustrated many times over from the famous *Quarterly Journal of Economics* Symposium (1966); here it will suffice to mention the Wicksellian, dated-labour example given in Samuelson's 'Summing Up' (Samuelson, 1966, pp. 569–71). Direct labour-use per unit of consumer good output is here equal to zero both for $0 \leq 42w \leq 3$ and for $4 < 42w \leq 6$, but it is equal to *six* for $3 < 42w < 4$.

Four years later, Garegnani (1970, pp. 428–34) provided examples involving infinitely many alternative techniques, each of the Samuelson–Hicks–Spaventa 'corn-tractor' type. Garegnani concentrated on the behaviour of net national income per worker and of the value of aggregate capital per worker, but it is easy to see how the direct use of labour per unit of output in the consumer good industry varies with the real wage, w. In the main example of Garegnani's text, as w falls from 0.200 to about 0.129 the labour-use rises (from 0.500 to about 6.391), but as w continues to fall to zero, the labour-use falls (back to 0.500). (The direct capital–output ratio in the consumer good industry is also non-monotonically related to the interest rate, but that is not our concern here.) Thus implicit in Garegnani's main example is a demonstration that, in an FIE context, the real wage and labour-use in a particular industry need not be inversely related.

The analyses referred to above ignored the use of land, but this was considered in Metcalfe and Steedman (1972) and in Montet (1979). While both these papers again centred on the economy as a whole and on 'vertically integrated' uses of land and labour, each of them had implicit in a numerical example the result that direct labour-use per unit of output in a particular industry was positively related to the real wage rate (see Metcalfe and Steedman, 1972, pp. 151–52; Montet, 1979, pp. 643–44). The former paper invoked reswitching but the latter did not, requiring only that the rate of interest be positive. Again, then, these papers contained implicitly an FIE analysis in which the real wage was not inversely related to labour-use in a particular industry.

In Steedman (2006) the focus on labour-use in a specific industry became explicit. It was shown that in three different kinds of model of production, the consumer good industry can use 'more labour per unit of output the higher is the real (consumer good) wage rate' (Steedman, 2006, p. 164), even when reswitching is completely excluded. However, because land was ignored in this paper, there were (necessarily) variations in the rate of interest as the real wage varied.

In the light of all the above, we now ask whether direct primary input-use in an industry can be unconventionally related to its real wage (or real rent) in an FIE analysis, even when reswitching is absent and even, perhaps, when the rate of interest is constant and zero. If the answer proves to be positive, then it might be thought that the earlier Sraffian critique of mainstream theory, stressing interest rate variations, reswitching and capital reversing, perhaps let conventional theorizing off too lightly.

5.3 A Wicksellian two-period case

We may begin with a particularly simple case in which reswitching could not possibly occur and in which we shall impose a constant and zero rate of interest throughout. Two primary inputs, land and labour, are used in two stages of production and we examine the effect of a change in the rent/wage ratio on the second stage, i.e. the consumer good industry. At the level of the whole economy everything will be entirely conventional and nothing 'unexpected' could ever happen (we need at least three periods for that), yet at the level of the consumer good industry input use/input price relations for labour and land may or may not be conventional, depending on the details of the example chosen.

Suppose that there are two distinct ways of producing one unit of the consumer good, the 'Roman' method and the 'Greek' method,

Table 5.1a *Two methods, fixed coefficients: individual industries.*

	Roman method		Greek method	
	Roman intermediate industry (R)	Consumer industry	Greek intermediate industry (G)	Consumer industry
Labour	1	2	3	1
Land	3	1	1	2
R/G Intermediate	0	1	0	1

Table 5.1b *Two methods, fixed coefficients: whole economy.*

	Vertically integrated consumer sector	
	Roman method	Greek method
Total labour	3	4
Total land	4	3

described by Tables 5.1a and 5.1b. Each method involves two stages and a specific intermediate.

At the level of the vertically integrated consumer sector we have the coefficients shown in Table 5.1b.

The Roman method will be used when the rent of land, r, is zero. Conversely, the Greek method will be used when the wage, w, is zero. (The switch between the methods occurs at $w = r = 1/7$.) Thus as r rises from zero (and w falls from its maximum value) the switch of method is from the Roman to the Greek method which means that, in the consumer good industry, land-use rises (from 1 to 2) and labour-use falls (from 2 to 1). The consumer good industry use of each primary input, per unit of output, is positively related to the corresponding real input price.

Simple variations in the numbers used in the example can produce cases illustrating each of the other eight logically possible combinations of positive, zero, or negative input use/input price relationships. Thus an FIE analysis of a particularly simple and familiar model of production shows that one can have no a priori expectation concerning the signs of dl/dw, etc.

Note that it is crucial to the example that the Roman and Greek methods involve different intermediates. If the intermediate were common to the two methods then there would be two further possible ways of producing the consumer good: use the Roman inputs for the first stage and the Greek inputs for the second stage, or vice versa. In fact, these 'composite methods' would dominate the Roman and Greek methods (other than at $w = r = 1/7$) and would exhibit the properties $(dl/dw) < 0 > (dt/dr)$. So we see here, once again, the important role of 'on/off' inputs, as in Section 2.8 (more on this in Section 5.5).

The kind of example given here, with just two distinct 'two-period' methods, is readily developed into one in which each of the four primary input quantities is a given function of a single continuous variable (defined over a certain range), so that there are infinitely many alternative methods (but not a full four-dimensional unit isoquant). That is, there is a continuum of qualitatively different produced inputs, each used only in the final stage/consumer industry, by analogy with Samuelson's 'Surrogate Production Function' (Samuelson, 1962). To each such produced input there corresponds a unique set of input coefficients $(l_0, t_0; l_1, t_1)$, where (l_1, t_1) produce one unit of such an input and (l_0, t_0) *use* one unit of it to produce one unit of the consumer good. For example, let us represent the various methods by the continuous variable θ in the interval $[0, 1]$, as shown in Table 5.2.

Table 5.2 *Infinitely many methods.*

	Intermediate industries	Consumer industry
Labour	$l_1 = 1 + \theta + \dfrac{\theta^2}{2}$	$l_0 = (1 - \theta)$
Land	$t_1 = 2 - 2\theta + \dfrac{\theta^2}{2}$	$t_0 = \theta$
θ-specific intermediate	0	1

We are still assuming that there is no interest, so that a change in method is provoked by a change in the $(r/w) \equiv z$ ratio. For any given $z \geq 0$, the best method is given by $\theta = z/(1 + z)$ and thus everything is known.

It is not difficult to prove that the real wage–real rent frontier is 'well behaved' (i.e. downward-sloping and convex from above) and that at

Table 5.3 *Smooth substitutability between land and labour in one method.*

	Roman method		Greek method	
	Roman intermediate industry (R)	Consumer industry	Greek intermediate industry (G)	Consumer industry
Labour	1	θ	1	7/18
Land	3	$1/\theta$	1	19/6
R/G intermediate	0	1	0	1

every point its absolute slope is the total land/total labour ratio: at the economy level, therefore, everything is conventional.

By contrast, at the consumer industry level we have

$$l_0 = \frac{1}{1+z}; \quad t_0 = \frac{z}{1+z}$$

We see at once that, like the real wage, also the direct use of labour in the consumer industry decreases as z increases; symmetrically, both the direct use of land in that industry and the real rent increase as z increases. Hence $(dl_0/dw) > 0 < (dt_0/dr)$, which is far from conventional. It should be stressed that a change in the (l_0, t_0) combination always involves here, as in the previous example, a qualitative change in the intermediate so that no possible 'isoquant' can be drawn in (l_0, t_0) space.

Let us revert to the case in which there are only two alternative intermediates, but we assume now smooth substitutability between land and labour in the consumer good industry when the Roman method is used. It might be expected that the introduction of substitutability eliminates the unconventional aspects present in the first example, but in fact we can see that, to the contrary, it adds a further unconventional aspect. Let land and labour use per unit of output using the Roman method be parametric functions of a positive parameter, θ, and let all other coefficients be fixed, as in Table 5.3.

It should be remarked that, differently from the previous case, we can now draw a (land, labour) isoquant curve on a plane where the use of the Roman intermediate is fixed to unity. It is readily shown that, using the Roman method, the best land and labour use is given by $\theta = \sqrt{r/w}$ and we have $w + 3r + 2\sqrt{wr} = 1$; using the Greek method we have $1.64w + 4r = 1$.

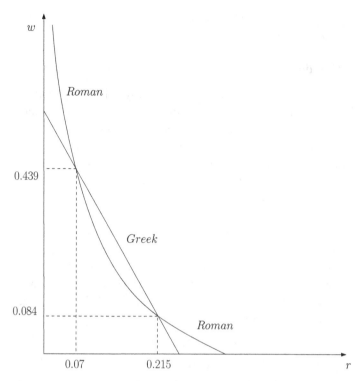

Figure 5.3 Recurrence of type of intermediate.

If the rent/wage ratio is very close to 0, the Roman method is used. As it increases, the Roman method uses a decreasing amount of land (and an increasing amount of labour). This is true both at the level of the consumer industry and at the level of the economy. At $r/w = 0.16$ the two methods are equally profitable: together with a unit of the Roman intermediate, the consumer good industry uses $(l_0 = 0.4; t_0 = 2.5)$ amounts of labour and land; together with a unit of the Greek intermediate, it uses $(\lambda_0 = 1/4 < l_0; \tau_0 = 3 > t_0)$ amounts of labour and land. As the r/w ratio increases further, the Greek method is chosen, so that, in the neighbourhood of the switch point, both labour and land use are positively related to their own real price, as in the previous examples. The peculiarity of the present example is that, at $r/w \geq 2.56$, the Roman method recurs, as we see from Figure 5.3, so that there cannot possibly be monotonic relations between the use of a Roman/Greek intermediate and prices. Such a 'recurrence' should not be confused with 'reswitching', because the land and labour use continuously changes with r/w within the Roman method.

5.4 A Nuti-model case

However many primary inputs and however many periods of production are allowed for in the Wicksellian model, it retains the unsatisfactory feature that production begins with 'unassisted' land and labour, which conjure an intermediate good out of thin air. That feature is somewhat mitigated in the 'Nuti' modification of the Wicksell model, in which the first-period land and labour are at least allowed to use some quantity of the final consumer good as a produced input (Nuti, 1970).

Suppose, then, that land and labour are used both in the final-stage consumer good industry and in a first intermediate-producing stage (as above), but that now the initial stage also involves some consumer good as an input. If wages and rents are paid *ex post* but interest must be paid on all capital advanced and if a is the amount of the final stage good used to produce an intermediate, we have

$$1 = wl_0 + rt_0 + (1+i)wl_1 + (1+i)rt_1 + (1+i)^2 a$$

The real wage–real rent–interest rate frontier is generally not a plane, obviously, but it becomes a plane if we impose the 'equal proportions' condition that

$$l_1 = l_0\sqrt{a} \quad \text{and} \quad t_1 = t_0\sqrt{a}$$

Then the frontier simplifies to

$$wl_0 + rt_0 = 1 - (1+i)\sqrt{a}$$

We make this special assumption for both the techniques in the following example, just in order to emphasize that even 'equal proportions' cannot eliminate the phenomenon to be considered. The two techniques, alpha and beta, are shown in Table 5.4.

Table 5.4 *A Nuti-model with equal proportions.*

	Alpha	Beta
l_0	2	1
t_0	3	1
a	1/10	1/2

With $i = 0$ throughout, alpha provides the higher wage (when the rent is zero) and beta provides the higher rent (when the wage is zero). Hence, as w falls and r rises there is a switch from alpha to beta (at w just under $2r$). However, l_0 is smaller for beta than for alpha so that labour-use in the consumer good industry is positively related to the real wage rate. (This with 'equal proportions', no reswitching and $i = 0$.)

The phenomenon of 'recurrence' can occur also in this Nuti-model with 'equal proportions'. Let there now be three alternative techniques:

Table 5.5 *A Nuti-model with equal proportions and recurrence.*

	Alpha	Beta	Gamma
l_0	1	2	3
t_0	3	2	1
a	1/4	1/9	1/4

It is easy to see that for $0 \leq r < 1/12$ technique alpha is used; for $1/12 \leq r \leq 1/4$ technique beta is used; for $1/4 < r \leq 1/2$ technique gamma is used.

However, a is the same for techniques alpha and gamma, while it is different for technique beta. Hence, as r/w varies, with $i = 0$ throughout, there is recurrence of the produced input quantity per unit of final output. (It is true, of course, that this input is not used directly in the production of the consumer good.)

A continuous example is

$$6\sqrt{a} = 6 - 4t + t^2$$
$$l = 4 - t$$

for

$$0 \leq t \leq 4$$

Here $t^2 z = (4 - t)^2$ and thus a first falls and then rises as z increases (the minimum being at $z = 1$ and $t = l = 2$, $9a = 1$). Every value of a in the range $1 < 9a < 9$ occurs for two distinct values of r/w.

It can be shown that

$$\sqrt{w} + \sqrt{r} = \sqrt{2/3}$$

Now let C be the total output of the consumer good in the stationary economy, with L and T representing the total use of labour and land (not just their use in the consumer good industry). It can be shown that, for the stationary economy as a whole,

$$3C = \frac{2LT}{L+T}$$

That is, we have a CES technology with elasticity $= 0.5$ and nothing unconventional will be observed at the aggregate level.

5.5 The corn-tractor (Samuelson–Surrogate) case

We now extend the famous surrogate model of Samuelson (1962) to include land (see also Opocher and Steedman, 2013). We retain Samuelson's assumption of 'equal proportions' in machine production and in the production of the consumer good. Indeed, we strengthen that assumption by supposing equal 'machine–land' ratios as well as equal 'machine–labour' ratios and examine the reaction of land and labour use to a change in the wage/rent ratio, at a constant rate of interest.

Because the type of machine is qualitatively different for each technique, there is no loss of generality in stipulating that, for every technique, one machine is used in the production of one unit of the consumer good. If the latter process also uses l units of labour and t units of land then the input–output matrix can be written as in Table 5.6.

Table 5.6 *A Samuelson–Surrogate case with labour and land.*

	Machine	Corn
Machine	a	1
Corn	0	0
Labour	al	l
Land	at	t

It is clear that the price of a machine in terms of corn is simply a, so that we have

$$lw + tr = 1 - a(1 + i)$$

as the real wage–real rent–interest rate plane. Obviously, no two such techniques could ever reswitch as i varies, whatever the r/w ratio might

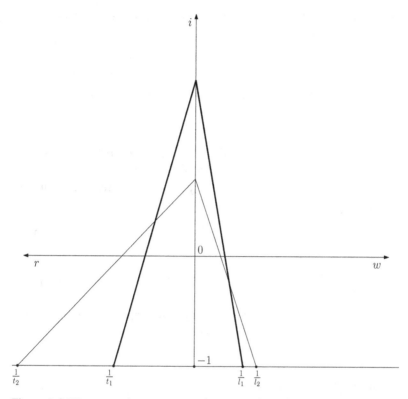

Figure 5.4 Wage–rent–interest rate relations with each machine type (thick lines for machine 1).

be. It certainly does not follow, however, that primary input-use in the consumer good industry must be conventionally related to real primary input-price, even when $i = 0$.

To begin, let there be just two machine types and two corresponding techniques (a_1, l_1, t_1) and (a_2, l_2, t_2), where

$$[(1 - a_1)/l_1] > [(1 - a_2)/l_2] \quad \text{and} \quad [(1 - a_1)/t_1] < [(1 - a_2)/t_2]$$

$$(5.3)$$

As w falls from its maximum value and r rises (the rate of interest remaining zero) there will be a switch from machine (technique) 1 to machine (technique) 2. However, if $a_1 < a_2$ then (5.3) is consistent with $l_1 > l_2$ and in this case $(dl/dw) > 0$ across the switch (see Figure 5.4).

The argument is now readily extended to n alternative techniques with

$$a_1 < a_2 < \cdots < a_n$$

$$t_1 > t_2 > \cdots > t_n$$

$$l_1 > l_2 > \cdots > l_n$$

and such that $dl/dw > 0$ holds at *every* switch.

Strong 'equal proportions' and a constant, zero rate of interest are thus perfectly compatible with $dl/dw > 0$.

A version of the above with infinitely many alternative techniques is given by supposing that

$$a = 2 - 6l + 6l^2 \qquad (5.4)$$

and

$$t = l^2 \qquad (5.5)$$

where $3 - \sqrt{3} < 6l < 3$. At a given wage rate, w, the rent is

$$r = \left[\frac{-1 + (6 - w)l - 6l^2}{l^2} \right] \qquad (5.6)$$

and this is maximized when

$$l = \left(\frac{2}{6 - w} \right) \qquad (5.7)$$

Thus as w rises from zero to its maximum value of $(6 - 2\sqrt{6})$, at which $r = 0$, l rises monotonically from $1/3$ to $1/\sqrt{6}$. The greater is the real wage rate, the greater is the direct use of labour per unit of output in the consumer good industry, even with strong 'equal proportions', no reswitching and $i = 0$.

It can also be shown from (5.4)–(5.7) that the real wage–real rent frontier is

$$w = 6 - 2\sqrt{6 + r}$$

and that, as w rises from zero to $(6 - 2\sqrt{6})$:

(i) t increases from $1/9$ to $1/6$
(ii) t/l increases from $1/3$ to $1/\sqrt{6}$
(iii) a falls from $2/3$ to $(3 - \sqrt{6})$.

We conclude our examination of this infinitely many techniques example by asking whether the possibility of unconventional outcomes at the level of the consumer good industry turns on the possibility of such outcomes at the level of the whole economy. It does not. Adopting the same notation as in the previous section, it is readily shown that

$$\left(\frac{C}{L}\right) = 6 - 6\left(\frac{T}{L}\right) - \left(\frac{L}{T}\right) \tag{5.8}$$

While (5.8) is not, perhaps, a familiar form of production function, it does have the required properties. As T/L rises from $1/3$ to $1/\sqrt{6}$, output per worker, C/L, rises from 1 to $(6 - 2\sqrt{6})$. C/L is always increasing, but at an ever-diminishing rate, and the derivative of C/L with respect to T/L, in (5.8), is always equal to r; moreover, the tangent to the curve cuts the C/L axis at w. Hence (5.8), defined over the relevant range for T/L, is a 'well-behaved' aggregate production function. Thus an economic system that is conventional at its aggregate level can display quite unconventional relationships at the level of a particular industry. (Note that everything said in this section, after i was set equal to zero, could be interpreted as referring to a literally one-commodity economy, in which a is the own-use capital/gross output ratio. Under this interpretation, indeed, it is easier to see how a transition could be made from one technique to another.)

5.6 An input–output case

We have so far considered an economy in which there is one consumer good industry which uses a produced input (chosen from a menu of qualitatively different intermediates). In fact, this was the benchmark of many important capital theoretic studies. Now we turn to an examination of input–output systems without any particular hierarchy among industries and without any on/off inputs.

In the following two-commodity, labour and land example, industry 1 has access to only one method of production, but industry 2 can use either method A or method B, as in Table 5.7 below.

Note that commodity 2 is the more land-intensive one for both technique A and technique B (so that no factor intensity reversal is involved) and that we set $i = 0$ throughout.

It is readily calculated that, when $r = 0$, technique A yields the higher wage and that, when $w = 0$, technique B yields the higher rent. Thus,

Table 5.7 *An input–output example with two techniques.*

	1	2A	2B
Commodity 1	0.2	0.8	2.0
Commodity 2	0.1	0.2	0.05
Labour	1.0	3.0	1.6
Land	1.0	6.0	4.0

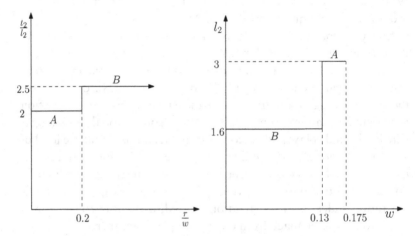

Figure 5.5 Unconventional input use/input price relationships in an input–output model.

as w falls and r rises there is a switch from A to B. (This occurs at $w = 5r$.)

Now $(t_2/l_2) = 2$ for technique A, while $(t_2/l_2) = 2.5$ for technique B; hence (t_2/l_2) rises as r/w rises. Moreover, $l_2 = 3$ for A but $l_2 = 1.6$ for B; hence l_2 falls as w falls. With respect to both the direct land–labour ratio and the direct labour–output ratio, industry 2 thus exhibits unconventional behaviour (see Figure 5.5). This establishes that our findings in the previous cases did not always depend on the presence of on/off inputs.

5.7 Recurrence of the complete input–output matrix

We have seen in Sections 5.3 and 5.4 that there can be 'recurrence', respectively, of intermediate types of input and in the quantity of a single intermediate as the rent/wage ratio changes. Now we examine

Table 5.8 *Recurrence of the complete input–output matrix.*

	1	2A	2B	2C
Commodity 1	0	1	0.4	1
Commodity 2	0.8	0.1	0.4	0.1
Labour	1	1	6	2
Land	1	2	6	1

the possibility that a complete material input–output matrix might recur.

Consider a two-commodity, labour and land system in which industry 1 has access to only one method of production but industry 2 has access to three alternative methods, as in Table 5.8.

It is easily seen that, with $i = 0$ throughout, the three possible complete techniques yield the following real wage–real rent frontiers (the numéraire being commodity 2).

$$140w_A + 210r_A = 7$$

$$160w_B + 160r_B = 7$$

$$210w_C + 140r_C = 7$$

Clearly, A will be chosen when the rent is zero and C will be chosen when the wage is zero. When the wage and rent rates are equal, B will be chosen. Thus, as w falls and r rises, the choice of technique will be $A \to B \to C$. The first switch occurs at $80(w, r) = (2.5, 1)$ and the second at $80(w, r) = (1, 2.5)$.

However, A and C have exactly the same material input–output matrix

$$\begin{pmatrix} 0 & 1.0 \\ 0.8 & 0.1 \end{pmatrix}$$

while B has a different one. Thus, the entire input–output matrix recurs; it is chosen at both 'low' r/w and at 'high' r/w, but not at intermediate values of r/w.

Needless to say, we are not dealing here with reswitching, for both labour-use and land-use differ as between techniques A and C.

Such a recurrence of the complete input–output matrix can be easily extended to n goods, with no choice for industries 1, ..., $(n - 1)$ and with three or more alternatives for industry n.

5.8 Concluding remarks

We have shown in this chapter that, under FIE, conventional behaviour in the economy as a whole by no means implies conventional behaviour in a particular industry. This is true both when we consider a variation in the rate of interest and when we consider a variation in relative primary input prices with a null rate of interest. In the first context, a small increase in the rate of interest (and decrease in the real wage) across a switch may well determine, in a particular industry, an increase in the capital–output ratio and a fall in employment per unit of output even though, at the economy level, the aggregate use of capital per unit of net output falls and that of labour increases. In the second context, we may say that in Wicksellian, Nuti, Samuelson–Surrogate and input–output models of production, one industry can exhibit the property $dl/dw > 0$ and/or $dt/dr > 0$. These possibilities have nothing whatever to do with unequal proportions, reswitching, capital-reversing or interest-rate effects of any kind. All that is necessary is that we suppose FIE both before and after the exogenous change considered. Taken seriously, the 'long run' does not ensure an inverse relation between primary input-use and input-price at the level of a particular industry (unless it be true both that technology is smooth everywhere and that all inputs are Hicksian substitutes, as in Chapter 4). This is so even when everything behaves 'normally' at the level of the economy as a whole.

The above findings should be of interest, we suppose, to any serious marginalist economist, because they undercut various common assumptions. At the same time, they imply an admonition of those critics of mainstream theory who narrowed the focus of Sraffa-inspired arguments down to the single issue of interest rate variations and their economy-wide effects when, as we have seen, there are many further criticisms of standard theory to be made, even when the interest rate is always zero. An exaggerated concern with a variable interest rate and with economic aggregates has, arguably, stood in the way of developing the full force of Sraffa's emphasis on the interdependence of industries and on FIE.

6 | The 'autonomous' components of input prices

The preceding chapters emphasized the mutual dependence of real input prices under FIE and analysed the 'collateral effects' brought about by an original parametric change in one price. We conceptualized the overall change in terms of a movement on the FIE frontier and stressed that the FIE comparative statics of the firm and the industry involve multiple input price changes.

However, we did not attempt to discuss adequately the important issue of the possible cause leading to a price change.

We must now recognize that a movement on the frontier is generally associated with some external shock, such as technological change or a change in taxation/subsidy policy. Such shocks regulate what may be called the 'autonomous' or 'exogenous' components of input prices (we borrow this terminology from Braulke, 1987, pp. 479 and 481, respectively), which frequently are the 'true' *primum movens* in the passage from one FIE to another.

To these autonomous components we now turn. Because a change in one of them determines, at the ruling input prices, either profits or losses in at least one industry, a comparison of different FIE will generally be across shifting frontiers: a shift in the frontier and a movement on it should be considered as two aspects of the same shock and we need some conceptual tools for distinguishing between them and assigning to each of them a specific effect.

The next two chapters study, respectively, a change in taxation and a change in technology and how they modify the autonomous components of input and output prices. (The specific role of the terms of trade in a small open economy has already been discussed in Appendix 2 to Chapter 2.)

As a prelude to such an analysis, we discuss in this chapter some common aspects of the different sources of a shifting FIE frontier, under the general heading (borrowed from Harberger, 1998) of 'real cost reduction' (RCR). (Needless to say, a negative RCR corresponds to a real cost increase.) Because wage dispersion is an important empirical issue which is often related to taxation and to technical progress, we replace land in this and the next two chapters by a second kind of labour.

In Section 6.1, we limit ourselves to the simple case of an 'isolated' industry, where the sources of RCR are necessarily internal to the industry itself; then, in Section 6.2, we examine the possibility that such a source may originate in another industry and be 'imported' via the relative price of a commodity input. Section 6.3 briefly compares RCR with the familiar concept of Total Factor Productivity. Section 6.4 draws some conclusions and introduces the more detailed analysis that will be presented in the next two chapters.

6.1 Real cost reduction in an isolated industry

Let us revert in this section to the isolated industry discussed in Chapter 2 and assume, for simplicity, that production requires two industry-specific kinds of labour and nothing else. The FIE frontier defines a trade-off between the two real wage rates, but the trade-off itself depends on some autonomous factors, which we have so far taken as given.

We call RCR any improvement in the industry's conditions which cuts costs at constant input prices and thereby makes room for an increase in both real wage rates. By definition, then, RCR is mirrored by an upward shift in the real wages frontier (and a negative RCR by a downward shift); its possible sources are a change in taxation and/or productivity increase, both within the industry.

Let us reformulate the indirect average cost function of Chapter 2, Equation (2.3), as

$$c(w_1(1 + t_1), w_2(1 + t_2); T)$$

where t_1, t_2 are tax/subsidy rates on labour (where a subsidy is a negative tax) and T is a time shift parameter.

Now let p be the output price; for simplicity, we assume that no tax is levied on this output. Maximum profits are null when

$$p = c(w_1(1 + t_1), w_2(1 + t_2); T)$$

By the homogeneity properties of $c(\ )$, we may express both input prices in terms of the industrial output, obtaining

$$1 = c(w_1(1 + t_1), w_2(1 + t_2); T) \tag{6.1}$$

Let us differentiate (6.1) totally, under the assumption that the tax rates are initially null; by Shephard's lemma, we have

$$0 = l_1(dw_1 + w_1 dt_1) + l_2(dw_2 + w_2 dt_2) + \frac{\partial c}{\partial T} dT \tag{6.2}$$

Now we may sensibly define the industrial RCR, as

$$RCR = -w_1 l_1 dt_1 - w_2 l_2 dt_2 - \frac{\partial c}{\partial T} dT \tag{6.3}$$

By (6.2), the 'other side' of RCR under FIE is that

$$RCR = w_1 l_1 \frac{dw_1}{w_1} + w_2 l_2 \frac{dw_2}{w_2} \tag{6.4}$$

The sum on the rhs of (6.3) gives the 'sources' of RCR, while the sum on the rhs of (6.4) gives its 'outcome'. The proportional rates of increase in the real wages may be the same or may differ, depending on the interplay of the specific sources of RCR with market mechanisms. For instance, skill-biased technical change is known to increase the wage of skilled labour relative to that of unskilled labour; a proportional increase in the tax wedge on wages may diminish more the wage of the labour in more elastic supply; and so on. All this should be studied case by case, and in the next two chapters we shall enter into the main details. For now, we examine the general properties of (6.4) in order to clarify how we can distinguish between a shift of the frontier and a movement along it.

When the ratio between the wage rates of the two kinds of labour remains constant, total RCR is simply a measure of the expansion (contraction) of the frontier on a certain ray, as $(w_1 l_1 + w_2 l_2) = 1$. However, as we said, nothing guarantees that an exogenous change is neutral with respect to w_1/w_2.

Fortunately, the frontier has the nice property that its absolute slope at a point is equal to the ratio of labour uses at that point. Let an initial pair (w_1^A, w_2^A) be at point P_A in Figure 6.1 and a second pair (w_1^B, w_2^B) be at point P_B: the two pairs differ both in the values of the real wage rates and in the ratios between them. We can find, however, a hypothetical pair (w_1^{AB}, w_2^{AB}) at point P_{AB} which is a linear

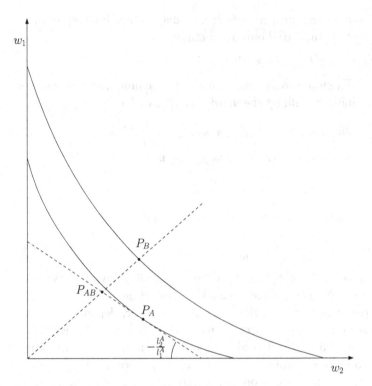

Figure 6.1 Real cost reduction in discrete time.

approximation of the real wages on the 'old' frontier and at the 'new' w_1/w_2 ratio. Setting $\Delta w_j = (w_j^B - w_j^A)$, $j = 1, 2$, it can be shown (see Section 8.1 for details) that

$$w_1^A l_1^A \frac{\Delta w_1}{w_1^A} + w_2^A l_2^A \frac{\Delta w_2}{w_2^A} = \frac{w_{1,2}^B}{w_{1,2}^{AB}}$$

For discrete variations, therefore, (6.4) approximates the proportional rate of increase in the real wage rates on the ray passing through P_B. This is a measure of the autonomous component of each wage change; the remainder is due to the change in relative wages.

6.2 Real cost reduction with interdependent industries

The autonomous components of the real wages in a certain industry under FIE may originate, however, outside the boundaries of the industry itself. As we know, over half of the cost of production in most industries is due to intermediate inputs and therefore a significant source of RCR in any industry is a change in the relative price of other industries' outputs. For example, much RCR in the computer industry is accounted for by a reduction in the semiconductor price (see Jorgenson *et al.*, 2005, Chapter 4). One should expect, therefore, that an industrial RCR depends on the rates of productivity increase and the changes in taxation/subsidy rates in a wide range of industries; and it also depends on the relative-output-price effect of changing relative primary input prices, which we have studied in the preceding chapters. Both the identification of the autonomous factors regulating the real input prices and the distinction between a shift of an FIE frontier and a movement along it are more complex than in the isolated industry. In the next two chapters we shall examine this matter separately for taxation and productivity increase, but it will be useful to consider now some basic common elements.

Let our consumer good industry, indexed 1, use also an intermediate input, indexed 2; in turn, this commodity input is produced by an industry which uses the same two kinds of labour as 'our' industry and nothing else. No interest is charged on the intermediate input. Taking the consumer good as the numéraire, FIE implies, in obvious notation, that

$$1 = c_1(w_1(1 + t_1), w_2(1 + t_2), p_2; T) \tag{6.5}$$

$$p_2 = c_2(w_1(1 + t_1), w_2(1 + t_2); T) \tag{6.6}$$

Differentiating (6.5) and (6.6) and assuming, once again, that initially $t_1 = 0 = t_2$, we obtain

$$0 = l_{11}(dw_1 + w_1 dt_1) + l_{21}(dw_2 + w_2 dt_2) + a_{21} dp_2 + \frac{\partial c_1}{\partial T} dT \tag{6.7}$$

$$dp_2 = l_{12}(dw_1 + w_1 dt_1) + l_{22}(dw_2 + w_2 dt_2) + \frac{\partial c_2}{\partial T} dT \tag{6.8}$$

RCR in the consumer good industry includes now the cost-changing effect of a changing p_2, so that (6.3) is replaced by

$$RCR = -a_{21} dp_2 - w_1 l_{11} dt_1 - w_2 l_{21} dt_2 - \frac{\partial c_1}{\partial T} dT \tag{6.9}$$

By (6.7) and (6.8), dp_2 depends, in turn, on the change in the ratio between the two wage rates and on the autonomous factors in both industries, or

$$dp_2 = F\left(\frac{dw_1}{w_1} - \frac{dw_2}{w_2}\right) + G(dt_1, dt_2; dT)$$

Specifically, we have

$$F\left(\frac{dw_1}{w_1} - \frac{dw_2}{w_2}\right) = (l_{21}l_{12} - l_{11}l_{22})w_1 w_2 \left(\frac{dw_1}{w_1} - \frac{dw_2}{w_2}\right)$$

$$G(dt; dT) = (l_{21}l_{12} - l_{11}l_{22})w_1 w_2(dt_1 - dt_2)$$

$$+ (w_1 l_{11} + w_2 l_{21})\frac{\partial c_2}{\partial T}dT$$

$$- (w_1 l_{12} + w_2 l_{22})\frac{\partial c_1}{\partial T}dT$$

Substituting dp_2 into (6.7) we finally get

$$RCR = -a_{21}F\left(\frac{dw_1}{w_1} - \frac{dw_2}{w_2}\right) - a_{21}G(dt; dT)$$

$$- \left(w_1 l_{11}dt_1 + w_2 l_{21}dt_2 + \frac{\partial c_1}{\partial T}dT\right) \tag{6.10}$$

Real cost reduction in the consumer good industry can therefore be split into three broad components, the first incorporating the specific effect of a possible change in relative wages, the second incorporating the indirect effects of the external shocks via the intermediate input, and the third incorporating the direct effect of the external shocks in the consumer good industry.

Once again, a graphical illustration may help. We may associate to each point on the FIE frontier (solid line) a constant-price curve (dotted line): as we move along the FIE frontier, the constant-price curve shifts outwards or inwards according to whether the relative price of the commodity input falls or increases. (The reader can easily verify that Figure 6.2 is but a transformation of the three-dimensional Figure 4.2.)

Let the initial and final equilibria be at P_A and P_B, respectively. Once again, we may conceptually divide the overall change into two steps, a movement on the initial FIE frontier, due to the change in relative wages (from P_A to P_C), and a proper shift of the frontier, due to the autonomous factors (from P_C to P_B). However, the passage from P_A to P_C itself involves some RCR in the consumer good industry, because (in the case depicted by the figure) p_2 decreases by the mere

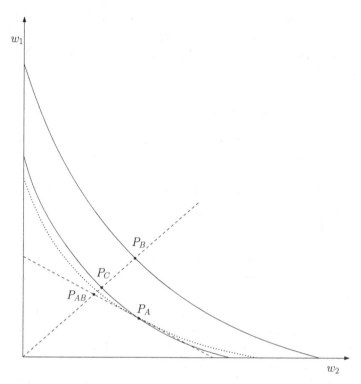

Figure 6.2 Real cost reduction with interdependent industries.

fact that w_1/w_2 increases. In order to isolate this component of RCR we should consider the constant-price curve related to P_A and subdivide the change from P_A to P_C into two components: the change from P_A to P_{AB}, which approximates the movement on the constant-price curve, and the change from P_{AB} to P_C, which reflects the effect of the new relative price, as determined at P_C.

If one is interested in RCR, not at the level of the industrial sector, but at that of the vertically integrated sector (rcr), things are much simpler. One may eliminate dp_2 from (6.7), obtaining immediately

$$
rcr = -a_{21}\left(l_{12}dt_1 + l_{22}dt_2 + \frac{\partial c_2}{\partial T}dT\right) - \left(l_{12}dt_1 + l_{21}dt_2 + \frac{\partial c_1}{\partial T}dT\right)
$$
$$
= (l_{11} + a_{21}l_{12})dw_1 + (l_{21} + a_2l_{22})dw_2
$$

Needless to say, rcr approximates (in its own different way) the radial shift in the frontier, because the absolute slope of the FIE frontier is the ratio between the two kinds of labour in the vertically integrated consumer good sector. Whereas RCR captures the developments in real, observable industries, rcr is useful for matters of aggregation. We shall return to this in Section 8.3.

6.3 Real cost reduction and TFP

Although total factor productivity (TFP) accounts were initially referred to the aggregate economy (the original source being, of course, Solow, 1957), there has been an increasing interest in TFP growth in each individual industry, due to the extreme variety of industry-level productivity performance (see Jorgenson and Stiroh, 2000, and Jorgenson *et al.*, 2005).

Because the growth-accounting measure of the rate of productivity growth also assumes competition, profit maximization and equality between revenues and costs, one may wonder how RCR relates to industry-level TFP.

The duality between cost and production functions suggests that the two notions are indeed intimately related. In Chapter 8 we shall discuss at length the symmetries between a measure of industrial productivity increase based on the technological sources of RCR and a measure based on conventional growth accounting, but some general remarks on the usefulness of our approach based on the cost function are in order here.

First, just as industrial TFP is aimed at discovering the industrial sources of aggregate economic growth, so RCR naturally clarifies the industrial sources of the increase in real wages. Competition forces each industry to adjust wages to changing real costs (as defined above), for otherwise there would be either losses or profits and it is somewhat artificial to measure RCR using TFP data, as is commonly done (e.g. Harberger, 1998), when we can measure it directly, on the basis of price data. In our framework, it is also quite natural to incorporate unevenness in the industrial sources of the change in real wages and to coordinate them with relative price changes.

Second, the current studies of wage dispersion rely heavily on technological change. It is often argued that progress in the production and use of Information Technologies materially changed the relative wages of workers characterized by different skills. In the presence of different speeds of real wage increase, then, it should be useful to distinguish between an overall rate of improvement (RCR) and a change in 'distribution', as we did in the previous sections.

Third, the 'precipitous IT price decline' is widely recognized as an important source of progress in a series of industries (e.g. Jorgenson *et al.*, 2005, pp. xvii–xxiii; Autor *et al.*, 2006, p. 192) and our approach is, of course, designed to take this into account.

A final wider consideration is in order. It is beyond doubt that, in a growth-accounting perspective, productivity increase is considered as a long-run phenomenon. In order to extract the trend component from the headline TFP accounts for the economy as a whole, using a production function approach, it is customary to calculate potential output using 'long-run' measures of the labour and capital inputs. However, 'long-run employment' is an eminently macroeconomic concept and simply cannot be referred to the individual industry; by contrast, the assumption of zero net profits distinctly captures a long-run tendency of the competitive industry, while short-run disturbances create losses or profits.

6.4 Concluding remarks

Under FIE, real wage rates are both mutually related and depend on some common autonomous factors. While it is certainly useful to study these two determinants separately, we must recognize that a change in an autonomous factor can affect relative wage rates; therefore the 'endogenous' and the 'autonomous' sources of real wage changes can and frequently do come together. We conceptualized the former source in terms of a movement along an initial FIE frontier and the latter source (which we have called Real Cost Reduction, RCR) in terms of a shift of the frontier itself and we have shown that, by the properties of the frontier, we can identify the role of RCR on the simple basis of the observable change in the real wages, just as TFP accounts identify productivity increase on the basis of the observable changes in input use per unit of output.

Because a major share of costs in any industry is due to the use of intermediate inputs, some sources of RCR are external to the industry under consideration and affect real wages via changing commodity prices. We have discussed this kind of dependence with reference to the simple case with only one commodity input, produced by means of primary inputs alone and with no particular specifications concerning the 'autonomous' changes involved. We must now enter into some details of the possible autonomous changes and study their effects in a more general analytical framework with many produced inputs and many industries. We shall relate a vector of specified changes originating in a series of industries to the changing structure of relative prices and thereby to RCR in any industry. The next chapter is devoted to taxation changes, while the following one concerns productivity increase.

7 | *The effects of taxation*

In an excellent textbook, Atkinson and Stiglitz (1980, pp. 160–61) distinguish between five main points of view on tax incidence, one of them being the incidence on the 'factors of production', which they particularly emphasize. Broadly speaking, the present chapter is entirely devoted to this latter point of view. By the zero-profit condition, a tax always reduces the real primary input prices, taken together, in terms of the output of the taxed industry; what, then, determines the size of this effect? How can we distinguish between it and the specific effects on each primary input? Do real wages also decrease in terms of untaxed commodities? Are uniform tax rates neutral for relative commodity prices? Do non-uniform tax rates determine a predictable change in the price structure? In this chapter we shall analyse these and other related questions in the framework of the FIE analysis developed above.

A series of fundamental studies of tax incidence are focused on the changes in equilibrium input and output prices and in equilibrium input and output quantities (e.g. Musgrave, 1953; Harberger, 1962; valuable surveys are Atkinson and Stiglitz, 1980, chapter 6; Fullerton and Metcalf, 2002); in our FIE analysis we adopt a strictly industrial standpoint and derive all our conclusions from the double equality between prices and average and marginal costs including taxes and from the uniformity of input prices, net of taxes, in the various industries.

Of course, our approach involves ignoring a series of aspects which traditionally belong to taxation theory. First, even though taxes are in fact a means to 'purchase' public goods and services, we follow many partial equilibrium studies of tax incidence in ignoring the distribution of the tax proceeds; more generally, the welfare implications of taxation (important as they are) are outside the scope of the present analysis. Second, the familiar treatment of tax incidence in terms of 'households' and 'producers' is of no interest in our context: it is totally irrelevant in FIE analysis whether a tax is 'shifted forward' by an increasing price or is 'shifted backward' by diminishing wages. When comparing FIE equilibria, it would be highly misleading to think of an *ad-valorem* tax in terms of a shifting 'flat supply curve', as seems to be implied in some studies (e.g. Fullerton and Metcalf, 2002, p. 1822). To repeat, we fully subscribe to the view that 'incidence is a matter of relative price changes and *real* income changes' (Mieszkowski, 1969, p. 1104). In this respect, we should also stress from the outset that our assumption of zero net profits leaves no room for the classical problems of a 'corporation tax': rather, we focus on output taxes and (differentiated) payroll taxes and their implications for relative commodity prices and real wages. Finally, unlike general equilibrium approaches, our analysis of taxation pays no special attention to preferences or factor supplies, in order to focus on other aspects, not least the interdependence in the industrial costs of production.

In our framework, we can only expect to determine the effects of taxation on the FIE frontier as a whole, that is, on the real input prices taken together, the distribution of the tax burden among the different primary inputs being conditional on alternative assumptions; we therefore isolate the effects of taxation that can be discussed regardless of preferences or endowments and depend solely on some fundamental competitive forces relating to production. This point of view can be justified by the wide recognition that in general equilibrium frameworks 'tax incidence results are generally ambiguous without additional restrictions on the precise nature of preferences and technology' (Kotlikoff and Summers, 1987, p. 1044).

The argument is organized as follows. The effect of taxation on real wages is first analysed in the case of an isolated industry (Section 7.1); in this simple context, we introduce an intermediate input assuming either that it can be imported at given terms of trade or that it consists of the industry's output itself. In Section 7.2 we introduce a second industry: the FIE effect of taxation on the relative price and on real wages – in terms of each commodity – is first examined in the familiar model with two kinds of labour; then we extend the analysis to the more realistic case with input–output relations. Section 7.3 generalizes to any number of industries. In Section 7.4 we discuss the possibility of unconventional FIE effects of either a subsidy on a specific kind of labour or a tax on an intermediate input. Section 7.5 concludes. Of course, various kinds of taxes will be considered (sales, value-added, uniform or differentiated payroll taxes) and we may also consider a subsidy as a negative tax. Moreover, with multiple industries, one should distinguish between a tax levied on just one commodity and a tax levied on all commodities (whether or not at the same rate): the analysis of taxation, alas, involves a somewhat baroque taxonomy and in this respect we beg the reader's patience.

7.1 An isolated industry

As usual, let us initially postulate an isolated industry whose output is produced by means of two primary inputs (two kinds of labour).

In the case of a sales tax, t, competitive pricing requires that

$$p = c(w_1, w_2)(1 + t) \tag{7.1}$$

By linear homogeneity of the cost function and setting $p = 1$, we have

$$1 = c(w_1(1 + t), w_2(1 + t)) \tag{7.1'}$$

where w_i now denotes a *net* real wage, as expressed in terms of our numéraire. Equation (7.1') has two immediate consequences: first, in such a simple case a sales tax (at rate t) is equivalent to a proportional income tax (at rate $t/(1 + t)$); second, the tax has no direct effect on input use per unit of output and on the long-run firm output, which are homogeneous functions of degree zero in the *gross* wages $w_i(1 + t)$. We notice, finally, that in this case the sales (*ad-valorem*) tax is indistinguishable from an excise (unit) tax, because the taxed commodity has been chosen as numéraire (see Fullerton and Metcalf, 2002, p. 1794 for details). Needless to say, if the burden of the tax is borne by the two kinds of labour in different proportions, the tax will have indirect effects on input use per unit of output and on the long-run level of output.

In terms of a net real wages frontier, we obtain

$$(1 + t)^{-1} = c(w_1, w_2)$$

Differentiating totally at $t = 0$, we have

$$-dt = w_1 l_1 \hat{w}_1 + w_2 l_2 \hat{w}_2 \tag{7.2}$$

The tax simply determines a radial contraction of the frontier, towards the point $(0,0)$, 'as if' both inputs decreased in efficiency units.

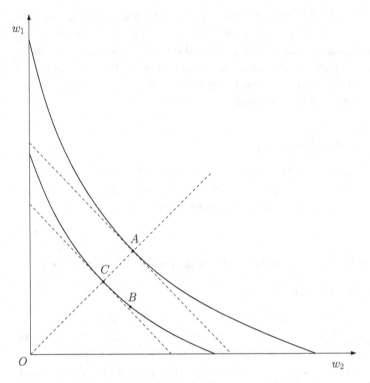

Figure 7.1 Incidence in a simple one-industry, two-primary-inputs model.

In Figure 7.1, let A be the initial equilibrium and let the tax determine a change to B. We can conceptually distinguish between a shift of the frontier (from A to C) and a movement along the new frontier (from C to B). The shift of the frontier is measured by the common hypothetical rate of reduction in the real wages, $\overline{CA}/\overline{OA}$, and is equal to the tax; the movement along the frontier satisfies a condition whose linear approximation is expressed by (7.2); notice that along any ray the gross primary input prices are constant and therefore the two frontiers have the same absolute slope, equal to relative input use.

It goes without saying that (7.2) alone cannot determine the reduction of each input price: it only provides a relationship between them. Different 'closures' are possible. If, say, the w_1/w_2 ratio remains constant, then $\hat{w}_1 = \hat{w}_2 = -dt$; conversely, if w_1 is constant, then $\hat{w}_2 = -(1/w_2 l_2)dt$.

A uniform payroll tax, t_w, would be indistinguishable from a sales tax. In the case of a differentiated payroll tax on, say, labour 1, we have

$$1 = c(w_1(1 + t_{w1}), w_2) \tag{7.3}$$

With w_1 on the vertical axis, the with-tax frontier is now a vertical contraction of the no-tax frontier. Setting $t_{w1} = 0$, the shift in the frontier is $-(w_1 l_1)dt_{w1}$. If the burden of the tax falls entirely on the taxed labour, the relative *gross* wages and the l_1/l_2 ratio will remain constant. Any shift of the tax towards labour 2 would determine an increase of the l_1/l_2 ratio.

Now let us extend our analysis by assuming that production also requires the use of a commodity input. Our industry is still the only domestic productive activity and the commodity input is imported at an international price P (relative to p), independent of internal taxes. We are thus briefly reverting to the small economy case examined in Appendix 2 of Chapter 2.

With a sales (excise) tax, we have

$$(1 + t)^{-1} = c(w_1, w_2, P) \tag{7.4}$$

Keeping the terms of trade, P, constant, an increase in the tax determines a contraction of the frontier, still determined by (7.2). However, we now draw different conclusions from it. An obvious difference is that the common proportional $\hat{w}_1, \hat{w}_2$ decrease in net real wages is greater than the increase in the tax rate, which we may call the 'magnification effect'. (Some partial-equilibrium empirical literature denotes by 'overshifting' of a sales tax, a situation in which, *ceteris paribus*, the price of the taxed commodity rises by more than the tax; see Poterba, 1996.) In Figure 7.2, the tax rate is $\overline{CA}/\overline{OA}$, while the hypothetical common reduction in real wages is $\overline{DA}/\overline{OA}$. A more subtle difference is that it is now impossible to keep the ratios of the three input prices unchanged: if, say, w_1/w_2 is constant, then P/w_i automatically increases and we can make no general prediction about the l_1/l_2 ratio.

From a geometrical point of view, the shift of the frontier is no longer radial, as is shown in Figure 7.2: if the burden of the tax falls on wages in the same proportion, then the ratio l_1/l_2 generally changes (and so does the firm's long-run output); if the labour use ratio is fixed (say, due to fixed and fully employed endowments), then the burden falls on wages in different proportions.

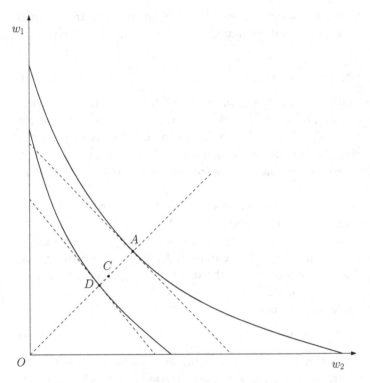

Figure 7.2 Incidence with a commodity input.

By contrast, a value added tax, t_v (or a uniform income tax), has no magnification effect and it does determine a radial shift in the frontier. In this case we have

$$1 = c(w_1(1 + t_v), w_2(1 + t_v), P) \tag{7.5}$$

and, at $t_v = 0$

$$-(w_1 l_1 + w_2 l_2)dt_v = w_1 l_1 \hat{w}_1 + w_2 l_2 \hat{w}_2 \tag{7.6}$$

If $\hat{w}_1 = \hat{w}_2$, then the gross wages, $w_1(1 + t_v)$, $w_2(1 + t_v)$, remain constant, like P: there would be no change in the input prices facing the firms and no effect whatever on the input intensities (or on the firm's long-run output).

The same conclusions hold if the commodity input, rather than being imported at fixed terms of trade, is produced by the industry itself, as can be seen by setting $P = 1$.

Quite different is the case in which a commodity input is drawn from another domestic industry, because its price would depend on taxation and on the distribution of the tax burden. To this we now turn.

7.2 Two industries

The presence of another domestic industry introduces a further dimension of taxation, the potentially changing relative commodity price. The relationship between tax rates and relative prices is a very important issue. First, in some cases it may be desirable that taxation raises the relative price of a certain commodity (due, for instance, to negative externalities), while in others it may be desirable that it is price-neutral. Second, when taxation modifies the relative commodity price, the question arises of whether a tax in one industry affects the real primary input prices as expressed in terms of the output of untaxed industries.

In the interest of simplicity, we shall adopt in this and the next section the so-called 'unit convention' (Fullerton and Metcalf, 2002, p. 1974), i.e. we take the unit quantities of commodities other than the numéraire to be such that their prices in terms of the numéraire are initially, in the pre-tax-change equilibrium, equal to one; another advantage of the 'unit convention' is that there is no distinction between (marginal) sales and excise taxes, whatever the industry in which they are levied. Of course we shall continue to assume that tax rates are initially equal to zero.

7.2.1 A tax on one commodity

Let us first consider the standard 2×2 model with two kinds of labour as the only inputs and assume that one industry (labelled 1) is taxed, its output being the numéraire. In the case of a sales tax we have

$$1 = c_1(w_1, w_2)(1 + t_1) \tag{7.7}$$

$$p_2 = c_2(w_1, w_2) \tag{7.8}$$

Differentiating totally at $t_1 = 0$ and under the 'unit convention', we obtain

$$-dt_1 = w_1 l_{11} \hat{w}_1 + w_2 l_{21} \hat{w}_2 \tag{7.9}$$

$$\hat{p}_2 = w_1 l_{12} \hat{w}_1 + w_2 l_{22} \hat{w}_2 \tag{7.10}$$

Assuming that the real wages change at the same rate, we have $\hat{w}_i = \hat{p}_2 = -dt_1$: the net real wages decrease in terms of the taxed commodity, the proportional decrease being the tax rate, and remain constant in terms of the untaxed commodity.

By (7.9) we see at once that the tax is entirely absorbed by labour in the taxed industry; by competition, however, workers in the untaxed industry bear the same burden and therefore the relative price of their output diminishes at the same rate as that of the tax. It should be stressed once again that the zero-net-profits condition both before and after the tax does not involve that the tax burden is ultimately shifted to the 'consumers'. To the contrary, precisely because profits are always null the burden of the tax falls on input prices, as Harberger (1962, particularly the numerical example in section 2) pointed out long ago.

Making the alternative assumption that, in terms of the taxed commodity, the real wage of labour 1 remains constant, we have

$$\hat{w}_2 = -(1/w_2 l_{21})dt_1, \quad \hat{p}_2 = -(l_{22}/l_{21})dt_1$$

Now the real wage of labour 1 increases in terms of commodity 2, while w_2 falls, not only in terms of commodity 1, but also in terms of commodity 2. Specifically, we have

$$(\hat{w}_1 - \hat{p}_2) = \frac{l_{22}}{l_{21}}dt_1; \quad (\hat{w}_2 - \hat{p}_2) = -\frac{w_1 l_{12}}{w_2 l_{21}}dt_1$$

A sales tax on one commodity the burden of which, in terms of the taxed commodity, is entirely borne by labour 2 in fact benefits labour 1. A graphical illustration is provided in Figure 7.3.

In terms of commodity 1, the tax determines a (radial) shift in the frontier for industry 1 and we are assuming that equilibrium moves from A to B: w_1 is constant and w_2 has decreased. In industry 2, by competition, there will be a movement on the frontier in which, in terms of commodity 2, w_2 decreases and w_1 increases. The practical sense of this conclusion is quite immediate if we express the change in terms of 'money' variables: let the money price of the taxed output and the money wage of labour 1 be unaffected by the tax, while the money wage of labour 2 net of taxes diminishes. The (money) wage of labour 2 in the untaxed industry will therefore fall as well, like the price of the untaxed commodity: in terms of that commodity, then, the real wage of labour 1 increases.

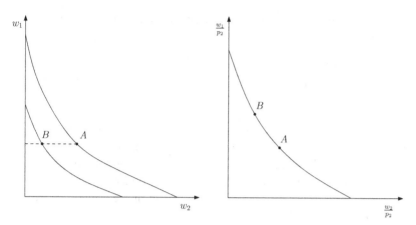

Figure 7.3 Incidence in terms of taxed or untaxed commodities.

Now let us introduce intermediate inputs, as in Steedman (1986). Let us assume first that commodity 2 is used as an input in industry 1. The effect of a sales (or a value added) tax naturally differs according to whether the input-using or the input-providing industry is taxed.

In the first case, (7.7) should be replaced by

$$1 = c_1(w_1, w_2, p_2)(1 + t_1) \tag{7.11}$$

Total differentiation gives

$$-dt_1 = w_1 l_{11} \hat{w}_1 + w_2 l_{21} \hat{w}_2 + a_{21} \hat{p}_2 \tag{7.12}$$

where a_{21} denotes the (initial) cost-minimizing use of commodity 2 in industry 1. By (7.10) and (7.12) and reverting to the assumption that the two real wage rates change at the same rate, we have $\hat{w}_1 = \hat{w}_2 = \hat{p}_2 = -dt_1$, as in the previous case, but now, by (7.12), the tax is only partially absorbed by labour in the taxed industry. The remainder, $(1 - w_1 l_1 - w_2 l_2)dt_1$, is absorbed by labour of the input-providing industry 2: they contribute positively to the payment of the tax.

If the input-providing industry 2 is taxed, we have

$$1 = c_1(w_1, w_2, p_2) \tag{7.13}$$
$$p_2 = c_2(w_1, w_2)(1 + t_2) \tag{7.14}$$

Differentiating under the usual assumptions and setting $\hat{w}_1 = \hat{w}_2 = \hat{w}$, we obtain

$$\hat{w} = -a_{21}dt_2 \tag{7.15}$$

$$\hat{p}_2 = (1 - a_{21})dt_2 \tag{7.16}$$

$$(\hat{w} - \hat{p}_2) = -dt_2 \tag{7.17}$$

We see at once that, with a_{21} positive, a sales tax on commodity 2 increases the relative price of the taxed commodity proportionally less than the tax and leads real wages to decrease not only in terms of the taxed commodity, but also in terms of the untaxed commodity.

If each commodity is used in the production of the other and a sales tax is levied on commodity 1, we have

$$1 = c_1(w_1, w_2, p_2)(1 + t_1) \tag{7.18}$$

$$p_2 = c_2(w_1, w_2, 1) \tag{7.19}$$

Our usual differentiation at $t_1 = 0$, setting $\hat{w}_1 = \hat{w}_2 = \hat{w}$, gives

$$\hat{w} = -\frac{1}{(1 - a_{21}a_{12})}dt_1 \tag{7.20}$$

$$\hat{p}_2 = -\frac{(w_1 l_{12} + w_2 l_{22})}{(1 - a_{21}a_{12})}dt_1 \tag{7.21}$$

$$(\hat{w} - \hat{p}_2) = -\frac{a_{12}}{(1 - a_{21}a_{12})}dt_1 \tag{7.22}$$

In this case, $|\hat{w}| \geq dt_1$: a sales tax determines a fall in wages, in terms of the taxed commodity, at a higher proportional rate than the tax rate – a magnification effect similar to that seen in Section 7.1. It will be noted that such an effect requires that both a_{21} and a_{12} be positive (in Sraffian terminology, it requires that both commodities be 'basic'). The relative price of the untaxed commodity always falls, as expected, and it can easily be proved that $|\hat{p}_2| \leq dt_1$, with strict equality if $a_{12} = 0$ (as we have seen). These two relations taken together imply, of course, that the real wages fall also in terms of the untaxed commodity (unless $a_{12} = 0$); if a_{12} is sufficiently high, it may even happen that $|\hat{w} - \hat{p}_2| > dt_1$.

A value-added tax does not avoid the 'disturbances' arising from the input–output relations. Let t_{v1} be a value-added tax levied on industry 1. We clearly have

$$1 = c_1(w_1(1 + t_{v1}), w_2(1 + t_{v1}), p_2) \tag{7.23}$$

$$p_2 = c_2(w_1, w_2, 1) \tag{7.24}$$

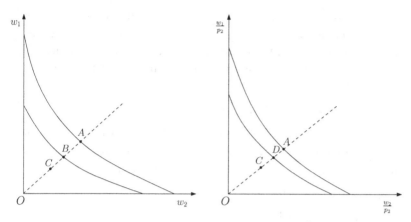

Figure 7.4 Incidence of a VAT on industry 1.

Again, let the tax be borne by the two kinds of labour in the same proportions. The reduction in net wages determines a reduction in the price of the untaxed commodity 2, by (7.24), which in turn leads to an increase in $w_1(1 + t_{v1})$, $w_2(1 + t_{v1})$. It follows that, differently from the case of a sales tax, the real wages, in terms of the taxed commodity, fall at a rate which is lower than the tax rate. Specifically, we have

$$\hat{w} = -\frac{(1 - a_{21})}{(1 - a_{12}a_{21})}dt_{v1} \tag{7.25}$$

$$\hat{p}_2 = -\frac{(1 - a_{21})}{(1 - a_{12}a_{21})}(w_1 l_{12} + w_2 l_{22})dt_{v1} \tag{7.26}$$

where, by the 'unit convention', both a_{12}, a_{21} are lower than one. A graphical illustration is given in Figure 7.4. In the diagram on the left, the VAT rate of industry 1 is $\overline{CA}/\overline{OA}$, while the inward shift in the frontier for industry 1 is 'only' $\overline{BA}/\overline{OA}$: we have here a sort of 'diminution effect'. In the diagram on the right, we also see that the frontier for the untaxed industry 2 shifts inwards, by $\overline{DA}/\overline{OA} < \overline{BA}/\overline{OA}$. A logical consequence, of course, is that the relative price of the untaxed commodity decreases proportionally less than $\overline{BA}/\overline{OA}$. Another aspect concerning both sales and value-added taxes is worth noting: because in both industries the wages fall relative to the price of the commodity input, a constant w_1/w_2 ratio generally involves changing input proportions: from a geometrical point of view, the inward shift of the two frontiers is not radial.

If the burden of the tax falls entirely on, say, labour 2 – in the sense that w_1 remains constant – we still have a positive effect on the wage of labour 1 as expressed in terms of the untaxed commodity similarly to the case without input–output relations earlier in this section.

7.2.2 A tax on all commodities

Now let us assume that both commodities are taxed (by the same kind of tax). With such a general taxation, sales and value added taxes have qualitatively different effects. In the case of a sales tax we have

$$1 = c_1(w_1, w_2, p_2)(1 + t_1)$$
$$p_2 = c_2(w_1, w_2, 1)(1 + t_2)$$

Making our usual assumptions, we have

$$\hat{w} = -\frac{dt_1 + a_{21}dt_2}{(1 - a_{12}a_{21})}$$
$$\hat{p}_2 = \frac{(w_1l_{11} + w_2l_{21})dt_2 - (w_1l_{12} + w_2l_{22})dt_1}{(1 - a_{12}a_{21})}$$

Two main observations are in order. The first is that the proportional fall in real wages is a weighted sum of the tax rates, with weights summing to more than one. This sum is higher the higher are the shares of produced inputs in the two industries: there is again a magnification effect, which ultimately depends on the fact that taxes are (marginal) fractions of the gross outputs, while wages are paid out of real value added. The second observation is that the qualitative change in the relative commodity price does not depend solely on the tax rates. Only if $dt_1/dt_2 = (w_1l_{11} + w_2l_{21})/(w_1l_{12} + w_2l_{22})$ is the relative price constant. Thus equal tax rates modify relative prices, except for the special case in which the shares of value added in gross output are the same. This is shown in Figure 7.5, where the tax rates $\overline{CA/OA}$ are the same in the two industries but the shift in the frontier of industry 1 $\overline{BA/OA}$ is greater than that of industry 2 $\overline{DA/OA}$. If, say, the shares of value added in the two industries are, respectively, 60% and 40%, a uniform sales tax of 5% reduces the real wages by 9.2% in terms of commodity 1 and by 10.5% in terms of commodity 2, because the relative price of the latter commodity increases by 1.3%. In the case of differential taxation, it may happen that the less heavily taxed commodity increases in relative price. If one wishes the relative

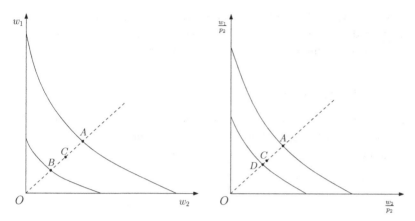

Figure 7.5 Incidence of a uniform sales tax.

prices to be unaffected by sales taxes, then the various commodities must be taxed at different rates.

A VAT has qualitatively different effects. It can easily be shown that, if relative wages remain constant, then

$$\hat{w} = -\frac{(1 - a_{21})dt_{v1} + a_{21}(1 - a_{12})dt_{v2}}{(1 - a_{12}a_{21})} \tag{7.27}$$

$$\hat{p}_2 = \frac{(w_1 l_{12} + w_2 l_{22})(w_1 l_{11} + w_2 l_{21})(dt_{v2} - dt_{v1})}{(1 - a_{12}a_{21})}$$

(It will be noted that (7.27) is not a symmetrical relationship, due to 'asymmetry' in our choice of numéraire.) The common rate of change in real wage rates is, in fact, a weighted average of the two tax rates and p_2 rises if $dt_{v2} > dt_{v1}$. We shall see in the next section, however, that this result does not generalize to any number of industries and commodities, in the sense that the ranking of relative price change does not necessarily correspond to the ranking of differential taxation.

In the case of equal VAT rates, we do have a neat (and general) result: relative prices are constant and the common hypothetical rate of change in wages (in terms of any commodity) is equal to that rate. In other words, uniform VAT rates (of t_v) correspond to a uniform general income tax (of $t_v/(1 + t_v)$). It goes without saying that non-proportional incidence would add a redistribution effect on relative prices and equal tax rates would not then ensure that they remain constant.

A differentiated payroll tax would leave relative prices constant only if its burden is borne by each kind of labour in proportion to its own tax rate, as the interested reader can easily verify.

7.3 Many industries

The extension to n industries is straightforward. Let us express all prices in terms of the general numéraire formed by a bundle s of commodities. In the case of sales taxes, we have

$$\mathbf{p} = \mathbf{c}(w_1, w_2, \mathbf{p})(\mathbf{I} + \tilde{\mathbf{T}})$$
$$\mathbf{ps} \equiv 1$$

where $\tilde{\mathbf{T}}$ is the diagonal matrix formed by the sales tax rates. As usual, let these rates be null initially and let dt be the vector of the newly introduced (marginal) rates. Moreover, let, in obvious notation, $\mathbf{c_w} = \mathbf{L}$, $\mathbf{c_p} = \mathbf{A}$. If we choose units such that initially $\mathbf{p} = \mathbf{u}$ (which also implies $\mathbf{us} = 1$), we have

$$\hat{\mathbf{p}} = (\mathbf{dwL} + \mathbf{dt})(\mathbf{I} - \mathbf{A})^{-1}$$
$$\hat{\mathbf{p}}\mathbf{s} = 0$$

The columns of matrix $(\mathbf{I} - \mathbf{A})$ have a 'double' meaning: they are at the same time vectors of *material* commodity 'netputs' per unit of gross output in the various industries and vectors of commodity 'netput' *shares* per unit of gross output. Each column sum is thus identically equal to the (equilibrium) value-added share per unit of gross output in the corresponding industry, so that matrix $(\mathbf{I} - \mathbf{A})$ is semi-stochastic. Denoting by $\boldsymbol{\sigma}$ the vector of such shares, we have then $\mathbf{u}(\mathbf{I} - \mathbf{A}) = \boldsymbol{\sigma}$ and of course $\mathbf{u} = \boldsymbol{\sigma}(\mathbf{I} - \mathbf{A})^{-1}$. Setting $\hat{w}_1 = \hat{w}_2 = \hat{w}$, we therefore have

$$\hat{\mathbf{p}} = \mathbf{u}\hat{w} + \mathbf{dt}(\mathbf{I} - \mathbf{A})^{-1}$$
$$0 = \hat{w} + \mathbf{dt}(\mathbf{I} - \mathbf{A})^{-1}\mathbf{s}$$

It follows that

$$\hat{w} = -\mathbf{dt}(\mathbf{I} - \mathbf{A})^{-1}\mathbf{s} \tag{7.28}$$
$$\hat{p}_j = \mathbf{dt}(\mathbf{I} - \mathbf{A})^{-1}(\mathbf{e}_j - \mathbf{s}), \ j = 1, 2, \dots n \tag{7.29}$$

We have here a generalization of the simple results obtained in the two-industry case. Because $(\mathbf{I} - \mathbf{A})^{-1}\mathbf{s}$ is a weighted average of the columns of $(\mathbf{I} - \mathbf{A})^{-1}$ and as each column adds to more than one, the (hypothetical) common proportional reduction in the real wages is generally a weighted sum of the tax rates, with weights adding, also, to more than one (unless $\mathbf{A} = 0$). It follows that, with a uniform tax rate, $\hat{w}$ is higher, in absolute value, than that rate. In the special case of uniform shares, σ, we have $\mathbf{u}(\mathbf{I} - \mathbf{A})^{-1}\mathbf{e}_j = 1/\sigma$. More generally, $1/\sigma_{\max} \leq \mathbf{u}(\mathbf{I} - \mathbf{A})^{-1}\mathbf{e}_j \leq 1/\sigma_{\min}, \forall j$.

As far as prices are concerned, let us first notice that $\mathbf{u}(\mathbf{e}_j - \mathbf{s}) = 0$. This implies that $\hat{p}_j = 0, \forall j$, only if $\mathbf{dt}(\mathbf{I} - \mathbf{A})^{-1}$ is proportional to $\mathbf{u}$. However, we know that $\sigma(\mathbf{I} - \mathbf{A})^{-1} = \mathbf{u}$. Thus, relative prices are constant only if $\mathbf{dt}$ is proportional to σ. A uniform sales tax rate will modify relative prices, except in the very special case of equal value-added shares in the various industries. On the other hand, if a system of sales taxes is used in order to increase, say, the numéraire price of a specific commodity having negative externalities, no simple rule, such as a higher sales tax rate for that commodity than for other commodities, can be used.

In the case of a value-added tax, competitive pricing requires that

$$p_j = c_j(w_1(1 + t_{vj}), w_2(1 + t_{vj}), \mathbf{p}), \quad j = 1, 2, \ldots, n$$

$$\mathbf{ps} = 1$$

Differentiating at $t_{vj} = 0$, we have

$$\hat{\mathbf{p}} = (\mathbf{dwL} + \sigma \mathbf{d}\tilde{\mathbf{T}}_v)(\mathbf{I} - \mathbf{A})^{-1}$$

$$\hat{\mathbf{p}}\mathbf{s} = 0$$

where $\mathbf{d}\tilde{\mathbf{T}}_v$ is the diagonal matrix formed by the new VAT rates. If $\hat{w}_1 = \hat{w}_2 = \hat{w}$, then we have, after substitutions

$$\hat{w} = -\sigma \mathbf{d}\tilde{\mathbf{T}}_v(\mathbf{I} - \mathbf{A})^{-1}\mathbf{s}$$

$$\hat{p}_j = \sigma \mathbf{d}\tilde{\mathbf{T}}_v(\mathbf{I} - \mathbf{A})^{-1}(\mathbf{e}_j - \mathbf{s}), \quad j = 1, 2, \ldots, n$$

Because $\sigma(\mathbf{I} - \mathbf{A})^{-1}\mathbf{s} = 1$, the hypothetical common rate of reduction in real wages is a weighted average of the industrial VAT rates. Because also $\sigma(\mathbf{I} - \mathbf{A})^{-1}\mathbf{e}_j = 1$, we see at once that prices are constant with uniform VAT rates.

It would be wrong, however, to infer from this that, with differential taxation, the ranking of the price changes is the same as the ranking of the VAT rates. Let $dt_{v1} > dt_{v2} > 0$ and $dt_{vj} = 0, j = 3, \ldots, n$. Now

$$(\hat{p}_1 - \hat{p}_2) = \sigma_1\{\mathbf{e}_1^T(\mathbf{I} - \mathbf{A})^{-1}(\mathbf{e}_1 - \mathbf{e}_2)\}dt_{v1}$$
$$- \sigma_2\{\mathbf{e}_2^T(\mathbf{I} - \mathbf{A})^{-1}(\mathbf{e}_2 - \mathbf{e}_1)\}dt_{v2}$$

But we know that $\sigma(I - A)^{-1}(e_1 - e_2) = 0$. It follows that, in general, differently from the case with only two commodities,

$$\sigma_1\{e_1^T(I - A)^{-1}(e_1 - e_2)\} \neq \sigma_2\{e_2^T(I - A)^{-1}(e_2 - e_1)\}$$

The fact that commodity 1 is more heavily taxed than commodity 2 does not predetermine the sign of $(\hat{p}_1 - \hat{p}_2)$: it may happen that p_1 falls relative to p_2. It should also be remarked that the prices of the untaxed commodities are far from remaining constant and that they change, in terms of the numéraire and relative to one another, in a direction which depends in a complex way on input–output relations.

7.4 The effects of taxation on input use per unit of output

Sometimes taxation is aimed at stimulating a more intensive use of a specific primary input (say, young or highly skilled labour) or a less intensive use of a specific commodity input (say, a polluting form of energy). It is commonly held that the desired incentives can be provided, respectively, by a subsidy and a tax. Microeconomic theory tells us that this is indeed the case when the modification affects the gross price of the subsidized/taxed input and no other input price. However, under FIE, many prices normally change at once and the question should be studied in more detail.

Let us reconsider the isolated-industry case of Section 7.1 with two kinds of labour and a commodity input, imported at given terms of trade. Starting from a no-tax FIE, let a negative payroll tax (a subsidy) be introduced on the use of 'labour 1'. We have therefore

$$1 = c(w_1(1 + t_{w1}), w_2, P)$$

with t_{w1} initially equal to zero and then negative.

Needless to say, this policy is completely ineffective if the subsidy is entirely absorbed by an increase in w_1, for in this case the gross real wage (the wage paid by the firms) remains constant. We must therefore assume that the subsidy determines a fall in $w_1(1 + t_{w1})$, as expected, thus triggering, under FIE, a compensating increase in w_2; to consider a simple case, we assume that both net wages (the wages received by the workers) increase and that the w_1/w_2 ratio remains constant; also P is assumed to remain constant. Notice that the gross real wage of the subsidized labour falls relative to all other input prices. No doubt,

Table 7.1 *Two fixed-coefficient techniques.*

	α	β
l_1	1.04	1.01
l_2	2.45	1
a	0.1	1

if labour 1 is a Hicksian substitute for both other inputs in the neighborhood of the pre-subsidy equilibrium, then a marginal decrease in both $w_1(1 + t_{w1})/w_2$ and $w_1(1 + t_{w1})/P$ ensures that l_1 increases, as is well known from marginalist theory (cf. Equation (2.15)). Otherwise, in the case of discrete variations, we cannot infer from the change in prices that the use of the subsidized labour necessarily increases: it might decrease, contrary to the desired effect, as the following examples show.

Let us initially assume that two fixed-coefficient techniques are available (of course, we are reverting to an assumption of strictly constant returns), labelled α and β, as in Table 7.1.

Let the no-subsidy wages and the commodity input price be, respectively, $w_1 = 0.23$, $w_2 = 0.29$, $P = 0.5$. Using technique α, the unit cost is 1, while using technique β it is 1.022. Now let the use of labour 1 be subsidized with a negative tax rate of -28.5% and the net wages increase to $w_1' = 0.252$, $w_2' = 0.318$, respectively, while the commodity input price remains constant. The gross wage of labour 1 has now fallen to $w_1'(1 + t_{w1}) = 0.18$. At the new input prices, the unit cost becomes 1.016 with technique α and 1 with technique β: the switch from α to β has determined a reduction in the use of the subsidized labour.

Some readers may be tempted to guess that this unintended effect is attributable to lack of substitution. Another example, however, shows that this is not the case. Let there be infinitely many possibilities of combining the two kinds of labour and the commodity input; moreover, let a second imported commodity input be able, together with the same kinds of labour, to produce the same output, again with infinitely many technological possibilities. The two commodity inputs characterize different 'technologies' and are therefore of the on/off variety – a case that we have already discussed at length.

Let P_1, P_2 denote the prices of the two imported commodities and let the two 'technologies' be described, respectively, by the unit cost functions à la Diewert

$$c_1 = 0.2\sqrt{w_1 P_1} + 1.8\sqrt{w_1 w_2} + 0.5\sqrt{w_2 P_1}$$
$$c_2 = 0.7\sqrt{w_1 P_2} + 0.2\sqrt{w_1 w_2} + 0.6\sqrt{w_2 P_2}$$

Therefore, the industry's cost function will be

$$c = \min(0.2\sqrt{w_1 P_1} + 1.8\sqrt{w_1 w_2} + 0.5\sqrt{w_2 P_1},$$
$$0.7\sqrt{w_1 P_2} + 0.2\sqrt{w_1 w_2} + 0.6\sqrt{w_2 P_2})$$

Notice that within each technology all inputs are Hicksian substitutes for one another. Let initially $w_1 = 1.095$, $w_2 = 0.11$, $P_1 = 1 = P_2$. The industry adopts 'technology 1', which has a cost lower than that of 'technology 2'; the uses per unit of output of the two kinds of labour and of the commodity inputs are, respectively, $l_1 = 0.381$, $l_2 = 3.594$, $a_1 = 0.188$, $a_2 = 0$. Now let a subsidy of about 6% be introduced on the use of labour 1. Suppose that, as a result, the real wages received by the two kinds of labour rise by some 4.5% to $w_1' = 1.145$, $w_2' = 0.115$ (their ratio remaining constant), while the gross wage paid for the use of labour 1 falls to $w_1'(1 + t_{w1}) = 1.076$; the international relative prices of the two commodity inputs are assumed to remain constant. The industry shifts to 'technology 2', which has a cost about 1% lower than that of 'technology 1': input uses per unit of output are now $l_1' = 0.370$, $l_2' = 1.191$, $a_1' = 0$, $a_2' = 0.465$. As in the previous example, the subsidy on one kind of labour has reduced that labour's use per unit of output (by nearly 3%) –and yet there were all kinds of substitution possibilities, within-technology and across-technologies! The 'trick' in this example is that, at the switch point, where commodity 2 replaces commodity 1, there is a sudden downward jump in the use of both kinds of labour – and this prevails over the conventional substitution effects. The interested reader may easily verify that a sufficiently high subsidy would trigger within-technology substitutions such that the use per unit of output of the subsidized labour would in fact increase.

In both examples, the gross price of the subsidized labour decreases relative to all the other input prices but these latter, in turn, change relative to one another. In such a situation (as we have noted in Section 1.4) the 'generalized substitution theorem' provides no qualitative restriction on the input price–input use relationship.

The case of an excise tax on a certain commodity input is similar. Let us assume that the relative wages remain constant. If commodity j, and no other commodity, is taxed we have from (7.28), (7.29) that

$$\hat{w} = -dt_j e_j^T (I - A)^{-1} s \tag{7.28'}$$

$$\hat{p}_j = dt_j e_j^T (I - A)^{-1} (e_j - s) \tag{7.29'}$$

$$\hat{p}_i = dt_j e_j^T (I - A)^{-1} (e_i - s) \tag{7.29''}$$

Because the diagonal terms of $(I - A)^{-1}$ are all greater than one and the off-diagonal terms are all lower than one, it is certain that the price of the taxed commodity increases relative to all other commodity prices and relative to the wages but the other input prices (and their ratios) change as well: under this point of view, a tax on a commodity input is symmetrical to a subsidy on a primary input and we cannot generally expect that the use of that input per unit of output falls.

Gehrke and Lager (1995) have shown in the context of a Sraffian model with circulating capital and a positive rate of interest that an environmental tax on a commodity input may increase the total use of the taxed commodity in the economic system as a whole. The foregoing analysis helps to clarify the microeconomic rationale of such an unconventional result and shows that at the level of the individual industry it by no means involves any capital-theoretic considerations and can be referred also to subsidies on primary inputs.

7.5 Concluding remarks

Under free competition, the burden of taxes on production falls entirely on real primary input rentals, for otherwise it would generate permanent losses. The most simple way to illustrate this fundamental long-run effect of taxation is by assuming only one industry: the imposition of a sales tax, a VAT, or payroll taxes determines an inward shift of the entire real wages frontier. The qualitative properties of such a shift differ according to economic circumstances and the kind of tax. A VAT determines a radial contraction of the frontier at a proportional rate equal to the new tax, so that a constant real wages ratio is associated with constant relative labour use: in this case, the tax is similar to a general income tax. By contrast, in the presence of (imported) produced inputs, a sales tax produces a magnification effect on real wages and it modifies the shape of the frontier: with proportional incidence, input intensities would change; if the relative labour use is to remain constant, then the tax would have to be associated with a movement along the new frontier.

The connection between taxation and real wages is naturally more complex in the presence of multiple industries having input–output relations with one another, because taxation in one industry affects real costs in other industries: not only, then, is the shift in the frontier for the taxed industry more complex than in the case with one industry, but the real wages change also in terms of the untaxed commodities. One should therefore determine the effect of taxation in one industry on the entire structure of competitive prices.

A related question is under what conditions uniform taxation keeps relative prices constant; we have seen that this is obtained by uniform VAT rates and by sales tax rates proportional to the industrial shares of value added. However, if the government aims at a certain change in the structure of relative prices, there is no simple rule for the required tax rates. We have also shown that under FIE a subsidy on one kind of labour may have counter-productive effects on the use of that input per unit of output.

8 | *Productivity increase*

A fundamental source of a changing price structure is technological progress in the various industries. It is a common understanding, for instance, that the recent pattern of progress has determined a sharp diminution in the relative price of computing power (e.g. Jorgenson *et al.*, 2005, p. xviii; see also Autor *et al.*, 2006, p. 192), an increase in the 'average' real wage and a change in the ratios among the wages of different kinds of labour (e.g. Goos *et al.*, 2009). The theoretical background of these investigations, and of many others, is solidly anchored to the traditional growth-accounting logic of Total Factor Productivity. By contrast, the present chapter looks at productivity increase directly from the standpoint of price and wage developments and argues that, in conditions of free competition, we can in principle extract from the system of long-run prices some useful information on the industrial rates of productivity increase. In so doing, we offer to the applied microeconomist a unified conceptual framework for empirical investigations in which relative price change, wage dispersion and the rates of productivity increase are all parts of the same theoretical system.

Technical improvements not only increase outputs relative to inputs, they also reduce output *prices* relative to input rewards. Under free competition, these aspects are two sides of the same coin and from a mathematical point of view they are 'duals' (a useful textbook presentation of the 'primal' and the 'dual' for a generic price-taking firm is in Chambers, 1988, chapter 6). In the decades dominated by attention to the contribution of the different industries to aggregate growth, comparatively little attention has been paid to the 'dual': the measures of productivity increase on the one side, and of output-deflated wage increase/dispersion on the other, still belong to different fields (growth theory and labour market analysis, respectively) and their mutual consistency must be checked explicitly.

Perhaps the recent revival of interest in income distribution in connection with productivity increase (e.g. Katz and Autor, 1999; World Bank, 2006, pp. 28–54; Atkinson, 2007; Checchi and García-Peñalosa, 2008, pp. 603–06) might stimulate a shift in focus from the 'primal' to the 'dual'? We think it should and the present chapter is our contribution in this direction.

In Section 8.1 we define the 'dual' measure in the simple case of an isolated industry, using two kinds of labour and no other input: we show that the 'primal' and the 'dual' give the same theoretical result, as expected. In this section we also introduce a commodity input, imported at an internationally given relative price, and identify a 'terms of trade' component of real earnings change, distinguished from productivity increase.

We shall then introduce in Section 8.2 other domestic industries. As in the case of taxation, the impact on relative prices is a central issue. In the simple case without commodity inputs and assuming constant relative wages, the analysis is straightforward and we shall see that the change in the structure of relative prices just mirrors the pattern of technical change; but when technical progress leads to a modification in relative wages, some further effects should be taken into account. In this multi-sectoral framework, we also deal with the important issue of the aggregate measure of productivity increase, in terms of real wage increase (cf. Steedman, 1983).

In Section 8.3 we consider the more general case of industries with input–output relations, stressing the inter-industry effects of productivity increase: to use Hulten's (1978, p. 514) terminology, a 'nominal' initial change must be distinguished from an 'effective' change which includes an inter-industry transmission of the gains from productivity increase. It will be shown that uniform rates of progress do not normally involve constant relative prices and the fact that one industry is more progressive than another does not ensure that the former's output price falls relative to the latter's. We shall also extend our method of aggregation of the industrial rates of productivity increase and compare it with the conventional method originated by Domar (1961).

In Section 8.4 we reconsider the TFP view, in both the 'gross output' and the 'value-added-output' versions, in the light of our findings. Section 8.5 contains some historical notes on early price-accounting descriptions of productivity increase. Section 8.6 concludes.

8.1 An isolated industry

In Chapter 7 we analysed the effects of the introduction of (marginal) tax rates under the obvious supposition that such rates were given parametrically. No similar supposition can be made with respect to productivity increase. That rate must be judged from its proximate economic effects. This is what Solow (1957) did on the basis of observable output and input changes and we must first of all define the dual counterpart, on the basis of observable changes in input and output prices.

In order to illustrate the basic rationale of the dual definition in the simplest possible context, let us start, once again, from a one-industry economy, in which production requires just two different kinds of labour, perhaps skilled and unskilled labour.

At given input prices, the indirect average cost is a function of (logical) time (T) and this reflects the operation of technical improvements. In the usual notation, we have then

$$p = c(w_1, w_2; T) \tag{8.1}$$

By the homogeneity properties of $c(\ )$, we may express both input prices in terms of the industrial output, obtaining

$$1 = c(w_1, w_2; T) \tag{8.2}$$

Equation (8.2) implicitly traces the 'real wages frontier', whose position depends on the shift parameter T.

Let us pause for a moment in order to translate the familiar definitions of 'neutrality' in terms of the 'real wages frontier'. Hicks-neutral technical progress determines a radial 'outward' shift of the frontier, with an unchanged slope (the skilled/unskilled labour ratio) associated with an unchanged w_1/w_2 ratio. In this case, the indirect average cost function is of the kind $c(w_1, w_2, T) = g(w_1, w_2) \cdot h(T)$ and productivity increase is analogous to the imposition of a negative sales tax (i.e. a subsidy). By contrast, a cost function $c(w_1 \cdot h(T), w_2)$ would represent labour-1-augmenting productivity increase. Taking labour 1 and labour 2 to represent skilled and unskilled labour, respectively, such a cost function would embody the assumption of 'skill-biased technical change'. (*Mutatis mutandis*, the interested reader may associate the cost functions $c(w_1 \cdot h(T), w_2)$ and $c(w_1, w_2 \cdot h(T))$ with Harrod's and Solow's symmetrical concepts of neutrality; see also Steedman, 1983.)

Now independently of whether technical progress is neutral (on any definition) or not, the rate of productivity growth, γ, can sensibly be defined as $(-)$ the partial logarithmic derivative of c with respect to T (see Chambers, 1988, p. 214), that is

$$\gamma \equiv -\frac{\partial c}{\partial T}\frac{1}{c} \tag{8.3}$$

Setting $\sigma_i = (w_i l_i / p)$ as the share of labour i, total differentiation of (8.1) gives

$$\hat{p} = \sigma_1 \hat{w}_1 + \sigma_2 \hat{w}_2 - \gamma \tag{8.4}$$

or

$$\gamma = \sigma_1(\hat{w}_1 - \hat{p}) + \sigma_2(\hat{w}_2 - \hat{p}) \tag{8.5}$$

The industrial rate of productivity growth is therefore a weighted sum of the rates of change in real input prices, in terms of the industrial output, using input shares as weights. In the terminology introduced in Chapter 6, the lhs of (8.5) can be interpreted as the source of industrial real cost reduction and the rhs as its outcome.

There is a clear analogy with Solow's growth accounting formula. Of course, Solow considered labour and capital, but he treated capital as if it were a primary input, so we can safely refer his argument to two different kinds of labour. For the reader's convenience, let us rewrite in obvious notation Solow's growth-accounting equation

$$\hat{Y} = \hat{A} + \sigma_1 \hat{L}_1 + \sigma_2 \hat{L}_2$$

A slight rearrangement gives

$$\hat{A} = \sigma_1(\hat{Y} - \hat{L}_1) + \sigma_2(\hat{Y} - \hat{L}_2) \tag{8.6}$$

Equation (8.5) is the precise dual of the more conventional Equation (8.6). Accordingly, the two equations give in principle the same result. To see this, let us first note that, by homogeneity of degree one of c in (w_1, w_2) and by Shephard's lemma, we have $w_1 l_1 + w_2 l_2 = c$ and

$$w_1 L_1 + w_2 L_2 = cY,$$

where $L_i = l_i Y, i = 1, 2$. Because $c = p$, we have by differentiation

$$\sigma_1(\hat{w}_1 + \hat{L}_1) + \sigma_2(\hat{w}_2 + \hat{L}_2) = \hat{p} + \hat{Y}$$

which, together with (8.5) and (8.6), clearly implies $\gamma = \hat{A}$.

From a practical point of view, however, one cannot rely on a complete knowledge of the cost function: only discrete variations in (logical) time are relevant and only actual real wages can be observed. The rate of productivity increase must therefore be estimated on the basis of a comparison of 'effective' points on different frontiers. To this end, let us reinterpret Figure 6.1 (reproduced here as Figure 8.1 on the next page) with the understanding that 'real cost reduction' is now specifically due to productivity increase. For ease of notation, we set $p = 1$, so that (w_1, w_2) here denote the real wage rates.

In discrete time, the rate of productivity increase, γ, is defined as $-\Delta c/c$, calculated at constant wages; from a geometrical point of view, therefore, it corresponds to the (proportional) expansion of the 'old' frontier on the same ray. Because the 'initial' and 'final' real wages are normally not on a ray, we can generate by linear approximation a pair of hypothetical wages on the old frontier and the new w_1/w_2 ratio, at P_{AB}; therefore, our approximate measure of the rate of productivity increase will be

$$\gamma \cong \frac{w_1^B}{w_1^{AB}} - 1 = \frac{w_2^B}{w_2^{AB}} - 1 \tag{8.7}$$

Because the slope of the frontier at P_A is $-l_2^A/l_1^A$, we have

$$\left(w_1^{AB} - w_1^A\right) = -\left(\frac{l_2^A}{l_1^A}\right)\left(w_2^{AB} - w_2^A\right)$$

Now $w_2^{AB} = (w_2^B/w_1^B)w_1^{AB}$, by construction. Taking into account that $w_1^A l_1^A + w_2^A l_2^A = 1$, it follows that, at P_{AB}

$$w_1^{AB} = \frac{1}{w_1^B l_1^A + w_2^B l_2^A}w_1^B; \quad w_2^{AB} = \frac{1}{w_1^B l_1^A + w_2^B l_2^A}w_2^B$$

Hence

$$\gamma \cong w_1^B l_1^A + w_2^B l_2^A - 1,$$

or

$$\gamma \cong w_1^A l_1^A \left(\frac{w_1^B}{w_1^A} - 1\right) + w_2^A l_2^A \left(\frac{w_2^B}{w_2^A} - 1\right) \tag{8.8}$$

which is the discrete-time counterpart of (8.5).

The interested reader may easily check our Figure 8.1 against figure 1 in Solow (1957): Solow's method distinguishes between a shift of

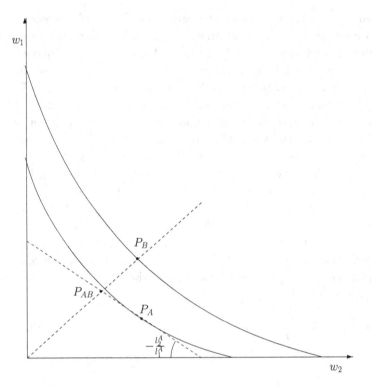

Figure 8.1 The measure of productivity increase, in discrete time.

the production function (per unit of labour) and a movement along it; our proposed method distinguishes between a shift of the (average) cost function and a movement along it.

The presence of a commodity input introduces some further aspects which are worth noting. Let us first assume that the commodity itself is used as input and that the interest rate is identically zero. The cost function and the real wages frontier become, respectively,

$$c = c(w_1, w_2, p; T)$$

$$1 = c\left(\frac{w_1}{p}, \frac{w_2}{p}, 1; T\right)$$

The main difference from the previous case is that now it is impossible that all three relative input prices remain constant, by the obvious fact that at least one of w_1/p and w_2/p increases. The very definition of Hicks-neutrality in industrial sectors is problematic. In particular, a separable cost function $c(w_1, w_2, p, T) = g(w_1, w_2, p) \cdot h(T)$ would not, in general, determine a radial shift of the frontier; even though the w_2/w_1 ratio remains constant, it generally happens that l_2/l_1 changes (likewise, also the long-run output of each firm generally changes). Equations (8.3) and (8.5) still hold; but now $\sigma_1 + \sigma_2 < 1$.

In discrete time, again setting $p = 1$, we have from (8.5)

$$\gamma \cong (\sigma_1 + \sigma_2) \left(\frac{w_i^B}{w_i^{AB}} - 1 \right), i = 1, 2 \tag{8.7'}$$

It follows that a radial measure of the 'upward' shift in the frontier would overestimate the rate of productivity increase: this measure should be reduced by the share of value added in the price. The absolute slope of the real wages frontier is still equal to relative labour use so that (8.8) also holds, *mutatis mutandis*.

Similar reasoning applies to the case in which another commodity is used as input and this commodity is imported at a given price P relative to the domestic commodity. Setting $\hat{p} = 0$ and denoting by a the cost-minimizing use of the imported commodity input, (8.5) should now be replaced by

$$\gamma - Pa\hat{P} = w_1 l_1 \hat{w}_1 + w_2 l_2 \hat{w}_2 \tag{8.9}$$

It is worth stressing that formally the imported intermediate input enters (8.9) as if it were a third primary input. However, in the economic interpretation, a change in the terms of trade should be considered as a factor analogous to productivity increase. Therefore, the change in real wages now has two sources and we can in principle distinguish between them on the basis of (8.9).

8.2 Many industries

When we turn to multiple industries, two main further problems arise. One is to analyse the effect of a certain pattern of industrial productivity increase on relative prices and, conversely, to infer from the latter an implied pattern of productivity change. The second problem is to develop a rational method of aggregation of the industrial rates, showing how each industry contributes to the overall change in wages.

It is convenient to assume at first that there are no produced inputs. The specific complications arising from input–output relations will be considered in the next section.

Assume that there are n industries which share the same two kinds of labour. In FIE we have

$$\mathbf{p} = \mathbf{c}(w_1, w_2; T) \tag{8.10}$$

As in the previous chapter, let us adopt the 'unit convention' so that initially $\mathbf{u} = \mathbf{p} = \mathbf{c}$, where $\mathbf{u}$ is the unit vector. Moreover, let $\mathbf{l}_i, i = 1, 2$ be the vector of the use of labour i per unit of output in the various industries. Differentiating (8.10) totally we get

$$\hat{\mathbf{p}} = w_1 \mathbf{l}_1 \hat{w}_1 + w_2 \mathbf{l}_2 \hat{w}_2 - \boldsymbol{\gamma} \tag{8.11}$$

It will be clear that, by the unit convention, $w_i l_{ij}$ is the share of labour i in industry j. It follows that, if $\hat{w}_1 = \hat{w}_2 = \hat{w}$, then $(\hat{p}_j - \hat{p}_s) = (\gamma_s - \gamma_j)$, $j, s = 1, 2, \ldots, n$, and, in terms of the industrial outputs, the wages increase at the industrial rate of productivity increase. Specifically, we have

$$\hat{\mathbf{p}} = \hat{w}\mathbf{u} - \boldsymbol{\gamma}$$

If $\hat{w}_1 \neq \hat{w}_2$ and the industries have different input shares, things are naturally more complex: uniform rates of productivity increase would be associated with a change in the relative prices of commodities; moreover, when such rates are not uniform, we can by no means be sure that in the 'more progressive' industry the relative price falls.

From the standpoint of the estimation of vector $\boldsymbol{\gamma}$, the discrete-time approximation discussed in the previous section can be referred to each individual industry, on the assumption that wages are uniform across industries. Specifically, we have

$$\gamma_j \cong w_1^A l_{1j}^A \left(\frac{w_1^B}{w_1^A} \frac{p_j^A}{p_j^B} - 1 \right) + w_2^A l_{2j}^A \left(\frac{w_2^B}{w_2^A} \frac{p_j^A}{p_j^B} - 1, \right)$$

$$j = 1, 2, \ldots, n$$

From knowledge of the output-deflated wages at two points of time and the 'initial' labour shares we can infer the rate of productivity increase in each industry.

Now let us express the real wages in terms of a commodity basket $\mathbf{s}$, so that $\mathbf{ps} = 1$. It should be noted that, initially, also $\mathbf{us} = 1$. By definition we have

$$\hat{p}s = 0 \tag{8.12}$$

Substituting $\hat{p}$ from (8.11) into (8.12), we have

$$w_1(l_1 s)\hat{w}_1 + w_2(l_2 s)\hat{w}_2 = \gamma s \tag{8.13}$$

Because $us = 1$, we also have $w_1(l_1 s) + w_2(l_2 s) = 1$, where $w_i(l_i s)$ is the average share of labour i, weighted by the commodity composition of the numéraire. Now one could define the aggregate rate of productivity increase, Γ, as the common hypothetical rate of increase of real wages, expressed in numéraire, that is

$$\Gamma = \gamma s \tag{8.14}$$

In this definition, the aggregate rate of productivity increase is a weighted average of the industrial rates, using as weights the shares of each commodity in the numéraire. Choosing a numéraire proportional to the value of industrial outputs, the weights correspond to the shares of each industry in the aggregate output, and Γ has the same theoretical value as the familiar aggregate Total Factor Productivity index. It is worth noting that, from a practical point of view, we can estimate Γ in two ways: we can estimate the industrial rates first, according to (8.11) and then aggregate them using (8.14); or we can directly use the observed changes in the numéraire-deflated wages and weight them using the average labour shares, according to (8.13). But, of course, whatever numéraire is chosen, the unfortunate fact is that Γ depends on the arbitrary choice of numéraire.

In the $\hat{w}_1 = \hat{w}_2$ case, the change in each commodity price, in numéraire, can be expressed as the difference between the aggregate and the industrial rates of productivity increase, that is

$$\hat{p} = (\Gamma u - \gamma)$$

Unfortunately, this nice property does not generalize to any distribution of the gains from productivity increase between wages. Only if the shares of the different kinds of labour are uniform across industries does a relative price change reflect exactly the differential rate of productivity increase; otherwise it also reflects a changing distribution. In particular, if, say, $\hat{w}_2 < \Gamma < \hat{w}_1$ and $l_{1j} < (l_1 s)$, then $\hat{p}_j < (\Gamma - \gamma_j)$: it may happen that industry j is performing worse than average and yet its product price in numéraire falls.

8.3 Many industries with input–output relations

The introduction of input–output relations modifies the conclusions reached so far in two main respects. First, the change in relative prices is no longer univocally determined by the industrial pattern of productivity increase, even in the absence of any 'redistribution' effect: the indirect effects of productivity increase in one industry on the costs in other industries may either reinforce or weaken the direct effect and the outcome depends in a complex way on the industrial shares of each commodity input. Second, the change in primary input prices, in any commodity numéraire, is no longer a simple weighted average of the industrial rates of productivity increase: there will be a magnification effect of the same kind as that discussed in Section 8.1 for the simple case with only one industry using as input its own output. In order to isolate these two complications, in this section we consider homogeneous labour, which is equivalent to assuming a constant wage ratio.

Competitive pricing requires

$$\mathbf{p} = \mathbf{c}(w, \mathbf{p}; T) \tag{8.15}$$

Let again $\mathbf{ps} = 1$ and $\mathbf{p} = \mathbf{u}$ at a given point of time. Denoting by $\mathbf{A}$ the matrix of (cost-minimizing) commodity inputs per unit of industrial gross output in the neighbourhood of equilibrium, we have by the usual differentiation

$$\hat{\mathbf{p}} = \hat{w}w\mathbf{l} + \hat{\mathbf{p}}\mathbf{A} - \boldsymbol{\gamma} \tag{8.16}$$

or

$$\hat{\mathbf{p}} = (\hat{w}w\mathbf{l} - \boldsymbol{\gamma})(\mathbf{I} - \mathbf{A})^{-1} \tag{8.17}$$

Of course, by the 'unit convention', $w\mathbf{l}$ is also the vector of the shares of value added in the different industries and $\mathbf{A}$ is also the matrix of the shares of produced inputs, with $w\mathbf{l} = \mathbf{u}(\mathbf{I} - \mathbf{A})$. Hence

$$\hat{\mathbf{p}} = \hat{w}\mathbf{u} - \boldsymbol{\gamma}(\mathbf{I} - \mathbf{A})^{-1} \tag{8.18}$$

If i, j is any pair of commodities, the change in their relative price is

$$\hat{p}_j - \hat{p}_i = \boldsymbol{\gamma}(\mathbf{I} - \mathbf{A})^{-1}(\mathbf{e}_i - \mathbf{e}_j) \tag{8.19}$$

Two special cases are of interest. First, $\boldsymbol{\gamma}$ may happen to be the positive left-hand eigenvector of $\mathbf{A}$; in this case $\boldsymbol{\gamma}(\mathbf{I} - \mathbf{A})^{-1} = (1/(1 - \Lambda))\boldsymbol{\gamma}$, where Λ is the dominant eigenvalue of $\mathbf{A}$, $0 < \Lambda < 1$ (as the terms in each column of $\mathbf{A}$ add to less than one) and (8.19) reduces to

$$\hat{p}_j - \hat{p}_i = \frac{1}{(1-\Lambda)}(\gamma_i - \gamma_j) \qquad (8.19')$$

The change in each relative price is an amplification of the pairwise differential rates of productivity increase. Second, γ may happen to be proportional to $w\mathbf{l}$, say $\gamma = \Omega w\mathbf{l}$; in this case, (8.19) reduces to

$$\hat{p}_j - \hat{p}_i = \Omega\mathbf{u}(e_i - e_j) = 0 \qquad (8.19'')$$

However diverse the industrial rates of productivity increase (and the shares of value added), the impact on relative prices is null.

It is worth remarking that if the value added shares are uniform and equal to σ, then the dominant eigenvalue is $\Lambda = 1 - \sigma$ and the two cases are indistinguishable.

More generally, however, we are left with no simple rule concerning relative price changes; (8.19) must be estimated case by case. It may even happen that the output price in a relatively 'progressive' industry rises relative to that of a relatively 'slow' one, as in the following example. Let there be three industries such that, at a certain time

$$\mathbf{A} = \begin{pmatrix} 0 & 0.2 & 0.15 \\ 0.2 & 0 & 0.25 \\ 0.4 & 0.3 & 0 \end{pmatrix}$$

and let the rates of productivity increase be $\gamma = (4.5\%, 5\%, 5.5\%)$. It is readily shown that $\hat{p}_1 - \hat{p}_2 = -0.38\%$, $\hat{p}_1 - \hat{p}_3 = -0.77\%$, $\hat{p}_2 - \hat{p}_3 = -0.39\%$; even though the first industry has the lowest rate of productivity increase, its price falls relative to every other price. The opposite happens in the third industry, which has the highest rate of productivity increase. The basic rationale of this perhaps counterintuitive example is that, relative to other industries, industry 1 has a lower share of value added, so that it benefits relatively more from progress in other industries and this outweighs its own lower industrial rate of productivity increase. More generally, we can consider the proportional fall in price, as deflated by the proportional increase in the wage (a Smithian 'real value'), $\hat{\mathbf{p}} - \hat{w}\mathbf{u} = -\gamma(\mathbf{I} - \mathbf{A})^{-1}$, as a measure of the 'advantage' that each industry gets from internal and external productivity increase. In order to distinguish between these two components, let us first notice that $(I - A)^{-1}$ is equivalent to $I + (I - A)^{-1}A$. We have therefore

$$(\hat{p} - \hat{w}u) = -(\gamma + \gamma(I - A)^{-1}A) \tag{8.20}$$

In general, each industry has its own ratio of the direct and indirect components, γ_j and $\gamma(I - A)^{-1}Ae_j$, respectively.

Equation (8.20) is the dual counterpart of the growth-accounting result that 'the change in sectoral factor efficiency creates, in general, extra output [...], which serves to increase both final demand [...] and intermediate deliveries. The increase in intermediate deliveries, however, serves further to increase output in those sectors using the intermediate good, and this further increases output, and so on' (Hulten, 1978, p. 514).

Now let us turn to the increase in the real wage. Multiplying the vector of price changes in (8.18) by the numéraire vector s and setting $\hat{p}s = 0$, we obtain

$$\hat{w} = \gamma(I - A)^{-1}s \tag{8.21}$$

That $\hat{w}$ is greater than a weighted average of the industrial rates of progress follows from the fact that $(I - A)^{-1}s$ is a weighted average of the columns of $(I - A)^{-1}$ and that each column adds to more than 1. In the case of uniform shares of value added, the terms of the vector $(I - A)^{-1}s$ add to $1/(1 - \Lambda)$. The 'magnification effect' is easily calculated in this case. If, say, productivity increases uniformly by 2% and in all sectors the share of value added is 1/2, the FIE reaction of real wages will be to increase (in any numéraire) by 4%.

The input–output relations will disappear, of course, if we replace the 'true' industries with vertically integrated sectors. All that is needed is to define the rates of productivity increase at vertically integrated level as $g = \gamma(I - A)^{-1}$: in terms of g, the simple rules discussed in the previous section would still hold and notably the relative price change would reflect the g differentials and the real wage increase would be a weighted average of the terms of g. It should be stressed, however, that g is a theoretical construction which is useful only in connection with the actual γ.

In our price-accounting perspective, $\hat{w}$ in (8.21) is also the aggregate rate of productivity increase, Γ. Needless to say, Γ can also be calculated directly, on the sole basis of data on (long-run) wage and price change as $\Gamma = \hat{w}_m - \hat{p}_m s$, where $\hat{w}_m$, $\hat{p}_m$ are now changes in money wages and prices.

We have known, of course, ever since Domar (1961), that a magnification effect must be accounted for in the presence of input–output relations. According to Hulten, 'the adjustment is found nearly to double the importance of technical progress as a source of growth' (1978, p. 512); uniform value added shares of 50% exactly double the importance of (uniform) technical progress as a source of real wage increase.

We can at this point establish a connection between our weights $(I - A)^{-1}s$ and the weights used in TFP aggregation on the basis of Domar (1961, pp. 720–21) and Hulten (1978, p. 514). It will be recalled that these latter weights are the ratios of gross industrial output to the economy's value added, that is $q/(py)$, where q is the vector of gross output and y is the vector of net output. If $s = y$, we have $py = 1$ and $(I - A)^{-1}s = q$ and the two weighting systems correspond. There is no special reason, however, to choose a numéraire equal to the net output vector and at least the numéraire is constant, unlike the composite net output. It should be remarked finally that, apart from the case of uniform value-added shares, the overall magnification effect in our price accounting is numéraire-dependent (just as the Domar–Hulten magnification effect depends on the output composition). This makes an aggregate measure of somewhat limited interest, unlike the industry-level measures.

8.4 Intermediate inputs, price accounting and TFP

We have seen in Section 8.1 that, in the absence of produced inputs, the rate of productivity increase calculated by price accounting is theoretically equal to that calculated by the familiar growth accounting. Equality holds also when we allow for produced inputs, provided that TFP is calculated on the basis of gross output and all physical inputs, whether primary or produced.

The extension of the result in Section 8.1 is straightforward. Let the (indirect) average cost function and the production function in industry j be, respectively, $c_j(w_1, w_2, p, T)$ and $Y_j(L_1, L_2, X, T)$, where p is the vector of commodity input prices and X is the vector of commodity input use. (Note that Y_j is now *gross* output.)

Setting $p_j = c_j$, total differentiation gives

$$dp_j Y_j = L_1 dw_1 + L_2 dw_2 + \sum_i X_i dp_i + \frac{\partial c_j}{\partial T} Y_j \qquad (8.22)$$

$$dY_j p_j = w_1 dL_1 + w_2 dL_2 + \sum_i p_i dX_i + \frac{\partial Y_j}{\partial T} p_j \qquad (8.23)$$

Now $w_1 L_1 + w_2 L_2 + \sum_i p_i X_i = p_j Y_j$. Hence

$$(L_1 dw_1 + w_1 dL_1) + (L_2 dw_2 + w_2 dL_2) + \left(\sum_i X_i dp_i + \sum_i p_i dX_i \right)$$

$$= (dY_j p_j + dp_j Y_j)$$

and

$$-\frac{\partial c_j}{\partial T} \frac{1}{p_j} = \frac{\partial Y_j}{\partial T} \frac{1}{Y_j}$$

A recognized drawback of the 'gross output' definition of TFP in (8.23) is that a large part of output growth is 'explained' by growth in commodity inputs (accounting as they do for over half of the output value and being in about constant proportions with gross output), which is hardly satisfying. For this reason it has become customary to define output as 'value-added' even at the level of the individual industry. Let $Y_j^{VA} = p_j Y_j - \sum p_i X_i$. The value-added growth can therefore be decomposed as

$$\frac{dY_j^{VA}}{Y_j^{VA}} = \frac{w_1}{Y_j^{VA}} dL_1 + \frac{w_2}{Y_j^{VA}} dL_2 + \left(\frac{\partial Y_j}{\partial T} \frac{1}{Y_j} \right) \frac{p_j Y_j}{Y_j^{VA}}$$

$$+ \left(Y_j dp_j - \sum_i X_i dp_i \right) \frac{1}{Y_j^{VA}} \qquad (8.24)$$

which of course includes the value-added TFP growth, defined as

$$\frac{\partial Y_j^{VA}}{\partial T} \frac{1}{Y_j^{VA}} = \left(\frac{\partial Y_j}{\partial T} \frac{1}{Y_j} \right) \frac{p_j Y_j}{Y_j^{VA}}$$

Not surprisingly, the value-added TFP growth is $p_j Y_j / Y_j^{VA}$ times higher than the gross-output TFP growth. Moreover, assuming constant relative prices, it corresponds to the difference between value-added growth and the growth component assigned to 'factor' growth. However, relative prices do in fact change, and they largely do so in response to the specific pattern of industrial productivity increase. We see at once from (8.24) that an 'average' decrease (increase) in the relative price of the commodity inputs would underestimate (overestimate) the 'true' rate of value-added TFP increase. By contrast, we have seen that our price-accounting approach naturally distinguishes between productivity increase proper and relative price effects. Thus, the price-accounting approach is not merely an alternative to the TFP approach at the industry level, but has some positive advantages over it.

8.5 Assessing productivity increase by price accounting: some historical notes

Solow's famous 1957 article laid the theoretical foundations for a host of later empirical studies on the contribution of productivity increase to aggregate growth. It mentioned a few previous contributions which measured technical progress by the increase of output per unit of input, but Solow's approach was more general and more sophisticated theoretically. Likewise, there had been some very early attempts at estimating the pace of technical progress by looking at price developments and they initially did so not at the aggregate level but at the industry level. It behoves us, therefore, to mention some leading early contributions; the interested reader is referred to Opocher (2010) for further details.

G.R. Porter was perhaps the first author to establish, in his *The Progress of the Nation* (1836), an empirical relationship between productivity increase and price changes. His work was facilitated by relatively stable 'gold' conditions in the bulk of the period that he considered (the first half of the nineteenth century); moreover, the temporary oscillations of general prices did not affect the long-run trends of individual prices. It is important to note that he was not concerned with the change in the output price in a certain industry per se, but in comparison with commodity input prices and wages for that industry. In modern language, he used relative prices and was most interested in the differential rates of progress. His concern for minute, detailed evidence of the improvements in the various branches of each industry and his keen interest in living standards (of the working classes in particular) almost inevitably made such relative changes transparent.

We can find many tables in which the average prices of a product (say, twist), a commodity input (raw cotton) and labour (wages of spinners) are brought together (e.g. Porter, 1851, pp. 183, 184, 227). His comment on the spectacular fall in the average price of twist in the 30 years from 1820 to 1849 is worth quoting at some length, because it shows that Porter was quite close to conceiving of the measure of productivity growth as the outcome of a price accounting exercise:

the average price [of white or plain cottons] per yard, which in 1820 was 12 ¾ d., [fell] in 1849 to 3 ⅔ d. [...] The average price of twist in 1820 was 2s 5 ½ d., and in 1849 was little more than 10 ¾ d. per pound. If, in addition to these values, we take account of the reduction that has occurred in the price of raw cotton, we may be enabled to form some judgment as to the economy which has been introduced into the process of manufacture during the last 30 years, and be besides able to apportion the degrees of that economy which appertain to the spinning and to the weaving branches of the manufacture respectively. [...] The diminution of value in the twist appears to amount to 63 per cent., and in the cloth to 73 ½ per cent.

(Porter 1851, pp. 179–81)

Interpreting 'judgment' in the sense of 'measure', we have here a clear statement of the idea that the industry-specific rate of productivity growth can be measured using the algebraic differences between the changes in the output price and the input prices. During the same period, the (money) wages of spinners and weavers remained roughly constant (Porter, 1851, pp. 184, 194). At the same time, the hours of work per week were shortened. In the case of spinners, they fell from 74 in 1804 to 69 in 1833 (Porter, 1851, p. 194), and this reinforces the evidence of technological improvements.

Porter's data are reported in Table 8.1, where prices have been indexed to 1820.

Porter did not develop his measure of productivity increase any further, nor did he provide a formal and general definition of it. Moreover, the absence of reliable data on the shares of wages and raw materials made further statistical elaborations impossible. It is tempting, however, to fill the gap with hypothetical data, just to figure out what the result might be. Assuming a wage share of 0.5 in both industries and no other inputs, Equation (8.16) would give rates of productivity increase, over 30 years, of 39% in the spinning industry and 41% in

Table 8.1 *Price developments of wages, raw cotton, twist and plain cottons, 1820–49.*

	Spinning industry			Weaving industry	
	1820	1849		1820	1849
Wages	About constant		Wages	About constant	
Price of raw cotton	1	0.5	Price of twist	1	0.36
Price of twist	1	0.36	Price of plain cottons	1	0.27

the weaving industry (on average, about 1.1% and 1.15% per year, respectively).

By the absence of a systematic direction of change in money wages, the simple long-run fall in money price in the period from the 1810s to about the middle of the century came to be considered as a fair approximation of the 'real' rate of cost reduction in a certain industry; a collateral fall in the price of raw materials used in that industry signalled, according to Porter, an overestimation, but a precise correction was beyond his possibilities.

Some 30 years after Porter, Robert Giffen inferred from the decline of an index of consumer prices relative to wages in the half century before the 1880s a rough measure of *aggregate* technical progress. In his own words, 'the *difference* between it [the fall in prices] and the fall in wages and incomes might represent the advance in the return to the industry of the community' (Giffen, 1888, p. 716; original emphasis). His estimation was that the improvement was 'at least between 50 and 100 per cent, and with an allowance for the shortening of the hours of labour, may be placed nearer the 100 than the 50, if not over the 100' (Giffen, 1888, p. 33). He regretted the 'want of records of wages', there being 'only records of isolated rates of wages, not weighted in any way' (Giffen, 1888, p. 728). His strategy, at least for the 20 years from 1867 to 1887, was to consider a proxy of the overall income per capita and he identified it in the records of the income tax, which were 'tolerably complete' (Giffen, 1888, p. 728). Of course, they admittedly represented mainly 'the earnings or profit on capital' (Giffen, 1888, p. 728), but he maintained that 'what we do know of wages points in the same direction' (Giffen, 1888, p. 729). Thus, for instance, he estimated that the index number of commodity prices of imports and exports in the 10 years from 1878 to 1887 fell by 16.5% (Giffen, 1888, p. 722; the table refers to the estimate made by 'Economist', which was Giffen's own pseudonym). At the same time, 'income-tax incomes' per capita rose by 13.3% (Giffen, 1888, p. 728). Under the assumption that wages also rose by about the same proportion (which would be realistic on the basis of the table; see Giffen, 1888, p. 731), the 10-year rate of productivity growth was about 30%, which amounted to a yearly average rate of 2.66%.

8.6 Concluding remarks

The 'price side' of productivity increase has received far less attention than the 'quantity side', both in theoretical models and in applications. Yet it is no less important. The different contributions of the individual industries to 'average' real wage increase, the change in relative prices and relative remunerations mirror the contributions of the different industries to aggregate growth, structural change and changes in input ratios. Even though the former side had been the first to be associated with productivity increase, in the first half of the nineteenth century, the quantity side has dominated since the late 1950s and has been developed much more both theoretically and empirically. A thorough knowledge of technical progress as a source of long-run relative price and relative wage variations (which are central in recent analyses), however, calls for a better understanding of the 'price side'.

In this chapter we have defined productivity increase in an individual industry as the hypothetical rate of reduction of the minimum average cost when all input prices are constant. With equality between output price and minimum average cost, our definition involves an outward shift of the industrial real (output-deflated) wages frontier. In a simple model with no commodity inputs, the rate of productivity increase corresponds therefore to a radial measure of such a shift and the change in each real wage can be decomposed into two parts, productivity increase and 'redistribution' (that is, a change in relative wages). In more realistic models with commodity inputs, the shift in the real wages frontier is determined also by a change in the output-deflated commodity-input prices and we can distinguish between this effect and productivity increase proper. When the commodity inputs are drawn from other domestic industries, themselves subject to progress, the change in the overall structure of relative prices can be determined in relation to the pattern of productivity increase: we have shown, in particular, that a relative price change reflects a pairwise differential in productivity increase only in a special case (even assuming constant relative wages). We have finally developed a theoretical measure of the aggregate rate of productivity increase, as an average increase in the real wage rates, expressed in terms of a composite numéraire, in which we can distinguish the contribution of each individual industry.

9 | *Full industry equilibrium in retrospect*

In earlier chapters we have referred to selected contributions to a theory of long-run industry equilibrium. Now it is time to reconstruct some lines of a historical evolution which may further illustrate the meaning and theoretical foundations of the analysis proposed in this book.

This chapter traces two fundamental lines of such an evolution. The first concerns the making of the theory of multi-input demand in the 50 years or so after 1938 and is presented in Sections 9.1–9.3. We argue that the various waves of studies originated by the seminal works of Hicks, Allen, Mosak and Samuelson conceptualized input demand with an increasing degree of inclusiveness, in which a two-dimensional relationship between input use and own- (or cross-) input price admitted of 'background' collateral changes in other variables. In the most recent formalizations, the analysis also includes equilibrium in other industries. A strict partial equilibrium input demand curve was considered only as a first step, preliminary to more interesting constructions. Even though the former became an agreed standard in textbooks and in some applications, it should be borne clearly in mind that it fails to capture the richness of the original contributions and the variety of developments which sprung from them.

The second line of evolution, presented in Sections 9.4–9.7, focuses on the interrelatedness among industries which characterized the older 'Marshallian' literature. We refer here mainly to the theoretical foundations of a long-run 'rising supply price' when factors in fixed supply are common to different industries. In this field too, a strict partial equilibrium approach was inadequate. We discuss in some detail Barone's and Sraffa's attacks on the Marshallian tradition and the Harrod–Robinson–Viner defence thereof. We also briefly examine Sraffa's shift, at the end of the 1920s, from interrelatedness due to the presence of common factors to interrelatedness due to the presence of produced inputs. Section 9.8 concludes.

9.1 The theory of multi-input demand in the formative period

Until the late 1930s the theory of input demand was rather fragmented and uncoordinated. On the one hand, an agreed standard was the case with only one variable input, subject to diminishing returns. This case was susceptible to a simple diagrammatic representation and the equality between the input price and the value-marginal-product provided all the necessary information for a (downward-sloping) input demand curve at the level of the individual firm (e.g Robinson, 1933, Chapter 20). On the other hand, Wicksteed and Wicksell had already shown by the turn of the century that in the long-run, when returns to scale are (at least locally) constant, the above equality holds for all inputs simultaneously; but no fully fledged analysis of 'multi-input demand' had been provided on that basis. The Marshall–Pigou laws of derived demand lacked a true mathematical substance and were based on verbal arguments (see Marshall, 1920, note XIV of the mathematical appendix), although it is true that the Appendix to Hicks' *Theory of Wages* (Hicks, 1932) offered a more sophisticated analysis, based on Euler's theorem.

Then, in a very concentrated time span (centred around the year 1938), three major works by Allen, Mosak and Hicks laid the foundations of the modern theory of input demand; a fourth work, Samuelson's *Foundations*, was under elaboration, took book form in 1941 and was published soon after the war. No doubt, this sudden flourishing had been greatly facilitated by the success of the new mathematical theory of consumer's choice put forward a few years earlier by Hicks–Allen themselves in London and, at about the same time, by Schultz in Chicago and Hotelling in New York.

9.1.1 R.G.D. Allen and the theory of derived demand

Allen's *Mathematical Analysis for Economists* (1938, pp. 372–74) was an early work that applied the method of total differentiation of the first-order conditions for a maximum profit as the key to a theory of multi-input demand. This contribution is still grounded on the Hicksian theory of derived demand and, in particular, is restricted to the case of a firm characterized by constant returns to scale, which is a price taker in input markets but not in the market for its output. (We recall that the 'imperfect competition revolution' was still making a strong impression at that time.) However, it developed a new technique of analysis (borrowed from the new consumption theory).

Given a demand function $\varphi(p)$ and a production function, $f(X_1, X_2)$, homogeneous of degree one and with continuous first- and second-order partial derivatives, a 'full competitive equilibrium' (Allen, 1938, p. 372), satisfies the following conditions (in obvious notation)

$$f(X_1, X_2) = \varphi(p), \ w_1 = p\,f_1, \ w_2 = p\,f_2,$$
$$\text{with} \quad f(X_1, X_2) = \frac{\partial f}{\partial X_1}X_1 + \frac{\partial f}{\partial X_2}X_2$$

The three latter equations are of course in the tradition of Wicksteed and Wicksell and imply that output price is always equal to both average and marginal cost. In this set of equilibrium conditions, w_1, w_2 are parameters, while X_1, X_2, p are the variables to be determined. Total differentiation determines a linear system in which the variations with respect to the input prices can be calculated at a certain point of equilibrium; economic theory provides restrictions/assumptions concerning the properties of the matrix involved. Specifically, differentiating the first three equations with respect to w_1 while holding w_2 constant, one gets

$$\begin{pmatrix} -\varphi' & f_1 & f_2 \\ f_1 & p\,f_{11} & p\,f_{12} \\ f_2 & p\,f_{21} & p\,f_{22} \end{pmatrix} \begin{pmatrix} \partial p/\partial w_1 \\ \partial X_1/\partial w_1 \\ \partial X_2/\partial w_1 \end{pmatrix} = \begin{pmatrix} 0 \\ 1 \\ 0 \end{pmatrix}$$

Each term of the (symmetrical) matrix on the lhs can be signed on the basis of meaningful economic assumptions: specifically, $\varphi' < 0, f_i > 0$, $f_{ii} < 0, f_{ij} > 0$. Solving the system, it is shown that $\partial p/\partial w_1 > 0$; that $\partial X_1/\partial w_1 < 0$; and that $\partial X_2/\partial w_1$ may be of either sign. Moreover, by the inverse relation between output demand and price, it is implicit that output, $f(X_1, X_2)$, falls as w_1 rises.

A few remarks are in order. The first is that Allen's argument does not automatically generalize to more than two inputs, because a third input would make room for possible technical complementarities in the Edgeworth–Pareto–Mosak definition ($f_{ij} < 0$ for a pair of inputs; see Mosak, 1938, p. 762) and this can modify some results. Second, Allen's study of the reaction of input use to a change in one input price takes into account the effect of collateral changes in the output level and in the output price: even though he expressed all of his results using 'curly derivatives', more than one variable was changing at a time and his analysis should not be confused with that of a partial equilibrium input demand curve. An increase, say, in w_1 leads to an increase in the long-run output price, which in turn reduces the equilibrium output: this latter change is responsible for the possibility that $\partial X_2/\partial w_1$ might be negative even though the two inputs are by definition substitutes. Finally, Allen introduced a neat and fundamental distinction between input demand constrained by a constant output and input demand associated with a variable output (see Allen, 1938, pp. 369–71). When positions of 'full competitive equilibrium' are compared, the second concept, not the first, is the relevant one.

9.1.2 *J.L. Mosak and the theory of the competitive firm*

It is well known that Allen collaborated with Hicks at the London School of Economics from the early 1930s and they certainly also influenced each other on the problem of the formation of input demand. We also know that before the publication of Allen's book, Hicks had already sketched the mathematical structure of his theory of the firm which was to appear in *Value and Capital*: his short book in French (Hicks, 1937) presents, in fact, much of the material reproduced in the mathematical notes of the 1939 book.

Before turning to Hicks' contribution, however, it is useful to consider now the contribution of Mosak, which was published soon after Allen's book and shortly before the appearance of *Value and Capital* and cites both Allen's book and Hicks' pamphlet. Interestingly, Mosak acknowledges the comments received from Allen in discussions at the University of Chicago and from another notable commentator: the young Paul Samuelson (see Mosak, 1938, p. 787), who graduated from the University of Chicago in 1935 and was granted a Social Science Research Council Fellowship at Harvard's Department of Economics. It was in that period that Samuelson conceived and drafted the book that 10 years later became his *Foundations of Economic Analysis* (cf. Samuelson, 1947, p. vii).

Mosak's analysis employs Allen's method of total differentiation, but places the problem of input demand in a different context. The firm is now assumed to be a price taker in both factor and product markets; this made it necessary, as we shall see, both to exclude constant returns to scale in favour of diminishing returns and to abandon the old path initiated by Wicksteed and Wicksell and initially followed by Hicks and Allen. All of Mosak's analysis converges towards the conceptualization of a mapping from 'price space' (input and output prices) to 'choice space' (input use and output level), which would become the standard methodological framework of the theory of input demand. He presented his argument following two routes, each in two stages, leading to the same results: one route starts from output maximization subject to a given expenditure and then determines the specific profit-maximizing expenditure; the other route, presented in the Appendix, starts from cost minimization subject to a given output and then determines the specific profit-maximizing output. The second route was adopted on the suggestion of Allen and Samuelson and, according to Mosak, 'was more in line with the classical treatment of production' and 'in some respects it is also a somewhat simpler treatment' (Mosak, 1938, p. 787). Mosak's preference for the first route reflected his opinion that 'it shows more clearly the relationship of the theory of production to the mathematical theory of consumer's demand' (Mosak, 1938, p. 787).

Mosak's analysis is very sophisticated from a mathematical point of view, made consistent use of the minimum value function concerning cost and distinctly anticipated Shephard's lemma (Mosak, 1938, p. 785; an early hint at the existence of indirect utility functions and profit functions whose partial derivatives with respect to prices determine an optimum quantity is to be found in Hotelling, 1932, p. 594, who remarks that 'the existence of such a function (. . .) heretofore does not seem to have been noticed'). It is not necessary here, however, to go through his series of linear systems of equations, aimed at making as transparent as possible the connections between the two stages of his argument and across the two different routes he followed. It will suffice to note that he distinguished between direct, indirect and total effects of a change in an input price: in the formulation based on cost minimization, the direct effect is calculated keeping output constant; the indirect effect isolates the change in input use brought about solely by the adjustment in output required to restore the equality between marginal cost and the given output price; the total effect is the sum of the two. Clearly, the 'indirect' effect cannot be calculated in the case of constant returns to scale and because only the total effect is relevant, that case is excluded (see Mosak, 1938, pp. 772–73, n. 8) and an increasing marginal cost is postulated (see Mosak, 1938, p. 765, n. 4). Like Allen, Mosak always adopted a 'curly derivative' notation for solutions (which might be questionable, of course), but found it compelling to indicate in a subscript the variables which are kept constant in each calculation (as we do below). His main results are the following:

(a) $(\partial X_j / \partial w_j)_{p, w_{i \neq j}} < 0$, that is, 'the slope of the demand curve for a productive service with respect to its own price is always negative' (Mosak, 1938, p. 777). It must be stressed that, although this result might look similar to Allen's result above, they are in fact different because the latter allowed for a compensating change in the output price;

(b) $(\partial X_i / \partial w_j)_{p, w_{i \neq j}} = (\partial X_j / \partial w_i)_{p, w_{j \neq i}}$, that is, the cross-price effects are symmetrical. Once again, Mosak's cross-price effects are not the same as Allen's, because they are based on different *ceteris paribus* stipulations. It is also worth remarking that Mosak did not attempt an analysis of their sign;

(c) denoting by q the output level, $(\partial q / \partial w_i)_{p, w_{j \neq i}} = -(\partial X_i / \partial p)_w$, that is, the effect of a change in input price on the output level is symmetric (with opposite sign) to the effect of a change in the output price on input use. Once again, Mosak did not extend his analysis to the respective signs: the subsequent literature would show that this requires a distinction between 'normal' and 'inferior' inputs.

9.1.3 J.R. Hicks: the contribution of Value and Capital

Hicks and Mosak adopted similar methodologies, placed the problem in a similar framework and came to similar conclusions; moreover, both of them insisted strongly on a parallelism with the theory of consumption. Having said that, Hicks' analysis is richer in economic insights than is Mosak's (and also than Allen's) and for good reason it became the main reference for further developments.

Even the basic mathematical structure in the Appendix to chapters VI and VII of *Value and Capital* has a personal touch of elegance. With any number of factors and goods (say, m factors and $n - m$ goods), the 'production function' (which in modern terminology would be called a 'transformation function') is expressed in implicit form as

$$f(X_1, \ldots, X_m, X_{m+1}, \ldots X_n) = 0$$

(where factors are treated as negative products).

Denoting by μ a Lagrange multiplier and by p_r the price of a factor $(r = 1, \ldots, m)$ or of a product $(r = m + 1, \ldots, n)$, the first-order conditions for a maximum profit are (for $= r = 1, \ldots, n)$

$$\mu f_r = p_r$$

Differentiating this system of equations with respect to p_r (no matter whether the price of a factor or of a product), we generate a linear system of the form $\mathbf{F}\mathbf{x} = \mathbf{e}_r$, where $\mathbf{e}_r$ is the rth unit vector, $\mathbf{x} = (\partial \mu / \partial p_r, \partial X_1 / \partial p_r, \ldots, \partial X_n / \partial p_r)$ and $\mathbf{F}$ is a square matrix whose determinant F and cofactors F_{rs} are the same as those of the bordered 'production function' Hessian. (Needless to say, in the case of single production, where $n = m + 1$, we have $f_n = 1$ and $\mu = p_n$.) At this point, the sensitivity of each choice of input use and output level to an isolated change in price can be generally expressed as $\partial X_s / \partial p_r = -F_{rs}/(\mu F)$ $(s = 1, \ldots, m)$ and $\partial X_s / \partial p_r = F_{rs}/(\mu F)$ $(s = m + 1, \ldots, n)$. Because $F_{rr} > 0$ and $F_{rs} = F_{sr}$, it is easy to see that these equations both yield Mosak's results with a variable output (the 'curly derivatives' having the same meaning as in Mosak) and extend them to the case of multiple outputs.

Like Mosak, Hicks explicitly remarks that this analysis cannot be referred to the case of constant returns to scale. For in this case the determinant F is null and 'it is not possible for the price of one factor (or product) to change, there being no change in the prices of all other factors and products, without upsetting equilibrium altogether. If the price of a product rises, output will become infinite; if the price of a factor rises, it will become zero. In the limiting case we are considering, our analysis threatens to break down altogether' (Hicks, 1939, p. 322). It is to be noted that in the often-quoted second edition, Hicks made no changes to the chapters concerning the theory of the firm, nor to the corresponding mathematical notes; even the page numbering happens to be precisely the same in the two editions).

Hicks' most important contribution, however, is an insightful verbal analysis of the economic relations which give rise to such results. Three related aspects, in particular, have been much discussed and developed in the subsequent literature which is referred to below as the 'second wave': the roles of complementary and of regressive inputs and the qualitative results obtained with nearly constant returns to scale. Before turning to this, however, we must briefly discuss the contribution that Samuelson was simultaneously elaborating.

9.1.4 The standardization of the theory of production: P.A. Samuelson

Samuelson's 'Comprehensive Restatement of the Theory of Cost and Production' (Samuelson, 1947, chapter IV) contains an elegant and insightful analysis of what he called the 'differential quotients' (Samuelson, 1947, p. 60). Like Allen, Mosak and Hicks, Samuelson traced a neat distinction between input demand which is conditional on a given output and input demand which is not. He laid particular stress on the first conception, because his principal aim was to establish all possible properties which could be referred to profit-maximizing firms, irrespective of the specific characteristics of the product market. Cost minimization is therefore at the centre of the chapter and the reception of Samuelson's contribution by second-wave developments (and beyond) was typically limited to a parametric output. Ferguson (1966), for instance, remarked that 'Samuelson studied the same problem [as Allen and Mosak] without the assumption of perfect competition in commodity and factor markets. However, he imposed a different restrictive condition, namely that the firm under consideration be confined to movements along a given production isoquant in response to changes in relative factor prices' (Ferguson, 1966, p. 454).

Nonetheless, Samuelson's chapter cannot be simply set aside here as a highly influential and elegant treatment of 'conditional' input demand. His 'Restatement', apart from contributing greatly to the shaping of the conventional view of partial equilibrium input demand, also goes well beyond that and it fully deserves a place in our narrative.

First, it laid the foundation for some important second-wave developments. In particular, Samuelson's analysis of the change in marginal cost due to a change in an input price implicitly contains the counter-intuitive result that the profit maximizing output might increase as an input price increases (see Bear, 1965, discussed below). In fact, Samuelson (1947, p. 66) proved that $(\partial^2 C/\partial q \partial w_i) = (\partial X_i/\partial q)_w$: this result was not in Allen–Mosak–Hicks. We shall see that, in Bear's definition, input i is inferior when $(\partial X_i/\partial q)_w < 0$: it follows at once that in the case of an inferior input – so defined – the marginal cost curve shifts downwards as w_i rises and the optimum partial equilibrium output must rise. Samuelson's priority is openly acknowledged (see Bear, 1965, p. 287).

Second, there are, in Samuelson's chapter, a few dense pages in which output is an object of choice. On the basis of any given product-market conditions, 'a new set of demand curves for factors of production' (Samuelson, 1947, p. 77) is presented: they are a generalization to the case of any product market conditions of the 'differential quotients' (as defined by Samuelson) in which his predecessors were interested. Their qualitative properties are not discussed in detail but, in the economy of that chapter, they are essential for putting previous results into the correct perspective.

Samuelson's chapter also provided fresh results and insights in new directions by considering corner solutions, discontinuity in partial derivatives and finite movements of any size. The so-called 'generalized substitution theorem', according to which the inequality $\Sigma \Delta w_i \Delta X_i \leq 0$ is implied by cost minimization alone, irrespective of the size of the movement, of whether a production function Hessian exists and of whether an input use may change from zero to positive (and conversely), is a remarkable achievement due to Samuelson (see Samuelson, 1947, pp. 70–74 and 80–81). He claimed that 'the method of finite increments appears to be mathematically simpler in the sense that it is possible to state the qualitative direction of changes without solving inversely for the actual demand functions' and was analogous to 'that which underlies Le Chatelier's principle in physics' (Samuelson, 1947, p. 81; the applicability of this method to economic theory was also stressed by Samuelson in his Nobel Memorial Lecture of 11 December 1970 and had been reportedly suggested to Samuelson by Professor E.B. Wilson, a mathematical physicist at Harvard University and Samuelson's revered teacher of mathematical economics and statistics: see Samuelson, 1972, p. 253; see also Weintraub, 1991, pp. 57–66). As we showed in Chapter 1, such a theorem is of much narrower applicability than is often believed, but it is still remarkable for its simplicity and generality. Also, Samuelson's interest in corner solutions and discontinuity is worth stressing here, because what we call 'on/off' inputs are an important case in which such matters are central; and Samuelson's famous 'Surrogate Production Function' (Samuelson, 1962) is of course a theoretical construction based on the presence of qualitatively different inputs which can replace one another altogether as the interest rate changes.

A final relevant aspect of Samuelson's contribution to the theory of input demand concerns his treatment of free entry. He rejected any a priori view of zero net revenue as a consequence of an arbitrary assumption of constant returns to scale: 'it is not on philosophical grounds that economists have wished to assume homogeneity, but rather because they were afraid that, if they did not do so, contradictions would emerge to vitiate the marginal productivity theory. This is simply a misconception' (Samuelson, 1947, p. 85). Null profits should be considered as a potential result of competition among firms. 'Free entry' is Samuelson's 'analytic definition for the case in which "competitive" conditions between firms are such that the demand curve of any firm will always shift until net revenue is equal to zero' (Samuelson, 1947, p. 87). In the case of 'pure competition' (horizontal demand), equilibrium can thus only occur at a point in which price equals both marginal and average costs. There is a precise hint here at further developments in the theory of input demand which would be developed by a third wave of studies (see Section 9.3).

9.2 Input complementarity, 'nearly constant' returns to scale and regression

As we said above, second-wave developments were concerned with questions raised, but not completely resolved, by Hicks (or Samuelson). In what follows, we restrict Hicks' analysis to the case of a single-product firm, as does most of the literature, and maintain our previous convention of denoting by w the m-vector of input prices, by p the output price and by q the output level of the firm.

9.2.1 Complementarity and 'nearly constant' returns to scale

It is well known that – differently from Edgeworth/Pareto/Mosak – Hicks defined substitution/complementarity with reference to the sign of the off-diagonal terms of what we now call the cost function Hessian (cf. Chapter 2, Appendix 1). Thus two inputs are complements when an increase in the price of one of them leads to a reduction in the use of the other keeping output constant (see Hicks, 1939, pp. 91–92). (Needless to say, input complementarity under this definition requires the presence of more than two inputs.) We can also find, however, in Chapter VII of *Value and Capital*, an extended definition of complementarity, which allows for the change in equilibrium output which normally follows a change in input price – a definition which Hicks seemed to prefer (see Hicks, 1939, pp. 95–96, n. 2). In this latter definition, there can be complementarity with only two inputs, as Hicks remarked. Adopting Mosak's usage of indicating in a subscript what is kept constant, inputs i and j are substitutes or complements in the narrower definition according to whether $(dX_i/dw_j)_{q,p,w_{i\neq j}}$ is positive or negative; in the broader definition, they are substitutes or complements according to whether $(dX_i/dw_j)_{p,w_{i\neq j}}$ is positive or negative.

This difference in definition came to be decisive for a 1950s debate between Hicks and Morishima on the 'dominance' of complementarity in the case of constant returns to scale. Even though, as Hicks remarked, the case of constant returns to scale is not amenable to an analysis which assumes the output price to be constant, this does not mean that nothing can be said about it, nor that it is uninteresting. Even in the model specifically designed for diminishing returns, constant returns to scale can still be studied as a limiting case (see Hicks, 1939, pp. 95–96, n. 2).

The most important implication of 'nearly constant' returns to scale consists in the 'dominance of complementarity', in the sense that $(dX_i/dw_j)_{p,w_{i\neq j}} < 0$ tends to prevail for all pairs of inputs, in the long run, as production tends to exhibit constant returns; and this is so even though for all such pairs it might well be that $(dX_i/dw_j)_{q,p,w_{i\neq j}} > 0$. This looked surprising, and in a later debate with Morishima (1953–54a and 1953–54b), Hicks admitted that in *Value and Capital* such a claim 'was decidedly obscure, and rather invited misunderstanding' (Hicks, 1953–54, p. 218). Nonetheless, his argument has been clarified, and confirmed, thanks to this debate. A further contribution is Rader (1968), who provided a clear definition of gross substitution or complementarity in relation to the sign of 'the response to changes in factor prices in the demand for factors by a competitive firm *before* any change in the price of the product or any other factor but *after* the firm has adjusted output to preserve equality between prices of the factors and the values of the marginal products' (Rader, 1968, p. 39; emphases added). He also noted that 'gross complementarity' contradicts the crucial assumption made by Arrow and Hurwicz (1958) in order to obtain their stability results.

The key to a correct understanding of the long-run dominance of gross complementarity consists in the fact that Hicks was not considering a production function homogeneous of degree one, but a production function nearly homogeneous of degree one (see Hicks, 1953–54,

p. 218) and a marginal cost which was increasing in output but nearly constant. Morishima (1953–54b) provided a mathematical proof. For the reader's convenience, however, it may be useful to restate the result in terms of our familiar cost function, $C(q, \mathbf{w})$.

Equilibrium requires of course $p = \partial C/\partial q$ (curly derivatives are used here in the proper sense of partial derivatives). Let w_i be the only price to change. Then $0 = (\partial^2 C/\partial q^2)dq + (\partial X_i/\partial q)dw_i$. The change in the use of an input different from i is of course $dX_j = (\partial X_j/\partial q)dq + (\partial X_j/\partial w_i)dw_i$. These two differential equations yield

$$\frac{dX_j}{dw_i} = \frac{\partial X_j}{\partial w_i} - \left(\frac{\partial X_i}{\partial q}\frac{\partial X_j}{\partial q}\right)\frac{1}{(\partial^2 C/\partial q^2)}$$

Assume that all inputs are non-inferior. If $(\partial^2 C/\partial q^2)$ is small then we can easily have

$$(dX_j/dw_i) < 0 < (\partial X_j/\partial w_i)$$

Then complementarity is certainly dominant among inputs, for sufficiently small $(\partial^2 C/\partial q^2)$, despite what is now usually called 'Hicksian substitution'.

9.2.2 Regression

Hicks defined 'regression' as 'a queer sort of inverted complementarity between factor and product' (e.g. Hicks, 1939, p. 93) in which a reduction, say, in one input price leads to a reduction in the equilibrium output, even though the use of that input necessarily increases; that is, input i is regressive when $(dq/dw_i)_{p,w_{j\neq i}} > 0$. This case is somewhat counterintuitive, as we said before, because it involves a downward shift in the marginal cost curve when an input price rises. For this reason, it attracted some interest and further studies provided more details. A fundamental step forward consisted in the definition of inferior and non-inferior inputs. Regression occurs if and only if an input is 'inferior'. Bear (1965) argued that $(dq/dw_i)_{p,w_{j\neq i}} = -(dX_i/dp)_w$ (as Mosak had already proved) and that negative definiteness of the production function Hessian implies, in turn, that $(dX_i/dp)_w$ has the same sign as $(dX_i/dq)_{p,w}$. Hence, an input is defined as inferior when $(dX_i/dq)_{p,w} < 0$ (cf. Bear, 1965, p. 288, n. 3). The way was now paved for an analysis of the conditions for inferiority. Bear proved that a sufficient condition for non-inferiority was homogeneity of the production function (hence, inferiority is excluded with constant returns to scale); a necessary condition for inferiority is that some off-diagonal terms of the production function Hessian be negative (which in turn implies complementarity); moreover, Bear argued that an input cannot be inferior at all output levels: this confirmed Hicks' intuition that regression concerns the fact that some inputs are suited to small-scale production and other, qualitatively different inputs, are suited to large-scale production (see Hicks, 1939, p. 96).

A further, counter-intuitive implication of input inferiority consists in the fact that, if the firm is a monopolist in the product market, then an increase in the price of an inferior input leads to a reduction in the equilibrium output price. This possibility obviously rests on a positive relationship between an input price and the output level, and was established by Ferguson (1966, p. 460). However, he seemed not to recognize that his result was a straightforward application of Hicks' concept of 'regression', nor did he mention Bear's article.

9.3 'Input demand' under industry equilibrium

The wave of contributions in the mid-1960s soon aroused a renewed interest in input 'demand' when account is taken of the change in the output price induced by a change in an input price. Saving (1963) remarked that 'it is useful to distinguish factor demand elasticities derived under conditions of: 1) constant product prices (. . .); and 2) allowing for the combined actions of all firms to affect the product price' (p. 555). In a comment on a faulty graphical illustration (Russell, 1964) of the Hicks–Mosak–Samuelson own input 'demand curve' with a variable output, Winch (1965) very explicitly remarked that 'a general proof of the proposition concerning the downward slope of the demand curve for a factor should take account of a consequent change in product price, and should also include the long-run case as well as the short run' (p. 856). These contributions, however, did not go much beyond what Allen had already proved.

It was not until a path-breaking article by Ferguson and Saving (1969) that a proper theory of the firm in a long-run industry equilibrium was sketched out in important analytical aspects, with reference to a firm characterized by a U-shaped average cost curve. In accordance with the tradition of Wicksell and Hicks' *Theory of Wages*, the 'condition for long-run equilibrium' is now that 'price equals marginal cost equals minimum average cost' (Ferguson and Saving, 1969, p. 775). This completely reshaped the Hicks–Bear problem of the output response to a change in an input price: rather than looking at the output which restores equality of marginal cost with a constant price, one has to consider the output at the new point of minimum average cost. Accordingly, a third kind of relation between input use and input price was introduced: a relation in which the output price is always equal to minimum average cost.

It is decidedly unfortunate that three distinct relations have all been called 'demand function (or curve)' (see Samuelson, 1947, p. 74 for the constant output, constant price framework; Mosak, 1938, p. 777 for the variable output, constant price framework; and then Ferguson and Saving, 1969, p. 782). In order to underline the qualitative difference between these three concepts, in this book we have always referred the phrase 'input demand function (or curve)' only to the first and most genuinely 'partial equilibrium' framework.

Now using the third concept, the existence of an inverse relation between input use and own input price had to be reconsidered. Ferguson and Saving proceeded in two steps. The first was to determine the variation of the minimum-average-cost output of the firm in relation to a variation in one input price. The interesting result is that, differently from the Hicks–Bear case, it is not inferiority or non-inferiority which matters but rather what Ferguson and Saving called '*expenditure elasticity*': that is, 'the proportional change in the use of a given factor divided by the proportional change in expenditure on all factors' (Ferguson and Saving, 1969, p. 777). Specifically, it is shown that $(dq/dw_i)_{w_{j \neq i}}$ is positive, null or negative according to whether the expenditure elasticity of input i is lower than, equal to or greater than one. In each case, it is shown that $(dp/dw_i)_{w_{j \neq i}} > 0$. At this point, it is certain that for a 'superior' input (elasticity greater than one) we have $(dX_i/dw_i)_{w_{j \neq i}} < 0$, but the same cannot be said for other kinds of inputs: 'the substitution effect is, of course, necessarily negative; but in this case [of a non-superior input] the expenditure effect may be positive. Thus in the long run an increase in factor price may result in an increase in the usage of the factor in question. [. . .] Note, however, that this result does not apply to the industry demand function since industry output necessarily declines when a factor price rises. It should further be noted that this is not a derived demand function of the conventional form. But it is interesting to observe that in shifting from one long-run equilibrium to another, a firm's usage of a factor may vary directly with its price' (Ferguson and Saving, 1969, pp. 782–83).

Other contributions, not referring to the article by Ferguson and Saving, are Bassett and Borcherding (1970a and 1970b). Clear progress in this field can be found in Silberberg (1974). Here, the comparative static properties of a long-run equilibrium are studied by means of the very powerful concept of an 'indirect average cost function', which replaced the old techniques of analysis based on the bordered production function Hessian. The main logic of Silberberg's argument has been presented in Chapter 2 as a natural starting point for our FIE analysis of input use. It will therefore suffice to remark here that not only did Silberberg succeed in formulating the Ferguson–Saving results in a simpler way and in more detail, but he also reached quite naturally a further important result – that the Ferguson–Saving 'curiosum' cannot obtain if referred to input use per unit of output (Silberberg, 1974, p. 736, corollary 2).

The approach to 'input demand' introduced by Ferguson–Saving and by Silberberg prompted a series of further studies on the mutual relationship between the equilibrium of the firm and that of the industry, with a special emphasis on the short run and on inter-firm diversity. In the presence of a certain shock, in fact, the other firms' reactions, as well as entry/exit processes, can affect the equilibrium of each firm, via a change in market-clearing conditions in output and input markets. The degree of inter-firm diversity is relevant here and the industry-level input use/input price relationship can be qualitatively different from that at the firm-level.

A fundamental study in this regard is Heiner (1982), based on the premiss that 'the law of demand for industry factor behavior cannot be established by aggregation of isolated firm responses' because 'a firm adjusts within a larger industry of firms whose collective output can affect output price' (Heiner, 1982, p. 55). A major methodological point is involved here: the analysis of the price-taking firm, established by Mosak, Hicks and Samuelson, cannot be transferred to the industry by mere aggregation. In fact, this new approach 'contradicts the older methodology associated with Paul Samuelson (1947) in which factor-demand responses are derived for firms acting in isolation from each other' (Heiner, 1982, p. 55). (An early recognition that the analysis of price-taking behaviour in a firm must presume no change in the other firms is in Sraffa, 1925, p. 301. Sraffa remarked that, for this reason, a sum of individual curves is generally absurd.)

Heiner's argument can be summarized as follows. Let the industry be formed by n firms (indexed $s = 1, 2, \ldots n$), generally different from one another. Each firm is individually a price taker in output and input markets and is characterized by the cost function $C_s(q_s, \mathbf{w})$, produced inputs being ignored. By contrast, for the entire industry, demand is inversely related to price (while inputs are still assumed, for simplicity, to be in infinitely elastic supply even for the industry; this assumption will be removed by later literature). Denoting by Q the aggregate output and by $D(p)$ output demand as a function of price, market equilibrium requires

$$Q = D(p)$$

In turn, each firm is in equilibrium when

$$\frac{\partial C_s}{\partial q_s}(q_s, \mathbf{w}) = p, \qquad \frac{\partial^2 C_s}{\partial q_s^2} > 0$$

$$\frac{\partial C_s}{\partial w_i}(q_s, \mathbf{w}) = X_{i,s}, \quad i = 1, 2, \ldots m; \, s = 1, 2, \ldots, n$$

where $X_{i,s}$ denotes the equilibrium use of input i by firm s. Now let the price of input 1 change slightly. Because there will be a response in the output of each firm, the market-clearing price changes by

$$dp = -\frac{1}{\eta}\frac{p}{Q} dQ$$

where $\eta > 0$ denotes the absolute value of the price elasticity of demand. The full reaction of each individual firm satisfies

$$dp = \frac{\partial X_{1,s}}{\partial q_s} dw_1 + \frac{\partial^2 C_s}{\partial q_s^2} dq_s$$

$$dX_{1,s} = \frac{\partial^2 C_s}{\partial w_1^2} dw_1 + \frac{\partial X_{1,s}}{\partial q_s} dq_s$$

In order to simplify notation, let $1/(\partial^2 C_s/\partial q_s^2) \equiv \gamma_s$. After substitutions and setting $dQ = \sum_{s=1}^{n} dq_s$, we obtain

$$\frac{dX_{1,s}}{dw_1} = \frac{\partial^2 C_s}{\partial w_1^2} - \gamma_s \left(\frac{\partial X_{1,s}}{\partial q_s}\right)^2 + \gamma_s \frac{1}{\eta}\frac{p}{Q}\left(\frac{\partial X_{1,s}}{\partial q_s}\right) \frac{\left(\sum \gamma_s \frac{\partial X_{1,s}}{\partial q_s}\right)}{\left[1 + (\sum \gamma_s)\frac{1}{\eta}\frac{p}{Q}\right]}$$

The first term on the rhs is the partial equilibrium own-price effect conditional on a constant output; the second term is the specific effect brought about by the change in the equilibrium output (at constant output price); the third term is the additional effect attributable to the change in the market-clearing output price. This latter effect depends, quite obviously, on the reaction of all the other firms. Now the sum of the first two terms is always semi-negative, as in Hicks–Mosak–Samuelson. The third term, however, is positive and can outweigh the former two if output demand is sufficiently rigid. Hence the Ferguson–Saving 'curiosum' yielding $dX_{1,s}/dw_1 > 0$ can occur even in the short run; it is readily seen that this can be so even if input 1 is normal for all firms (cf. Heiner, 1982, p. 557). The possibility that $dX_{1,s}/dw_1 > 0$ can be better analysed (going somewhat beyond Heiner's own findings) by slightly rearranging the above equation (referred now to the first firm):

$$\frac{dX_{1,1}}{dw_1} = \frac{\partial^2 C_1}{\partial w_1^2} - \frac{\gamma_1\left(\frac{\partial X_{1,1}}{\partial q_1}\right)}{\left[1 - \left(\sum \gamma_s\right)\frac{1}{\eta}\frac{p}{Q}\right]}$$
$$\times \left\{\left(\frac{\partial X_{1,1}}{\partial q_1}\right) + \frac{1}{\eta}\frac{p}{Q}\left[\sum \gamma_s \left(\frac{\partial X_{1,1}}{\partial q_1} - \frac{\partial X_{1,s}}{\partial q_s}\right)\right]\right\}$$

If input 1 is normal for firm 1, so that $(\partial X_{1,1}/\partial q_1 > 0)$, then $\sum_{s=2}^n \gamma_s\left(\frac{\partial X_{1,1}}{\partial q_1} - \frac{\partial X_{1,s}}{\partial q_s}\right) < 0$ is a *necessary* condition for $dX_{1,1}/dw_1 > 0$; conversely, if input 1 is inferior for firm 1 $(\partial X_{1,1}/\partial q_1 < 0)$, that necessary condition becomes $\sum_{s=2}^n \gamma_s\left(\frac{\partial X_{1,1}}{\partial q_1} - \frac{\partial X_{1,s}}{\partial q_s}\right) > 0$. When either of these conditions is satisfied, a sufficiently rigid output demand makes the second term on the rhs positive. At this point, a sufficiently high γ_1 (that is, a sufficiently 'flat' marginal cost curve in firm 1) ensures $dX_{1,1}/dw_1 > 0$. In general, the sign of this second term dominates with 'nearly' constant returns to scale in firm 1. Broadly speaking, the necessary condition for the unconventional result in a certain firm is that the (X_1, q) relation be 'weaker' in that firm than in 'most' other firms. In this light, it is quite easy to understand the basic rationale of Heiner's further result according to which, for the entire industry, we have $\left(\sum dX_{1,s}\right)/dw_1 < 0$ on the sole condition that the output demand curve be downward-sloping. The interested reader can easily verify that this holds also for each firm if firms are identical.

Braulke (1984 and 1987) extended Heiner's analysis of short-run industry equilibrium to the case of input markets characterized by less than infinitely elastic supplies; the second article also allowed for long-run entry/exit processes while maintaining the assumption of firm heterogeneity. This extension was most welcome, because the assumption that an entire industry is a price taker in all input markets can hardly find a general justification. Much turns on the question 'What proportion of total supply of each factor is employed by the industry under consideration?' and it is evident that the answer may be sensitive to the industry/factor definitions employed. However, unless an industry is defined very finely, and an input very grossly, input demand by the industry may be a sizeable fraction of total input demand. Note, however, that produced inputs are again ignored.

Braulke's extension required a comparative static analysis which was even more 'inclusive' than that of Heiner: the 'full' or 'net' effect of a parametric change was to be studied subject to market clearing not only in the industry under consideration but also in related (output and input) markets. In particular, Braulke included the case in which the industry's reaction to an exogenous shock (such as taxes or subsidies) might trigger a change in other industries' output prices, due to demand-side effects or to the presence of common factors. Moreover, output supply by the industry is also studied explicitly along with input demand within the same framework of 'equilibrium functions' (as they are called by Chavas and Cox, 1997, p. 500).

An important consequence of the wider scope of Braulke's study of industry equilibrium is that the industrial output demand can no longer be expressed, as it was in Heiner's article, as a function of the output price alone. When the whole structure of relative commodity prices is amenable to change in response to an exogenous shock, one must consider the entire 'demand function'.

Braulke therefore had to introduce a new concept of 'normality' referred to output demand (and input supply): not only is it assumed that the own-price effects are negative, but also that they outweigh the cross effects (Braulke, 1984, p. 751; see also Braulke, 1987, p. 482). More formally, denoting by X the vector of output-market demand for the industrial outputs and input-market supply of the inputs (where inputs are negative outputs) and by p the vector of output and input prices, Braulke's 'normality' consists in negative semi-definiteness of the Jacobian $X_p(p)$ (see Braulke, 1987, p. 482, equation 7). Assuming normality, he proved that 'aggregate supply and demand will obey the traditional law of [output] supply and [input] demand' (Braulke, 1987, p. 484) at the level of the industry. This result holds both in the short run, with a given number of firms, and in the long run, under free entry and exit. With respect to the long run, Braulke retained the

assumption of firm heterogeneity and generalized an earlier analysis by
Panzar and Willig (1978). By contrast, firm-level full reactions remain
unpredictable, in the presence of firm heterogeneity, as they were in
Heiner's model.

It should be stressed, however, that Braulke's 'normality' is more
restrictive and much more complex than the mere condition that the
own-price effects on demand be negative. His result should be treated
with care and further analysis was needed. A significant step forward
was the Slutsky-like equation, defining compensated and uncompensated demand/supply functions, in Chavas and Cox (1997, pp. 508–
10): it is shown that the uncompensated matrix $X_p(p)$ is generally neither negative semidefinite nor even symmetric, unless income effects
happen to be null. Braulke's 'normality', therefore, cannot be assumed
without explicit justification.

These studies of industry behaviour under competitive market
equilibrium offered both the stimulus and the theoretical basis for
a series of applied studies in many different fields: agricultural
economics (e.g. Wohlgenant, 2001; Reed *et al.*, 2005), taxation theory
(e.g. Braulke and Endres, 1985; De Meza, 1988) and welfare analysis
(e.g. Thurman and Wohlgenant, 1989; Thurman, 1991). In fact,
spillover effects must always be considered, to say the least, when
practical conclusions (concerning economic policy, for instance) are
drawn from theoretical studies. Just to take two examples, a tax or
subsidy does have spillover effects on other prices and 'when price
changes spill over, the welfare effects of interventions spill over as
well' (Thurman, 1991, p. 508); or 'technical change in an industry
[...] is expected to affect prices in related markets' (Chavas and
Cox, 1997, p. 501): for example, technical progress in the computing
industry leads to 'a precipitous decline in the price of computing
power' and this spills over onto the labour market, because it 'lowers
the price of routine task input' (Autor *et al.*, 2006, p. 192).

9.4 Industrial interdependence in the traditional theory of supply

The latest developments in the theory of input demand (and output
supply) are the outcome of a gradual evolution on the basis of
the mathematical approach started in the 1930s. However, it is
well known that inter-industry relationships were certainly also

contemplated in the older literature on the Marshallian 'supply curve'. Marshall himself theorized a dependence of input prices upon the size of the industry, due to the fact that raw materials and primary inputs are frequently supplied at increasing cost (e.g. Marshall, 1920, p. 415), while produced inputs are frequently supplied at diminishing cost (e.g. Marshall, 1920, p. 371). Barone (1894) analysed output supply curves under general equilibrium conditions (as Braulke and others did about one century later) and argued that 'common factors' can undermine the meaning of output supply curves. Pigou (1928) reformulated the Marshallian construction, recognizing that 'we should need to step outside the industry primarily under review and investigate the conditions of production in the others' (pp. 249–50). In the closing pages of his 'Notes on Supply', Harrod (1930, pp. 240–41) appeared to take account, when demand increases in one industry, of a corresponding fall in demand in other industries, for he argued that every industry faces a rising supply price unless either it is a small factor user or it uses factors (at the margin) in the same proportions as other industries, which are releasing factors. Whether or not this really was Harrod's meaning, it was certainly that of Robbins four years later when he wrote, with reference to 'particular equilibrium analysis', that 'The change in the data which is characterized by the increase in demand here must be accompanied by a diminution of demand elsewhere and this may be such as to release factors of production in such measure as to permit the necessary extension at constant, or even diminishing cost. Once the data change, there is no presumption that an increase in output of a particular kind must be accompanied by more than proportionately increased outlay' (Robbins, 1934, p. 8). In 1941, Joan Robinson was equally explicit, complaining that Marshall's problem of a one-industry change in demand was just not the appropriate problem to pose in value theory, which should be concerned with the supply response to a shift in demand, factors being released as well as absorbed (Robinson, 1941, p. 2). In his supplementary notes of 1953 – to the famous 'Cost Curves and Supply Curves' (1953) – Viner accepted this view and concluded that 'all industries must tend to be subject to "external net pecuniary diseconomies of large production" when they expand *relative to the economy* of which they are a part' (Viner, 1953, p. 228, emphasis added).

We need not enter here into the overall conceptions of industry equilibrium which we find in this Marshallian tradition: for a recent survey, the interested reader is referred to Opocher and Steedman (2008b). It will suffice here to consider some selected aspects which are of special importance for the present book.

9.5 The role of common factors

Barone argued that Marshall's succinct mathematical analysis of supply (in Marshall, 1920, Mathematical Appendix, note XIV *bis*) can be referred only to industries using entirely specific factors (see Barone, 1992 [1894], equation at the bottom of p. 34 and footnote on p. 36) and that extensive changes were needed in the more general case, stressing the fact that the equilibrium prices of 'common factors' depended on all industrial outputs. His argument was based on a simple two-by-two model with fixed coefficients, which can be sketched as follows.

Let l_j, t_j be the amounts of labour and land per unit of commodity j ($j = 1, 2$). The demand for the two factors is

$$
\begin{aligned}
L &= l_1 Q_1 + l_2 Q_2 \\
T &= t_1 Q_1 + t_2 Q_2
\end{aligned}
\tag{9.1}
$$

Assuming factor market equilibrium at prices (rentals) $w(L), r(T)$ we have, by substitution

$$
\begin{aligned}
w &= w(l_1 Q_1 + l_2 Q_2) \\
r &= r(t_1 Q_1 + t_2 Q_2)
\end{aligned}
$$

The long-run supply prices of the two commodities are

$$
\begin{aligned}
p_1 &= l_1 w + t_1 r \\
p_2 &= l_2 w + t_2 r
\end{aligned}
\tag{9.2}
$$

Under factor market equilibrium, then, the supply price of each commodity is (indirectly) a function of both Q_1 and Q_2, unless factors are specific (say, when $l_1 = 0 = t_2$). In order to relate the long-run price of an output to that output level, the other output should be assumed constant. However, such an assumption 'is equivalent to assuming not only that the demand for all products remains unchanged (except for the product directly affected by the disruptive force), but also that these product prices remain unchanged, and this could be a serious mistake' (Barone, 1992 [1894], p. 33).

Barone's 'negative' conclusion received little attention. According to Ricci (1906) and Sraffa (1925, p. 325), similar conclusions could also be referred, *mutatis mutandis*, to demand curves. It was not immediately clear what constructive theory (other than general equilibrium analysis) could be built on that basis. Yet, in the course of time, the 'common factor' model became a powerful tool.

Harrod (1930), Robinson (1941) and Viner (1953) maintained, differently from Barone, that one can still formalize a rising supply price when the common factors, in fixed supply, are used by the various industries in different proportions (at the margin) and can be (marginally) substituted for one another.

The analytical kernel of their (verbal) argument can be easily formalized by a suitable reinterpretation of (9.1) and (9.2) above, with the understanding that now L and T are constant and that l_j, t_j are functions of w/r.

Let us assume that industry 1 is relatively labour-intensive (in the neighbourhood of equilibrium), so that $\det[l_j, t_j] > 0$.

Differentiating (9.1) totally, we obtain

$$\begin{pmatrix} dQ_1 \\ dQ_2 \end{pmatrix} = -\frac{(\hat{w} - \hat{r})w}{\det[l_j, t_j]} \begin{pmatrix} t_2 & -l_2 \\ -t_1 & l_1 \end{pmatrix} \begin{pmatrix} \partial l_1/\partial w & \partial l_2/\partial w \\ \partial t_1/\partial w & \partial t_2/\partial w \end{pmatrix} \begin{pmatrix} Q_1 \\ Q_2 \end{pmatrix}$$

Now $\partial l_j/\partial w < 0 < \partial t_j/\partial w$. It follows that dQ_1 always has the same sign as $(\hat{w} - \hat{r})$ and a sign opposite to that of dQ_2: an expansion of industry 1 is met by drawing factors from industry 2 in a labour/land ratio lower than required and this would determine an increase in w/r and a substitution of land for labour in both industries (cf. Harrod, 1930, p. 240; Robinson, 1941, p. 4; Viner, 1953, p. 228). The implication of an increase in Q_1 for the output price p_1, is readily shown by differentiating Equations (9.2) totally. By the envelope theorem, we obtain

$$(\hat{p}_1, \hat{p}_2) = (\hat{w}, \hat{r}) \begin{pmatrix} \dfrac{wl_1}{p_1} & \dfrac{wl_2}{p_2} \\ \dfrac{rt_1}{p_1} & \dfrac{rt_2}{p_2} \end{pmatrix} \tag{9.2'}$$

which yields

$$(\hat{w} - \hat{r}) = \frac{p_1 p_2}{wr} \frac{1}{\det[l_j, t_j]} (\hat{p}_1 - \hat{p}_2) \tag{9.2''}$$

Unsurprisingly, because we are discussing here the familiar 2×2 model, the latter equation, as referred to an open economy, is a formulation of the Stolper–Samuelson theorem, of course (see Chapter 2, Appendix 2). The price of the commodity produced by the expanding industry rises in terms of the other commodity (notice that this is still so when $\det[l_j, t_j] < 0$, because in this case the sign of $(\hat{w} - \hat{r})$ is reversed). Moreover, it can be readily shown on the basis of Equations (9.2′) that, when 'our' industry is labour-intensive, this price rises also in terms of land but it falls in terms of labour (the reverse would hold if the industry was land-intensive).

9.6 Supply curves, relative prices and the numéraire

The above-mentioned authors were interested in extracting a supply curve from the overall relative price realignment and to this end they expressed the industrial prices in terms of a numéraire. Harrod seems, implicitly, to take the 'average' input bundle as the standard of value, for he wrote that the expanding industry 'can only get increasing quantities of [the scarce factor] at an enhanced price in terms of [the other factor(s)]. But since, *ex hypothesi*, it uses more than an average amount of [the scarce factor], it can only get an increase in the sample of factors required for a unit increase of its output at an enhanced price' (1930, p. 240). Joan Robinson more explicitly held that factor prices were the appropriate standard: 'The obvious solution is to measure prices in terms of a composite unit of resources, the factors being weighted by the proportions in which they are found in industry as a whole. So long as we are assuming a fixed supply of each factor this measurement is quite unambiguous' (1941, p. 5). Likewise, Viner (1953, p. 229) takes 'total national income' as the standard (or, more precisely, he stipulated that the latter had a constant money value).

It is clear that a composite of input prices weighted by the fixed factor supplies always yields the desired result, just because an expansion of 'our' industry will tend to raise the relative price of the factor which it uses in above-average proportion. This can easily be seen on the basis of (9.2′) setting $\hat{w}wL + \hat{r}rT = 0$. We can equally see, however, that both prices fall in terms of a numéraire formed by an input bundle L', T' with $L'/T' > l_1/t_1$ (and both rise if $L'/T' < l_2/t_2$). This ambiguity in the measurement of 'real' commodity prices when relative factor prices change had been noted by Pigou (1927, p. 191).

The fact that the supply price may be rising or falling according to the specific standard of value chosen should alert the economic theorist to the doubtful significance of a supply curve taken in isolation, with no reference to the overall price realignment. Only if a price rose or fell in terms of any possible numéraire would one be entitled to speak of the change in that price in isolation and in terms of an arbitrary numéraire, with no reference to other collateral changes; but this is not the case for the 'industry supply curve'. The same economic outcome can be represented by curves with slopes of opposite signs and none of them is a full representation of that outcome, as we argued at length in Opocher and Steedman (2008a).

9.7 Sraffian interdependence(s)

Like Barone, Piero Sraffa maintained that a rising supply price is well-defined only when factors are industry-specific but is logically defective in the presence of common factors. (His criticism of a falling supply price due to increasing returns need not concern us here.) This view has a very solid ground and was agreed by later authors. Samuelson (1971, pp. 12–18), for example, formulated the 'Rigorous foundations of partial equilibrium' in terms of a model in which 'each good is produced by transferable labour working on lands that are, respectively, completely-specific to the industry in question' (Samuelson, 1971, p. 12).

As compared to Barone's contribution, Sraffa's famous 1925 and 1926 articles adopted a simpler and, we suggest, deeper argument, which remains valid even after the Harrod–Robinson–Viner theory and, of course, after Samuelson's delimitation of consistent partial equilibrium analysis.

If an industry was a significant user of a factor in inelastic supply, Sraffa argued, its expansion would raise the costs of other industries and hence change the prices supposedly given in constructing the demand curve for the industry under consideration (cf. Sraffa, 1925, pp. 323–24, and Sraffa, 1926, p. 539). A movement along 'our' supply curve thus causes a shift of 'our' demand curve and the method of particular equilibrium analysis is inapplicable.

Sraffa's argument only requires that one 'fixed' factor, like land, be shared by different industries and can be easily formalized if we express all prices in terms of the other factor, 'labour'. Differentiating the second equation in (9.1), we have

$$t_1 dQ_1 = -(t_2 dQ_2) - (dt_1 Q_1 + dt_2 Q_2)$$

A small increase in Q_1 can be met by drawing marginal doses of land from industry 2 (the first term on the rhs) and/or by using land more intensively in both industries (the second term). In turn, the change in land intensity in both industries is brought about by an increase in the (intensive) rent. Differentiating (9.2) keeping w constant, we have

$$\hat{p}_1 = \frac{r t_1}{p_1} \hat{r}$$

$$\hat{p}_2 = \frac{r t_2}{p_2} \hat{r}$$

The first mechanism prevailed when the expanding industry used a 'small part' of total land and involved a 'negligible' increase in rent; the second mechanism prevailed when it used a 'considerable part' of total land and involved a sizeable increase in rent. Whatever the relative importance of the two mechanisms, Sraffa pointed out that they 'operate in a like degree upon all the industries' (Sraffa, 1926: p. 539; see also Sraffa, 1925, p. 324), thus determining a change in both prices. It is not essential to the argument that the shares of land (and labour) in the two industries be different: it only matters that the *ceteris paribus* assumption made on demand is contradicted by the logic of the 'supply curve'. If $r t_1 / p_1 < r t_2 / p_2$, the price of the second good would increase proportionally more than p_1: a downward-sloping demand curve drawn on the same diagram as the upward-sloping 'supply curve' would be rather enigmatic in this case!

When industry 1 is relatively labour-intensive, an expansion of this industry leads therefore to the following changes in (labour-commanded) prices: $0 < \hat{p}_1 < \hat{p}_2 < \hat{r}$. The fact that p_1 increases relative to the wage but decreases relative to the rent (and the other commodity) is a confirmation of the correctness of Pigou's and J. Robinson's concerns about measurement.

The two articles by Sraffa had also a *pars construens*, of course. In 1925 he advocated a return to the old constant-cost view of the industry, while in 1926 he proposed to 'abandon the path of free competition and turn in the opposite direction, namely towards monopoly' (Sraffa, 1926, p. 542). Despite the impressive impact that the latter article had on both the Marshallian tradition and the new wave of studies on imperfect competition, we know that, in 1927, he started thinking about industrial interdependence in a new way, emphasizing its most direct source, which is the presence of produced inputs. Commodities are now both products and inputs and economic activity is conceived as a circular process. This perspective was formalized in its purest form in the so-called 'first equations' and 'second equations' (which would eventually become the core of chapters 1 and 2 of Sraffa, 1960: see Gehrke and Kurz, 2006 for details): land scarcity is not considered and labour is implicitly assumed to be 'produced' by the consumption of commodities. Economic activity is reduced here to production and exchange of commodities by interdependent industries. In this setting, it is no wonder that the industrial system and the proportions of prices (and outputs) which keep the system in equilibrium became the main object of analysis. The subsequent explicit introduction of a labour input and a variable wage ('third equations'), of land, fixed capital, joint production, etc., maintained a focus on the system rather than the individual industry and so did the Sraffian literature following the publication of *Production of Commodities by Means of Commodities*, to which we referred towards the end of Chapter 4 and in Chapter 5.

The shift of emphasis from the individual industry to the entire system somewhat overshadowed the precise implications that the mere presence of produced inputs has for the comparative static properties of industry equilibrium: like 'common factors' in fixed supply, produced inputs determine a series of collateral effects which can and should be studied (also) from the standpoint of the individual industry. As the FIE analysis presented in this book has shown, they undermine certain results obtained from partial equilibrium analysis even when there are constant returns to scale and demand linkages are not considered. There is a logical continuity, therefore, between Sraffa's early criticism of partial equilibrium and his later studies focused on interdependence due to produced inputs.

9.8 Concluding remarks

Schumpeter (1954, pp. 990–98) suggests, reasonably enough, that the defining postulate of partial analysis is that there should be only negligible feedback from the industry (firm, household, etc.) to the economy as a whole. However, as he goes on to point out, there is no sharp, clear-cut borderline between partial and general equilibrium methods, by which we take him to mean that any analysis takes some things as given (independent of that which is studied), so that an element of judgement is always involved as to which 'indirect effects' (Marshall, 1919, Appendix A) may reasonably be ignored. In a similar vein, Viner introduced his analysis of the industry supply curve by alerting the reader to the fact that 'Like all partial equilibrium analysis, including the allegedly "general" equilibrium theories of the Lausanne School, it rests on assumptions of the *ceteris paribus* order which posit independence when in fact there is some degree of dependence' (1953, p. 199).

The literature on input demand and output supply by the competitive firm and industry, which has been reviewed in this chapter, is a good example of the wisdom of Schumpeter's and Viner's remarks. It is true that microeconomics textbooks encourage students to think of a firm-level partial equilibrium input demand (or output supply) curve as the outcome of an intellectual experiment in which the price of that input (or the output price), and nothing else, is variable; and that, even worse, they also encourage students to think about partial equilibrium industry-level 'curves' as a sum of independent firm-level curves. Yet, on this understanding, partial equilibrium has not always been taken too seriously. Both the theory of multi-input demand and the theory of supply, under competitive conditions, evolved in the sense of an increasing inclusiveness and interdependence. Even the early studies of input demand by the price-taking firm considered the combined effect of at least two connected variations (an input price and the output level) and this had important consequences for phenomena that strict partial analysis cannot detect (like the dominance of gross complementarity under nearly constant returns to scale, or a possible negative relation between an input price and marginal cost). However, the bulk of the long tradition of studies in the theory of multi-input demand was concerned with the deeper and more complex problem of the relationship between the competitive firm and its industrial environment. In the short run, the reaction of other firms to a common shock feeds back on the firm under consideration in the form of changing output and input prices; in the long run, an effect of a similar kind is brought about by freedom of entry and exit. Likewise, even the older studies of supply in the Marshallian tradition did not fail to take into consideration many feedbacks (on input prices and other commodity prices) of an initial expansion or contraction of an industry.

Despite the different degrees of inclusiveness which characterized these various industrial studies, the idea that, in one specification or another, one can always end up with an inverse relation between input use and own input price and a positive relation between output level and output price had a singular persistence. For instance, in Silberberg's model, while the traditional 'law of demand', referred to the long-run equilibrium of the firm, may not hold in 'absolute' terms, it does always hold in 'per unit of output' terms; in Heiner's model, it may not hold in a short-run equilibrium of the firm, but does always hold for the industry provided that the price elasticity of output demand is negative; in Braulke's generalization, it may not hold under Heiner's conditions, but it does hold under other (stronger) 'normality' conditions.

The present book is inscribed in this long tradition of microeconomic studies of 'input demand'. Full industry equilibrium is in fact a version of the many 'less partial' views of the industry and it shares with them the premiss that a crude partial equilibrium conception is of no practical use. Differently from them, however, we cast doubt on the 'traditional law'. It is notorious that the comparative statics results in Arrow–Debreu general equilibrium models have few qualitative restrictions: the Heiner–Braulke–Chavas–Cox results without 'normality' are hardly surprising, therefore. However, the traditional law can be violated even with no effects stemming from output demand and factor supply. We have shown over and over again, in many different specifications, that in an FIE one cannot rely on a long-run downward-sloping input use/own input price relationship.

10 | Conclusions

If microeconomic theory is to provide a solid foundation for the examination of the permanent effects of, say, the imposition of a tariff, or of some significant technical advance, then it must include the comparative statics of alternative long-period, zero-net-profit equilibria. Now such alternative equilibria can never be such that all but one of the prices stand in the same ratios to each other, only one price bearing a different ratio to the others. Yet conventional 'long-run' theory of input demand and output supply does turn, precisely, on changing just one price at a time. Consequently, it does not provide the solid foundation just referred to. To take a leading example, Samuelson's 'generalized substitution theorem' offers no useful guide to the comparative statics of firms which earn zero net profits both before and after a shock: albeit perfectly correct, it is, alas, of little use in a long-run competitive context. The familiar inference from the theorem – that an input use is inversely related to its price – has in fact been disproved both by the 'long-run theory of the firm' of the 1970s and by the Sraffian long-period theory of production (as considered from the standpoint of an individual industry). A serious long-run analysis of the input price–input use relationship should be consistent with the theorem and seek such regularities as there are, while acknowledging that they may be few in number.

The long-run theory of the firm developed in the 1970s introduced an innovative way of thinking about microeconomic equilibrium, aware of the effects of competition. Such an approach provided the basis for a series of interesting studies concerning the relations between the firm, the industry and the economic system. Yet this long-run theory of the firm did not go far enough, even in the narrow framework of an 'isolated industry'. The mere assumption that the industrial output may be used as an input by the same industry introduces significant variations and makes it clear that the input rental–input use relationship for a produced input is qualitatively different from the input rental–input

196

use relationship for a primary input. Under FIE, it is often impossible for the rental of a commodity input to increase or fall relative to all other inputs; rather, it may increase relative to some inputs and fall relative to others. In such a case no significant input rental–input use relationship exists, because its slope could be arbitrarily manipulated by mere choice of numéraire. By contrast, there *is* a significant input rental–input use (per unit of output) relationship for a primary input; however, the latter is subject to no general qualitative restrictions. To be sure, if all inputs are Hicksian substitutes *and* the cost function is twice-differentiable everywhere, then there is an inverse relationship for primary inputs, but if either assumption is removed, we are left without any specific regularity. Of special interest, in our context, are the implications of what we called 'on/off' inputs – that is, inputs which can entirely replace one another. They often consist in produced means of production associated with alternative 'technologies', such as wind turbines and photovoltaic panels. There may be input substitutability within each technology, as fine as we like, yet a price change determining a switch from one 'technology' to the other modifies input use per unit of output in a way which cannot be predicted by the conventional input demand curves: across the switch, even a primary input can be positively related to its own price.

The 'long-run theory of the firm' was concerned with single-output, multi-input firms. The symmetric case with one input and multiple outputs yields equivalent results: under FIE a firm's 'absolute' output may decrease when its price increases and the zero-profit condition determines a compensating increase of an input price. By contrast – in the simple case of no produced inputs and of disjoint groups of commodities – the ratios of inputs and outputs behave in the conventional way.

Both in the case of an 'isolated industry' and in the more general context of multiple industries we have shown over and over again that produced input use can react to a given shock in qualitatively different ways as compared to primary inputs. Even assuming utterly conventional cost functions in all industries, such as those of the CES variety, the behaviour of commodity inputs is undetermined a priori. This 'negative' result is independent of whether the rate of interest is taken as constant (and possibly null) or as variable. It has therefore no essential relation to capital-theoretic issues and everything to do with the more fundamental properties of FIE equilibria. Nonetheless, we have also analysed the industrial capital/(gross) output ratios in relation to the rate of interest thus touching on some capital-theoretic issues from the standpoint of an individual industry and proved that, even with CES cost functions, such ratios need not be inversely related to the rate of interest.

To make more transparent the connection between the results with a variable rate of interest and the famous capital theory debates of the 1960s and 1970s, we reconsidered from the standpoint of an individual industry some selected models which featured prominently in that literature. We had nothing to add to (or subtract from) long-settled results relating to the economy as a whole; nor did we stress the obvious fact that unconventional aggregate results imply unconventional behaviour in at least one individual industry. Rather, we have shown that, under FIE, conventional behaviour in the economy as a whole by no means implies conventional behaviour in every industry. This is true both when we consider a variation in the rate of interest and when we consider a variation in relative primary input prices with a null rate of interest. In the first context, a small increase in the rate of interest (and hence decrease in the real wage) across a switch may well determine, in an industry, an increase in the capital–output ratio and a fall in employment per unit of output even though, at the economy level, both variables behave conventionally. But also in the second context, with a null rate of interest, one industry can exhibit the property of a positive relationship between a primary input use and its price. These possibilities have nothing whatever to do with 'unequal proportions', reswitching, capital-reversing or interest-rate effects of any kind. All that is necessary is that we suppose FIE both before and after the exogenous change considered. We hope that the above findings would interest marginalist microeconomists and that they will develop FIE analysis in their own way. We hope, too, that our results will encourage Sraffa-inspired economists to pay much more attention both to individual industries and to the effects of exogenous changes other than changes in the interest rate.

The results mentioned so far take a change in income distribution to be entirely parametric. However, the change in the price system may depend in a predictable way on some specific shock, which modifies what we called the 'autonomous' components of prices. New taxes or subsidies, productivity increase in the various industries, or a change in international prices may bring about important modifications in each industry, which can be claimed to be fully accomplished only when zero excess profits have been restored by a new price system. The FIE comparative statics is therefore of potential interest for the applied microeconomist.

The connections between, for example, the various kinds of taxation, real primary input prices, relative commodity prices and input use per unit of output are quite complex in the presence of multiple industries having input–output relations with one another, because taxation in one industry affects real costs in other industries. Nevertheless, some regularities can be found. First, the effect that sales taxes have on real primary input prices is magnified by the presence of produced inputs: a rational estimation of such a magnification is based on the breakdown of costs in each industry. Second, assuming no impact of taxes on relative primary input prices, a certain industrial pattern of sales taxes leaves relative commodity prices unchanged not when the tax rates are the same, but when they are proportional to the industrial shares of value added; by the same token, equal tax rates generally modify the structure of relative prices. In particular, the relative price of a commodity taxed more heavily than the others does not necessarily increase, as compared to a no-tax situation: 'carbon taxes', for example, may have an ambiguous effect on the use of 'carbon' per unit of output in each industry.

Mutatis mutandis, similar results are obtained for productivity increase. Differently from taxes, however, the industrial rates of productivity increase are not observable and must be inferred from their economic outcomes. Whereas the familiar industry-level Total Factor Productivity calculations are based on the accounting of input and output change, an FIE perspective focuses on the accounting of input and output price change. Such an alternative method has some potential advantages. First, we may distinguish between the effects of technical progress on the average primary input prices and on distribution, which is highly desirable when the former has important effects on wage dispersion, as does skill-biased technical change; second, an FIE price accounting provides a theoretical definition of the long-run, or trend, component of productivity increase in an individual industry, which is lacking in the TFP method; finally, we may distinguish between the change in the average primary input prices due to productivity increase in the industry under consideration and the change brought about by productivity increase in other industries via a change in the prices of produced inputs; still another source of real wage increase, which can be singled out by price accounting, is an improvement in the terms of trade.

The presumption of downward-sloping input demand curves had a singular persistence in the making of the microeconomics of production. Many different versions were characterized by different *ceteris paribus* stipulations, each providing a different proof of the same property. Yet these proofs were by no means all of the same strength: Samuelson's conditional input demand curves are unassailable within their narrow limits; the Hicks–Allen curves of 'derived demand' were proved to be downward-sloping only under some regularity assumptions concerning output demand and in the case with two inputs; the partial equilibrium Hicksian input demand curves with an adjusting output were admittedly invalid in the case of constant returns to scale; the Ferguson–Saving–Silberberg long-run input demand curves with an adjusting output price were proved to be downward-sloping only when expressed in per unit of output terms. Other weaknesses characterized the many versions of a supply curve in the Marshallian tradition.

The deep-rooted beliefs in the existence of general 'laws' of demand and supply have been nurtured by an equally deep-rooted attitude to making a clear-cut distinction between partial equilibrium and general equilibrium methods, neglectful of Schumpeter's plea for more nuanced views. The Full Industry Equilibrium analysis proposed in this book rejects the crude logic of strict partial equilibrium on the ground that it is inconsistent with the long-run tendency of net profits (or losses) to vanish. At the same time, it does not pursue any general equilibrium argument (in the common understanding of that term). We make no claim to originality in the exploration of a method which is intermediate, so to speak; to the contrary, we have insisted that many significant episodes in the history of the theory of production developed one aspect or the other of what we call FIE analysis. However, perhaps a unified and systematic view of FIE was previously lacking. We hope that our book will offer to the microeconomic theorist a useful account of the zero-net-profit comparative statics and to the applied microeconomist a sound theoretical basis for a coherent long-run analysis of industrial shocks.

References

Allen R.G.D. (1938), *Mathematical Analysis for Economists*, London, Macmillan.

Arrow K.J. and Hurwicz L. (1958), 'On the Stability of Competitive Equilibrium', *Econometrica*, 24 (4): 522–52.

Atkinson A.B. (2007), 'The Distribution of Earnings in OECD Countries', *International Labour Review*, 146 (1–2): 41–60.

Atkinson A.B and Stiglitz J.E. (1980), *Lectures on Public Economics*, Maidenhead, McGraw-Hill.

Autor D.H., Katz L.F. and Kearney M.S. (2006), 'The Polarization of the US Labor Market', *American Economic Review*, 96 (2): 189–94.

Bain J.S. (1956), *Barriers to New Competition. Their Character and Consequences in Manufacturing Industries*, Cambridge, MA, Harvard University Press.

Barone E. (1992) [1894], 'On the Analysis of Dynamic Problems', in L.L. Pasinetti (ed.), *Italian Economic Papers*, Vol. I, pp. 17–38. Bologna, Il Mulino/Oxford University Press.

Bassett L.R. and Borcherding T.E. (1970a), 'The Firm, the Industry, and the Long-Run Demand for Factors of Production', *Canadian Journal of Economics*, 3 (1): 140–44.

Bassett L.R. and Borcherding T.E. (1970b), 'Industry Factor Demand', *Western Economic Journal*, 8 (3): 259–61.

Bassett L.R. and Borcherding T.E. (1970c), 'The Relationship between Firm Size and Factor Price', *Quarterly Journal of Economics*, 84 (3): 518–22.

Baumol W.J. (1982), 'Contestable Markets: An Uprising in the Theory of Industrial Structure', *American Economic Review*, 72 (1): 1–15.

Baumol W.J., Panzar, J.C. and Willig J.C. (1988)[1982], *Contestable Markets and the Theory of Industrial Structure*, second edition. New York, Harcourt Brace Jovanovich Publishers.

Bear D.V.T. (1965), 'Inferior Inputs and the Theory of the Firm', *Journal of Political Economy*, 73 (3): 287–89.

Bhagwati J. (1994), 'Free Trade: Old and New Challenges', *Economic Journal*, 104 (March): 231–46.

Braulke M. (1984), 'The Firm in Short-Run Industry Equilibrium: Comment', *American Economic Review*, 74 (4): 750–53.

Braulke M. (1987), 'On the Comparative Statics of a Competitive Industry', *American Economic Review*, 77 (3): 479–85.

Braulke M. and Endres A. (1985), 'On the Economics of Effluent Charges', *Canadian Journal of Economics/Revue Canadienne d'Economique*, 18 (4): 891–97.

Burmeister E. and Turnovsky S.J. (1972), 'Capital Deepening Response in an Economy with Heterogeneous Capital Goods', *American Economic Review*, 62 (5): 842–53.

Chambers R.G. (1988), *Applied Production Analysis. A Dual Approach*, Cambridge, Cambridge University Press.

Chavas J-P. and Cox T.L. (1997), 'On Market Equilibrium Analysis', *American Journal of Agricultural Economics*, 79 (2): 500–13.

Checchi D. and García-Peñalosa C. (2008), 'Labour Market Institutions and Income Inequality', *Economic Policy*, 23 (56): 601–49.

Cornes R. (1992), *Duality and Modern Economics*, Cambridge, Cambridge University Press.

De Meza D. (1988), 'The Efficacy of Effluent Charges', *Canadian Journal of Economics/Revue Canadienne d'Economique*, 21 (1): 182–86.

Diewert W.E. (1971), 'An Application of the Shephard Duality Theorem: a Generalized Leontief Production Function', *Journal of Political Economy*, 79(3): 481–507.

Diewert W.E. (1982), 'Duality Approaches to Microeconomic Theory', in K.J. Arrow and M.D. Intriligator (eds.), *Handbook of Mathematical Economics*, Vol. II, pp. 535–99. Amsterdam, North Holland.

Domar E.D. (1961), 'On the Measurement of Technological Change', *Economic Journal*, 71 (December): 709–29.

Dorfman R., Samuelson P.A. and Solow R.M. (1958), *Linear Programming and Economic Analysis*, New York, McGraw-Hill.

Edgeworth F.Y. (1913), 'Contributions to the Theory of Railway Rates – IV', *Economic Journal*, 23 (June): 206–26.

Ferguson C.E. (1966), 'Production, Prices, and the Theory of Jointly-derived Input Demand Functions', *Economica*, 33 (November): 454–61.

Ferguson C.E. and Saving T.R. (1969), 'Long-run Scale Adjustments of a Perfectly Competitive Firm and Industry', *American Economic Review*, 59 (5): 774–83.

Flux A.W. (1923) [1904], *Economic Principles: An Introductory Study*, London, Methuen & Co.

Fullerton D. and Metcalf G.E. (2002), 'Tax Incidence', in A.J. Auerbach and M.Feldstein (eds.) *Handbook of Public Economics*, Vol. 4, pp. 1787–872. Amsterdam, North-Holland.

Gamberoni E., Lanz R. and Piermartini R. (2010), 'Timeliness and Contract Enforceability in Intermediate Goods Trade', WTO, Staff Working Paper ERSD-2010-14.

Garegnani P. (1970), 'Heterogeneous Capital, the Production Function and the Theory of Distribution', *Review of Economic Studies*, 37 (3): 407–36.

Gehrke C. and Kurz H.D. (2006), 'Sraffa on von Bortkiewicz: Reconstructing the Classical Theory of Value and Distribution', *History of Political Economy*, 38 (1): 91–149.

Gehrke C. and Lager C. (1995), 'Environmental Taxes, Relative Prices and Choice of Technique in a Linear Model of Production', *Metroeconomica*, 46(2): 127–45.

Giffen R. (1888), 'Recent Changes in Prices and Incomes Compared', *Journal of the Royal Statistical Society*, 51 (4): 713–815.

Goos M. and Manning A. (2007), 'Lousy and Lovely Jobs: The Rising Polarization of Work in Britain', *Review of Economics and Statistics*, 89 (1): 118–33.

Goos M., Manning A. and Salomons A. (2009), 'Job Polarization in Europe', *American Economic Review*, 99 (2): 58–63.

Haberler G. (1936), *The Theory of International Trade, with its Applications to Commercial Policy*, London, William Hodge & Co. Ltd.

Harberger A.C. (1962), 'The Incidence of the Corporation Income Tax', *Journal of Political Economy*, 70 (3): 215–40.

Harberger A.C. (1998), 'A Vision of the Growth Process', *American Economic Review*, 88 (1): 1–32.

Harrod R.F. (1930), 'Notes on Supply', *Economic Journal*, 40 (June): 232–41.

Heiner R.A. (1982), 'The Theory of the Firm in "Short-Run" Industry Equilibrium', *American Economic Review*, 72 (3): 555–62.

Hicks J.R. (1932), *The Theory of Wages*, London, Macmillan.

Hicks J.R. (1937), *Théorie Mathématique de la Valeur en Régime de Libre Concurrence*, Paris, Herman & Cie Éditeurs.

Hicks J.R. (1939), *Value and Capital*, Oxford, Oxford University Press.

Hicks J.R. (1953–4), 'A Note on a Point in *Value and Capital*: A Reply', *Review of Economic Studies*, 21 (3): 218–21.

Hotelling H. (1932), 'Edgeworth's Taxation Paradox and the Nature of Demand and Supply Functions', *Journal of Political Economy*, 40 (5): 577–616.

Hulten C.R. (1978), 'Growth Accounting with Intermediate Inputs', *Review of Economic Studies*, 45 (3): 511–18.

Jorgenson D.W. and Stiroh K.J. (2000), 'US Economic Growth at the Industry Level', *American Economic Review*, 90 (2): 161–67.

Jorgenson D.W., Ho M.S. and Stiroh K.J. (2005), *Information Technology and the American Growth Resurgence*, Cambridge, MA, MIT Press.

Katz, L.F. and Autor, D.H. (1999), 'Changes in the Wage Structure and Earnings Inequality', in O. Ashenfelter and D. Card (eds.), *Handbook of Labor Economics*. Volume 3, pp. 1463–555. Amsterdam, Elsevier.

Kotlikoff L.J. and Summers L.H. (1987), 'Tax Incidence', in A.J. Auerbach and M. Feldstein (eds.), *Handbook of Public Economics*, Vol. 2, pp. 1043–92. Amsterdam, North-Holland.

Kurz H.D. and Salvadori N. (1995), *Theory of Production: A Long-Period Analysis*, Cambridge, Cambridge University Press.

Marshall A. (1919), *Industry and Trade*, London, Macmillan.

Marshall A. (1920), *Principles of Economics*, eighth edition, London, Macmillan.

Mas-Colell A., Whinston M.D. and Green J.R. (1995), *Microeconomic Theory*, Oxford, Oxford University Press.

McFadden D. (1978), 'Cost, Revenue, and Profit Functions', in M. Fuss and D. McFadden (eds.), *Production Economics: A Dual Approach to Theory and Applications*, Volume I, pp. 3–109. Amsterdam, North-Holland.

McKinnon R.I. (1966), 'Intermediate Products and Differential Tariffs: A Generalization of Lerner's Symmetry Theorem', *Quarterly Journal of Economics*, 80 (4): 584–615.

Metcalfe J.S. and Steedman I. (1972), 'Reswitching and Primary Input Use', *Economic Journal*, 82 (March): 140–57.

Mieszkowski P. (1969), 'Tax Incidence Theory: The Effects of Taxes on the Distribution of Income', *Journal of Economic Literature*, 7 (4): 1103–24.

Montet C. (1979), 'Reswitching and Primary Input Use: A Comment', *Economic Journal*, 89 (Sept.): 642–47.

Morishima M. (1953–4a), 'A Note on a Point in Value and Capital', *Review of Economic Studies*, 21 (3): 214–17.

Morishima M. (1953–4b), 'A Note on a Point in Value and Capital: A Rejoinder', *Review of Economic Studies*, 21 (3): 222.

Mosak J.L. (1938), 'Interrelations of Production, Price, and Derived Demand', *Journal of Political Economy*, 46 (6): 761–87.

Musgrave R.A. (1953), 'On Incidence', *Journal of Political Economy*, 61 (4): 306–23.

Musgrave R.A. (1985), 'A Brief History of Fiscal Doctrine', in A.J. Auerbach and M. Feldstein (eds.), *Handbook of Public Economics*, Vol 1, pp. 1–59. Amsterdam, North-Holland.

Neumann J. von (1945–6), 'A Model of General Equilibrium', *Review of Economic Studies*, 13 (1): 1–9.

Nuti D.M. (1970), 'Capitalism, Socialism and Steady Growth', *Economic Journal*, 80 (March): 32–57.

Opocher A. (2002), 'Taking Marshallian Long-Period Equilibrium Seriously', *Journal of Economics*, 75 (1): 63–93.

Opocher A. (2010), 'Measuring Productivity Increase by Long-Run Prices: The Early Analyses of G.R. Porter and R. Giffen', *European Journal of the History of Economic Thought*, 17 (5): 1271–91.

Opocher A. and Steedman I., (2008a), 'Long-Run Rising Supply Price and the Numéraire', *Metroeconomica*, 59 (1): 74–84.

Opocher A. and Steedman I. (2008b), 'The Industry Supply Curve: Two Different Traditions', *European Journal of the History of Economic Thought*, 15 (2): 247–74.

Opocher A. and Steedman I. (2009), 'Input Price–Input Quantity Relations and the Numéraire', *Cambridge Journal of Economics*, 33 (5): 937–48.

Opocher A. and Steedman I. (2011), 'On/off Inputs and their Rentals', in N. Salvadori and C. Gehrke (eds.), *Keynes, Sraffa and the Criticism of Neoclassical Theory. Essays in Honour of Heinz Kurz*, London, Routledge.

Opocher A. and Steedman I. (2013), 'Unconventional Results with Surrogate Production Functions', *Metroeconomica*, 64 (3): 539–46.

Panzar J.C. and Willig R.D. (1978), 'On the Comparative Statics of a Competitive Industry with Inframarginal Firms', *American Economic Review*, 68 (3): 474–78.

Pasinetti L.L. (1977)[1975], *Lectures on the Theory of Production*, London, Macmillan.

Pigou A.C. (1927), 'The Laws of Diminishing and Increasing Cost', *Economic Journal*, 37 (June): 199–97.

Pigou A.C. (1928), 'An Analysis of Supply', *Economic Journal*, 38 (June): 238–57.

Porter G.R. (1851)[1836], *The Progress of the Nation*, second edition, London, J. Murray.

Portes R.D. (1971), 'Long-Run Scale Adjustments of a Perfectly Competitive Firm and Industry: An Alternative Approach', *American Economic Review*, 61 (3): 430–34.

Poterba J.M. (1996), 'Retail Price Reactions to Changes in State and Local Sales Taxes', *National Tax Journal*, 49 (2): 165–76.

Rader T. (1968), 'Factor Inputs are Never Gross Substitutes', *Journal of Political Economy*, 76 (1): 38–43.

Reed A.J., Levedahl J.W. and Hallahan C. (2005), 'The Generalized Composite Commodity Theorem and Food Demand Estimation', *American Journal of Agricultural Economics*, 87 (1): 28–37.

Ricci U. (1906), 'Curve Piane di Offerta dei Prodotti', *Giornale degli Economisti*, 17 (September): 223–40.

Robbins L. (1934), 'Remarks Upon Certain Aspects of the Theory of Costs', *Economic Journal*, 44 (March): 1–18.

Robinson J.V. (1933), *The Economics of Imperfect Competition*, London, Macmillan.

Robinson J.V. (1941), 'Rising Supply Price', *Economica*, 8 (February): 1–8.

Robinson J.V. (1953), 'The Production Function and the Theory of Capital', *Review of Economic Studies*, 21 (2): 81–106.

Russell R.R. (1964), 'A Graphical Proof of the Impossibility of a Positively Inclined Demand Curve for a Factor of Production', *American Economic Review*, 54 (5): 726–32.

Samuelson P.A. (1947), *Foundations of Economic Analysis*, Cambridge, MA, Harvard University Press.

Samuelson P.A. (1962), 'Parable and Realism in Capital Theory: The Surrogate Production Function', *Review of Economic Studies*, 29 (3): 193–206.

Samuelson P.A. (1966), 'A Summing Up', *Quarterly Journal of Economics*, 80 (4): 568–83.

Samuelson P.A. (1971), 'An Exact Hume–Ricardo–Marshall Model of International Trade', *Journal of International Economics*, 1 (1): 1–18.

Samuelson P.A. (1972), 'Maximum Principles of Analytical Economics', *American Economic Review*, 62 (3): 249–62.

Saving T.R. (1963), 'Note on Factor Demand Elasticity: The Competitive Case', *Econometrica*, 31 (3): 555–7.

Schumpeter J.A. (1954), *History of Economic Analysis*, New York, Oxford University Press.

Shephard R.W. (1970), *Theory of Cost and Production Functions*, Princeton, Princeton University Press.

Silberberg E. (1974), 'The Theory of the Firm in Long-Run Equilibrium', *American Economic Review*, 64 (4): 734–41.

Solow R.M. (1957), 'Technical Change and the Aggregate Production Function', *Review of Economics and Statistics*, 39 (3): 312–20.

Spence M. (1983), 'Contestable Markets and the Theory of Industrial Structure: A Review Article', *Journal of Economic Literature*, 21 (3): 981–90.

Sraffa P. (1925), 'Sulla Relazione tra Costo e Quantità Prodotta', *Annali di Economia*, Vol. II: 277–328. English edition: L.L. Pasinetti (ed.) (1998) *Italian Economic Papers*, III, pp. 323–63. Bologna, Il Mulino/Oxford University Press.

Sraffa P. (1926), 'The Laws of Returns Under Competitive Conditions', *Economic Journal*, 36 (December): 535–50.

Sraffa P. (1960), *Production of Commodities by Means of Commodities. Prelude to a Critique of Economic Theory*, Cambridge, Cambridge University Press.

Steedman I. (1983), 'On the Measurement and Aggregation of Productivity Increase', *Metroeconomica*, 35 (3): 223–33.

Steedman I. (1985), 'On Input "Demand Curves"', *Cambridge Journal of Economics*, 9 (1): 165–72.

Steedman I. (1986), 'Produced Inputs and Tax Incidence Theory', *Public Finance/Finances Publique*, 41 (3): 331–49.

Steedman I. (1988), 'Sraffian Interdependence and Partial Equilibrium Analysis', *Cambridge Journal of Economics*, 12 (1): 85–95.

Steedman I. (1998), 'Produced Input Use per Unit of Output', *Economics Letters*, 59 (2): 195–99.

Steedman I. (2005), 'Comparative Statics of Industry-Level Produced Input Use in HOS Trade Theory', *Review of Political Economy*, 17 (3): 465–70.

Steedman I. (2006), 'Long Run Demand for Labour in the Consumer Good Industry', *Metroeconomica*, 57 (2): 158–64.

Steedman I. (2009), 'Many Capital–Output Ratios Increasing with the Rate of Interest: An Industry-Level Analysis', *Metroeconomica*, 60 (1): 150–61.

Steedman I. (2013), 'Sraffian Thoughts in Full Marginalist Dress', *Metroeconomica*, 64 (4): 598–606.

Stolper W.F. and Samuelson P.A. (1941), 'Protection and Real Wages', *Review of Economic Studies*, 9 (1): 58–73.

Thurman W.N. (1991), 'Applied General Equilibrium Welfare Analysis', *American Journal of Agricultural Economics*, 73 (5): 1508–16.

Thurman W.N. and Wohlgenant M.K. (1989), 'Consistent Estimation of General Equilibrium Welfare Effects', *American Journal of Agricultural Economics*, 71 (4): 1041–45.

Tirole J. (1988), *The Theory of Industrial Organization*, Cambridge, MA and London, MIT Press.

Vanek J. (1963), 'Variable Factor Proportions and Inter-Industry Flows in the Theory of International Trade', *Quarterly Journal of Economics*, 77 (1): 129–42.

Viner J. (1953)[1931], 'Cost Curves and Supply Curves', in G.J. Stigler and K.E. Boulding (eds.), *Readings in Price Theory*, pp. 198–232. London, Allen and Unwin.

Weintraub E.R. (1991), *Stabilizing Dynamics. Constructing Economic Knowledge*, Cambridge, Cambridge University Press.

Wicksell K. (1934)[1901], *Lectures on Political Economy*, London, Routledge.

Winch D.M. (1965), 'The Demand Curve for a Factor of Production: Comment', *American Economic Review*, 55 (4): 856–61.

Wohlgenant M.K. (2001), 'Marketing Margins: Empirical Analysis', in B. Gardner and G. Rausser (eds.) *Handbook of Agricultural Economics*, Vol. 1, pp. 934–70. Amsterdam, Elsevier.

World Bank (2006), 'Equity and Development', *World Development Report 2006*.

Index

aggregate quantities
  aggregation of the industrial rates of productivity increase, 149, 150, 157, 160, 161
  and total factor productivity, 126, 127, 163
  assumed to behave conventionally, 6, 100, 103, 107–8, 112, 115, 118
  in the Sraffian literature, 1, 89, 104, 118
  not a major issue in FIE analysis, 1, 100, 118, 198
Allen, R.G.D., 168, 169–71, 172, 173, 175, 180, 200
Arrow, K.J., 195
average cost curve
  bottom of, 8, 10, 18, 26, 27, 81, 181
  U-shaped, 8, 10, 14, 15, 18, 23, 26, 27, 81, 101, 180, 181

Barone, E., 168, 188–89, 191
Bear, D.V.T., 175, 179, 180, 181
Braulke, M., 184–86, 187, 195
Burmeister, E., xvi

Cambridge debates, 1, 7, 98, 100, 102, 104–5, 198
capital reversing, 98, 104, 105, 118, 198
  at industry level, 94–97, 99, 103
capital theory, xv, 7, 115, 197; see also Cambridge debates
capital/output ratio, 1, 93–94, 96–97, 98, 101, 103, 104, 118, 198
  preferred to capital/labour ratio, 102
CES cost function. See indirect average cost function; unit cost function
CES production function. See production function

Chavas, J.-P., 195
circulating capital, 92, 93–94, 96–97, 101, 110, 118, 147
common factors. See inputs
comparative statics
  need for a less partial, xv, 2, 6, 9, 10, 17, 195
  of FIE, 2, 4, 5, 17, 20–21, 22, 30–33, 39, 47, 65–67, 69–74, 76, 83–86, 119, 199
  Sraffian, 13, 15
competition, 12, 136, 196
  and free entry and exit, 8, 17, 18, 43, 58, 176, 177, 184, 185, 194
  free, xv, xvi, 9, 12, 14, 22, 66, 147, 149, 192
  in Bertrand equilibrium, 8, 18
  in contestability theory, 58
  perfect, 12
complementarity
  alternative concepts of complementarity and substitution, 32, 44–47, 59, 74–76
  effects of, 33, 36, 39–40, 43, 170, 174
  Hicks on prevalence of, 44, 45, 76, 178–79, 194
  not necessary for unconventional results, 6, 84, 86, 89, 97
constant returns to scale
  local, 24, 59, 68, 81, 101, 169
  nearly, 45, 174, 177–79, 184, 194
  strict, 14, 15, 20, 39, 41, 44, 47, 101, 145, 169, 171, 172, 174, 177, 180, 192
contestable markets theory, 5, 8, 10, 18, 58, 61, 68; see also competition

209

Printed in the United States
By Bookmasters